June 13, 1987

Dear Mike, Phillip, Randal & Guy

I bought this book since I
was lucky enough to go to the
Mets & Pittsburg game with
David, Brandy & Robin (my cousins) It
was great - Digue had been there & tried
to get Gary Carter to sign it for you, but
as luck would have it she didn't get
there in time - By the way the Mets lost -
Strawberry got into a fight & got
thrown out of the game -
I love you all
Mom

A
Dream
Season

A
Dream
Season

◆

GARY
CARTER
& John Hough, Jr.

Harcourt Brace Jovanovich, Publishers

San Diego   New York   London

Requests for permission to make copies of
any part of the work should be mailed to:
Permissions, Harcourt Brace Jovanovich, Publishers,
Orlando, Florida 32887.

The authors are grateful for permission
to quote from the song:
"New York State of Mind,"
copyright © 1975, Blackwood Music, Inc.

Library of Congress Cataloging-in-Publication Data

Carter, Gary, 1954-
A dream season.

1. Carter, Gary, 1954-
2. Baseball players—United States—Biography.
I. Hough, John T.   II. Title.
GV865.C319A3   1987   796.357′092′4 [B]   87-230
ISBN 0-15-126571-2

Designed by Michael Farmer
Printed in the United States of America
First edition
A B C D E

To my 1986 teammates for making the dream come true.
And, to my loving family—Sandy, Christy, Kimmy, and D.J.

Gary Carter

To Melanie

John Hough, Jr.

The authors would like to thank the following, who were there when we needed them: Matt Merola, Mead Chasky, Mets Public Relations Director Jay Horwitz, his assistant Dennis D'Agostino, Agnes and Wally Kiriloff, Kate Hough, Robert Fields, and Linda Sheridan.

Special thanks to our editor, B.J. Robbins. She's the best.

A
Dream
Season

1

I keep thinking about Ernie Banks.

Nineteen years in the major leagues, 512 home runs. Twice he led the National League in home runs. Twice he was named Most Valuable Player. He retired in 1971, and six years later was welcomed into the Hall of Fame. And I keep thinking how this Hall of Fame shortstop, this franchise player with the long career and the amazing statistics, never played in a World Series.

Ernie must have figured, after a while, that he'd never get there. He played for the Chicago Cubs, who finished as high as fourth only once in Ernie's nineteen years. This was before free agency; the Cubs owned Ernie, and they weren't about to part with one of the most brilliant shortstops who ever played the game. Somewhere along the line, Ernie Banks had to let go of the dream of playing in a World Series. I try to imagine that, and can't.

Baseball, with its dreams, began for me in the alley behind our house in Fullerton, California. The game, at first, was Whiffleball. The alley was our Dodger Stadium. The apartment building towering along one side, the garage doors, the garbage cans—they didn't exist. The sun shone on green grass, and crowds cheered. A garage was the left-field grandstand: lift one up onto our roof, home run.

We were Maury Wills, Wes Parker, Sandy Koufax, Don Drysdale, Tommy Davis. We set scenes: three and two, two outs, last of the ninth. Mickey Mantle at the plate. I loved Mickey Mantle, though he played for the Yankees—wrong league, and thousands of miles away. We were always emulating somebody, me, my older brother, Gordy, the rest of the neighborhood kids. And the biggest scene, the ultimate fantasy, was the World Series.

Seventh game of the World Series. Ninth inning. Two down. And here comes Mickey Mantle. You couldn't invent anything bigger. I remember those games, and I think of all the kids in all the alleys as spring comes on, playing with their Whiffleballs, or tennis balls, or scuffed-up hardballs. It's the World Series. Bruce Hurst on the mound, Darryl Strawberry at the plate. Hurst pitching to Strawberry, to Keith Hernandez, to Gary Carter. It's the World Series, baseball's dream of dreams.

I think of Ernie Banks, and know that I am one of the lucky ones.

I almost got there in 1981. I'd signed out of high school with the Montreal Expos in 1972, and at the end of the 1974 season I jumped from triple A to the majors and stayed. In 1980, we lost the race for the Eastern Division championship on the next-to-last day of the season. In 1981, the year of the players' strike, we won it.

The long strike had split the season in half. Baseball's solution was to declare first- and second-half winners in each of the divisions, and send them against each other in a best-of-five series. We won the second half and faced the Philadelphia Phillies, the previous year's division champions. We beat them in five games. The Championship Series in those days was best-of-five. Our opponent was my boyhood team, the Dodgers. Three wins, and we'd be there: the World Series.

That Championship Series went the full five games, and if there's any one pitch in my career I regret calling most, it's the fastball I asked Steve Rogers—we called him Cy—to throw to Rick Monday in the ninth inning of that close fifth game. We were playing at home, Olympic Stadium. We entered the ninth inning tied, 1–1. Now our manager, Jim Fanning, called Cy in to pitch. Cy was our best. He pitched two quick outs, and up came Monday.

Monday worked us to three balls and a strike. I worried that the breaking ball would miss; you don't want to walk anybody late in a tie ball game. So I asked for the fastball. It was supposed to drop, to stay away from Monday. It didn't, and Rick launched it to right center field. I threw the mask off and watched Andre Dawson chase the drive toward the fence. I thought Andre might get to the ball, but it was gone, and so was the game and with it the chance to get to the World Series. In the bottom of the ninth I worked Fernando Valenzuela to a two-out walk, but that was the end of it. We couldn't get that run back, and it had come on just one pitch, the fastball to Monday.

I thought a lot about that pitch, and I'd get thinking, too, about how we'd lost the year before, 1980, on the last, wet Saturday of the season. Again: one pitch, a questionable fastball, and a home run. We were neck and neck with the Phillies coming into that final weekend, and it happened that they were to play three games in Montreal. Whoever won two would be division champs.

It was a night game, and the artificial turf had been rained on. At about eleven o'clock, the game went into the eleventh inning, tied, 4–4. Stan Bahnsen was throwing for us at this point. Two out, runner on second, and up came the great Mike Schmidt. We got behind, two balls, no strikes. I wanted to stay cautious, walk him if we had to. I asked for the curve, but Bahnsen shook his head. I asked him for the slider; Stan shook his head. He wanted to throw his fastball. I didn't like it, but a catcher can't—or shouldn't—prevent a pitcher from using what he thinks is his best pitch. Stan insisted on his fastball, threw it, and Schmidt hit it out of the park. We couldn't score in the bottom of the inning, and the Phillies were division champs. A couple of weeks later, they won the World Series.

After '80 and '81, the World Series became something like an obsession. The memory of that pitch to Monday, and the one to Schmidt, wouldn't let me alone. It was getting to feel like a lifelong frustration, wanting to be part of a World Series, any World Series.

3

•

When I was in Little League, I was on an all-star team that had a chance to play its way to the Little League World Series in Williamsport, Pennsylvania. We didn't make it. Then in Pony League, same thing, a California all-star team shooting for the Pony League World Series in Williamsport. That was some summer, some team. We almost got there. We were one game, one win, from Williamsport, and got beaten.

The Expos finished third in 1982, and again in 1983. In 1984, we fell to a dismal fifth, eighteen games behind the winner. Then I was traded. I was traded for four good ballplayers—Hubie Brooks, Herm Winningham, Floyd Youmans, and Mike Fitzgerald—to the New York Mets, and suddenly I was with a contender. I was with a contender in the biggest, noisiest, most exciting city in the world. That year, 1985, we finished second, alive until the next-to-last day of the season. The city wrapped its noise and excitement around us, and in 1986 we finished first in a romp.

Some numbers from 1986:

We took the division championship on the night of September 17 with a victory over the Cubs in Shea Stadium. No team in the division had ever sewn it up this early. We finished the season with 108 wins and 54 losses, the best record in the twenty-five-year history of the team. Our nearest rivals, the Phillies, finished twenty-one and a half games behind us. The season's attendance at Shea was 2,762,417, a record for New York City. We beat the Houston Astros in the League Championship Series in six close games.

And so in my twelfth year in the major leagues, I got there: the World Series. Our young manager, Davey Johnson, had been there in his playing days, and so had four of our coaches. Our first baseman, Keith Hernandez, had played with a World Series winner in 1982. Infielder Howard Johnson had gotten there with the Detroit Tigers in 1984, but had only pinch-hit. For the rest of us Mets, it was all brand-new, a dream begun in an alley, a back yard, a dusty playground. Our opponents were the Boston Red Sox, a young team, like us. It was a good Series, a thrilling Series, and we won.

It was a dream season.

4

•

2

Our regular season ended on Sunday, October 5, in Shea Stadium, where we beat the Pittsburgh Pirates, 9–0. The win was our fifth straight and our third in a row against the Pirates. They'd been pests the year before, but this year we'd licked them seventeen times against a single loss. On June 6 in Pittsburgh we'd gotten into a brawl with them, a big one, and there wasn't any love between us.

Darryl Strawberry, twenty-four years old and tagged for greatness, hit a grand-slam home run that final Sunday. Veteran Ray Knight hit one out, and so did I. It was my 24th home run, my 105th run batted in. If I can hit 20 home runs and drive in 100 runs in a season, I'll go home figuring I've done my job.

When the game ended, the big crowd stood and cheered. The guys came up out of the dugout, and we scattered over the field and sailed our hats up into the stands. It had been Frank Cashen's idea; he's our general manager. We'd done the same thing a year ago on our own. We'd been eliminated from the race the day before, and even so the crowd had given us a standing ovation. Thank you, they were saying. Great season. So the next day we'd sent our hats into the stands. Thanks for coming, thanks for cheering. Frank wanted to thank them again, more than ever, and so did we.

The Championship Series was to begin Wednesday night out in Houston. On Monday we held a workout at Shea. It was a bright day, cool, with that autumn sharpness that gets the blood going, and we were relaxed and happy. The press had been kept out, and we were loose. We're always loose when the reporters aren't around. It's just family then. We frisked around like kids, slapped palms, talked as crazy as we wanted, and enjoyed being division champs.

The wind was blowing to left, and Dwight Gooden, the young ace of our pitching staff, hit some balls up into the wind that found their way out. Dwight had batted .086, but he's an all-around athlete and is always telling us what a terrific hitter he is. Now he was lifting them out of Shea on the back of that wind, and he was gloating like a kid. I'm gonna hit one out in the Dome, he kept threatening. Yeah, I'm gonna hit one *out.* I remember, too, rookie Kevin Mitchell hitting some bombs.

That night, we flew to Houston.

We rode a bus in to the city. As we were getting in, Keith, who was sitting up front, began wailing lines from the movie *Poltergeist*: "We're here. . . . We're back. . . ." We're back and we're going to get you was the implication. His low, spooky wail floated through the darkened bus, zany and yet carrying a message: we're going to beat you, Houston. It brought a big laugh, an appreciative laugh.

On Tuesday the Astros worked out under the Dome, and so did we. We, of course, wanted to get reacquainted with AstroTurf. Joe McIlvaine of our front office watched both sessions. He said the Astros looked tight, uneasy. The reporters were swarming around, and I wouldn't be surprised if the attention, the hype, made them nervous. Playing in New York, you get used to the carnival atmosphere, even during the regular season. The Astros weren't used to having an army of reporters nosing around. McIlvaine said we looked loose and confident. He said the comparison was like night and day.

The series should have begun in New York. A year ago, it had opened in the Western Division ball park, which meant it was the

Eastern winner's turn. But a weekend football game in the Astrodome forced us to open in Houston—and finish there, if it went six or seven games. Nice break for the Astros. They'd beaten us four out of six in the Astrodome. They are a team designed to play in that ball park. It's tough to beat the Astros under the Dome. It always has been. If there's any place I dislike playing baseball, it's the Astrodome.

I'm paid to drive in runs and hit balls over fences, and it's hard to do that in the Astrodome. The foul lines run 340 feet, and the outfield swells to 400 feet in deepest center. Death Valley. You're indoors; so there's never a breeze to push a ball out, or annoy an outfielder. And then there's the air itself, heavy somehow under that gray latticed dome, as if they'd squeezed more air in than belonged. A long ball seems to die in there. I'd hit two home runs in the Dome in '86; I really smoked both of them, and yet they barely climbed out. Glenn Davis, the Astros' first baseman, had hit a total of thirty-one, the first Astro in twenty years to hit more than thirty.

Other than Davis, the Astros were short-ball hitters. They would rap the ball off that bouncy AstroTurf, and leg out doubles and triples. Scratch a run here, a run there. And let the pitchers do the rest.

And what pitchers! Jim Deshaies. Bob Knepper. The strike-out artist Nolan Ryan, who'd been pitching as long as most of us could remember. Mike Scott, soon to be named winner of the Cy Young Award. Especially Mike Scott, who may or may not always play the game exactly according to the rules. I'll get to Scott in a bit.

The ball club said our wives could fly with us in the charter to Houston. If I could, I'd take Sandy, my beautiful and beloved wife of twelve years, on every road trip. She's not only my best friend, but we're a team. She's special. I might as well say, while I'm at it, that the days and weeks away from my three kids are as hard on me as being away from Sandy. My enthusiasm for my family—and for baseball, and other things, too—strikes some people as a bit too much. My happiness maybe crowds people a little.

7

•

Sandy and I slept late that big Wednesday. We ordered from room service and took our time over breakfast and the morning papers. They were full of that night's game. Back in July, four of our guys— Tim Teufel, Ron Darling, Rick Aguilera, and my Long Island neighbor Bobby Ojeda—had been arrested in a Houston bar after a fight with a couple of off-duty cops. This didn't endear us to the city. The newspapers resurrected the fight. They also reminded everybody that I'd accused Mike Scott, who was pitching that night, of cheating. What I'd said was: "It is the consensus around the league that Mike Scott cheats." And it was. It was the consensus around the league that he doctored the ball with sandpaper.

In the afternoon, we drove a rental car to a Steak and Ale we knew. It was quiet in the restaurant and we were left alone. It was nice being together that way. We talked some more about the game. We talked about the kids.

Sandy had taken our two-year-old, Douglas James—"D.J.," we call him—back to our off-season home in West Palm Beach, Florida, on August 5, and our girls, Christy and Kimmy, who are eight and six, followed a few weeks later. I saw the girls only once more in August, and I wouldn't see D.J. again until October 30. And *that* reunion would be short. I'd agreed to go to Japan a couple of days after the World Series with a group of ballplayers from both leagues and our wives to play some exhibition games with a Japanese all-star team. The tour was to last ten days. Davey Johnson was going to manage the Americans, and he'd asked me and Dwight Gooden to go along.

Soon, too soon, it was time for us to get back to the hotel and then to the ball park.

I rode to the Astrodome around three o'clock with my friend Mead Chasky, who lives in Queens. A lot of the guys know Mead. He's in his mid-twenties, very city-wise, and over the years he's done a lot of favors for members of the ball club. Sandy and I consider him a member of our family, a sort of kid brother. Mead was his usual cheerful self. I wasn't nervous so much as anxious to get playing, to get on with it.

8

•

It was raining. Gray sky, kind of gloomy. The parking lot attendant came out of his booth as we pulled up.

"I got Charlie Kerfeld here," Mead told him.

Kerfeld is the young oddball relief pitcher for the Astros. The
attendant didn't think this was so funny. He waved us in with a grim
smile.

Mead let me out, wished me luck, and I went through an employ-
ees' entrance and down a flight of stairs to the visitors' clubhouse.
Right away I noticed how quiet it was. I remembered: there were
no reporters allowed in the clubhouse. That was going to be the
rule, Championship Series and World Series. No press in the clubhouse pregame. They couldn't get at us till we went out to hit,
which would be at ten after six. About ten of the guys were there,
a card game was going, and the TV fed the noise of the American
League game into this strange silence.

I said hello to everybody and found my locker. My uniform, number eight, waited on a hanger. Charlie Samuels, our equipment manager, had ordered brand-new uniforms for the play-offs. Charlie takes
a lot of pride in the appearance of his ball club. The number on your
back matters; we all have our ideas, our hunches, about certain
numbers. I was born April 8, 1954. Sandy and I were married Feb-
ruary 8, 1975. When I came up with Montreal I was thinking about
number five, which was worn by the great Johnny Bench, my idol
then and always. But the Expos gave me eight, my birthday, our
wedding day, and it seemed just right.

I got out of my street clothes, pulled on shorts and a T-shirt, and
stepped into my shower shoes. Then I sat down to play casino with
Wally Backman and later with Rafael Santana. Raffy is our shortstop.
The classic shortstop: lean, swift, graceful. Wally, our second baseman, is a speed man, and a terrific bunter. We were hoping he'd lay
down a bunt or two against Scott, maybe rattle him a little. We
played cards and watched the ball game, Red Sox and California
Angels in Fenway Park. The Angels had won the night before, but
the Red Sox were getting one back today. The wind was blowing
the ball around, and everything was falling right for the Sox. It couldn't

happen in the Astrodome. We played cards and chatted off and on about the Astros, though there wasn't much new to say. The scouting reports, a sheet for every player, were laid out on the table, but we knew the Astros; we'd played them twelve games this year. As a catcher, I'd been studying most of those guys' hitting habits for years.

The first hour seemed to slip by quickly. I remember looking at the clock on the wall: 4:30, still three hours till game time. It got close to five, and I left the card game, wandered into the trainer's room and got in the whirlpool. The hot water massaged my right knee, my bad knee, pressed heat into it, loosening it. Five minutes. Then I got taped. The knee, both ankles, my left thumb. The assistant trainer, Bob Sikes, wraps them before every game.

Steve Garland is the head trainer, but Bob has been my man for as long as I've been a Met. By chance, he was available the first time I needed taping in spring training, and he's been wrapping me ever since. There's luck in those wrappings, and he knows precisely how to do it. I can't tell you how important his taping is in preventing injuries. Bob has the touch.

The knee thing goes way back. I was a quarterback in high school, and in a scrimmage my senior year I was carrying the ball and got cut down through the right knee. The ligaments were torn on the inside. They had to be operated on. The knee had been hurt again over the years. There'd been two more repair jobs, surgery, after the '84 and '85 seasons. I'd sprained some ligaments in my thumb in August, and spent two trying weeks on the disabled list. I hate wearing anything on my hands except batting gloves. I started playing with the thumb taped, then forgot the tape. Two games later, one of Dwight's fastballs had caught the thumb, and I'd almost wept from the pain. So I went back to tape. As for my ankles, they're just plain weak.

In twenty minutes Bob's job was done. I was ready for battle.

The team bus arrived, bringing everyone who hadn't found his own way to the ball park. The big clubhouse was full, but still quiet without the reporters carrying their questions around and the players gabbing back at them.

10

•

You like to get out on the field about ten minutes before batting practice. Take in the scene, get comfortable, do some stretching. It was getting close to six, finally. Time for the next private ceremony, dressing.

From the beginning: two jocks, then the cup. Catcher's precaution. Next, the stretchy white sanitary hose, tight-clinging to the knees. Then the stirrup stockings, Mets blue, a T-shirt, and the uniform.

We drifted out, down the stairs, to the rattle and crunch of cleated shoes. The crowd was thin yet. The reporters were everywhere. We take batting practice in groups of four. Each gets about twenty swings: eight, another round of six, and six more. I hit with the long-ball men: Keith, Darryl, and Ray.

Well, I felt good. Buddy Harrelson, our third-base coach, was throwing batting practice. Buddy had been down this road. He'd been the Mets' shortstop when they won the World Series in 1969, and when they lost it in 1973. Buddy was tossing those fat batting-practice pitches, and I was banging them all over the place. I felt good, I felt strong. I was excited. We hadn't played for two days, which can seem like a week.

Between swings we stood behind the cage, Mex, Straw, Ray, and I, and talked about Mike Scott. We can hit this guy, we said. Over the years I was ten for thirty-one off him, with a home run. We compared notes: Mex was twenty for fifty-three off Scott. We remembered that Wally was ten for twenty, batting .500 off the guy. We'd faced him only once this year, and it was under the Dome. He'd owned us for eight innings, two hits and no runs, and in the ninth we'd shelled him for four runs.

Hey. We can beat this guy.

Mike Scott had pitched a no-hitter against the Giants under this Dome the night the Astros became Western Division champs. He'd pitched better and better as the season came down to what we call "the stretch drive." He finished with eighteen wins and 306 strike-outs. Three hundred and six strike-outs is a very big number. It's a lot of people swinging and missing.

Scott's career record makes one of the more interesting pages of the *Baseball Register*. He used to pitch for the Mets, for one thing. The Mets traded him for Danny Heep in 1982. In his four years in New York, Scott won fourteen games and lost twenty-seven. He never struck out more than sixty-three in a season. He continued to log so-so numbers in Houston. In two years, he won fifteen, lost seventeen. He has said that he began to think he might have come to the end of the road.

He hadn't. In 1985, Mike Scott was one of the best pitchers in the game. He won eighteen, lost eight, struck out 137. What had happened? According to Scott, it was Roger Craig who provided the missing ingredient. Old Roger was a member of the original Mets in 1962; his picture, with Dwight's, was on the cover of the Mets' 1986 *Information Guide*. Roger Craig, Scott had explained, taught him to throw the split-fingered fastball. And it made a new pitcher of him.

I have hit, or tried to, a good split-fingered fastball. Bruce Sutter used it to help the Cardinals win the World Series in 1982. The pitch is what it says it is: a fastball thrown with the first two fingers splayed wide over the ball. The ball will drop, and hard. It's a nasty pitch, but it can be hit. You have to look for it in a certain zone, and hit it in that zone. What I'm saying is, you have an idea where the ball is going. You know where to be looking, more or less.

When Scott throws *his* split-fingered fastball, you don't know where it's going. It explodes—in, away, down, anywhere and everywhere. The ball is alive, unpredictable, unhittable.

I'd begun to wonder about Scott the year before, after one particular at-bat with runners at the corners. Two strikes, and he threw me a fastball that took off, and that I missed so completely that it baffled me. I'm a pretty good contact hitter, and I couldn't understand how I could swing and miss like that. (Next time I was up, he threw me a less lively one, and I hit it out of the park.) In the recent All-Star game—in Houston, coincidentally—I was catching when Scott fanned Jesse Barfield, the Toronto Blue Jays' big slugger, with a pitch that must have shot sideways four feet. Barfield took this huge wild cut and missed by a mile. Bob Feller couldn't have thrown that pitch. Or Dwight Gooden, who sends it well over ninety miles an hour and who has greatness in his arm.

I remember Steve Rogers, and how he loved to get hold of a ball that had been nicked and scuffed. Cy was a fine pitcher and an articulate man, and he didn't hesitate to say he loved a cut ball. He could make it drop, he could make it rise. A scratched-up baseball will turn certain big-league pitchers into magicians.

Right after Mike Scott threw his no-hitter against the Giants, a writer came up to me in Shea and asked me my opinion of Scott. That's when I said, "It is the consensus around the league that Mike Scott cheats." I'd heard it here, I'd heard it there. I also reminded the writer that Leon Durham, the Cubs' first baseman, had found a little piece of sandpaper near the pitcher's mound after Scott had been out there. The reporter took it all down, and out went the story. It reached Houston, of course. Gary Carter says Mike Scott scuffs the ball. The Houston fans were waiting for me. I probably ought to have thought of that and kept my mouth shut.

I'd only seen the place this full once, during the All-Star game in July. Over the years, the Astros haven't exactly packed them in. I'd played here in front of mostly thin, polite crowds, but on this night the ball park was rocking. When the cheering is for you, it's a happy sound; it gets into your blood, it strengthens you. When it's against you, it's a shrill sound, and hard to play through when the going is rough. As I say, the fans were waiting for me.

Lenny Dykstra, our little center fielder, bats lead-off. Lenny is our other speed man, and he did the reasonable thing, which was to test them with the bunt. If nothing else, it would give them something to think about. He dropped the bunt, and on that hard AstroTurf it scooted down to Davis at first, and Lenny was out. Scott walked Wally. He struck out Keith, and it was my turn.

Well, the crowd let loose on me, a real windstorm. Here we go.

13

•

Scott is a large man, expressionless on the mound. Almost sleepy-looking. He threw, the ball veered, and I swung and missed. The crowd loved it.

And already I was pressing. I wanted this so badly; wanted to win that night, and the next day and the next, wanted to get this over with and play in the World Series. I wanted to hit the ball hard—then, next time, and the next. I was all anxiousness, and I was pressing.

Scott threw me a fastball that seemed to vanish as I swung at it. I couldn't believe my eyes, and there I made another mistake. I asked the home-plate umpire, Doug Harvey, to examine the ball.

Doug Harvey. "The Lord," he's called. He's tall, with thick white hair and a face as stern as rock. He's one of the premier umpires, and he's never wrong. I mean, he knows *everything*. A pitch will come in, a ball, and Harvey will say, "That one missed by half an inch." Half an inch? What eyes! He tries to be helpful. He'll study your stance, your swing, and say, "You know, son, you're not holding your hands back enough." He calls every ballplayer "son."

So I asked Harvey, "Could you check that ball?"

The umpire has to when the hitter asks. Harvey plucked the ball out of Alan Ashby's mitt, rolled it around in his hands, offered me a quick look at it, and chucked it back to Scott. So that was that. The boos came raining down. I shook my head. Scott threw me another slippery fastball, and I waved and missed, strike three. The ovation was deafening. Take that, Carter. I'd looked bad, awful, and I walked back to the dugout shaking my head, wondering.

In the top of the second, Darryl led off, and Scott fanned him. It was about then that we realized it wasn't going to be quite as easy as it had seemed Monday in Shea Stadium, with that cocky feeling in us all and Dwight knocking balls into the seats. Darryl came back shaking *his* head. "The guy's unhittable," he said.

Dwight was pitching for us, and he, too, had brought his stuff with him. He set them down in the first, but in the second inning Davis hit a home run over the valley in left center. I didn't think he'd hit it hard enough, but the ball kept sailing. 1–0, Houston. It was Doc's only bad pitch of the night.

14

•

It worried us, but we felt we could get to Scott later. We remembered how we'd shelled him in the ninth inning in that July game, and told ourselves his magic wouldn't hold up. But he got tougher. And tougher. Guys would come back to the dugout dragging their bats, scrunching up their faces, amazed. "He's *unhittable*," they'd say. We were all saying it.

Meanwhile, Doug Harvey kept sharing his thoughts with me concerning Scott. Between hitters, during the pauses. "If this split-fingered fastball becomes an everyday pitch," said the Lord, "you're gonna find good hitters struggling just to hit .225. You're gonna find guys hitting .250 leading the league."

"Doug," I'd say, up over my shoulder, "I just don't believe it. He's got to be doing something to the ball."

And Harvey would say, "Son, I've umpired behind the plate with Scott pitching five or six times, and I've never found anything."

"I just don't believe it."

"I've never found a thing, son."

If he did find something, he'd be obliged to toss Scott out of the game. The league would be obliged to fine and maybe suspend him. Some years ago, Doug Harvey had thrown Don Sutton, then with the Dodgers, out of a ball game for using sandpaper. Now Doug kept rambling on about the greatness of Mike Scott, and I didn't buy it.

But whatever he was doing, the effect was tremendous. He struck me out again. Then I wanted it more, and pressed more. He struck me out again. The crowd ate it up.

I wasn't alone. He struck Mex out three times, Doc twice, Ray twice. He struck out fourteen in all, to set a League Championship Series record. We did scatter five harmless base hits. Lenny, Mex, Straw, Ratty, and Danny Heep, who pinch-hit for Doc in the eighth.

My last time up, all I wanted to do was put my bat on the ball. I'd been missing so badly, looking so horrible. Thinking, Is this really happening to me? I'd struck out three times in a game maybe eight, ten times in my career. I'd struck out four times only once. But Scott had baffled me, he'd embarrassed me, and I went up there in the ninth inning thinking it would be a victory if I could just hit the ball fair somewhere, anywhere. And I did. I tapped a ground ball to

Denny Walling at third base, an easy out. The crowd whooped it up, and I was done for the night.

Astros 1, Mets 0.

I had struck out four times in a game in Dodger Stadium my rookie year, 1975. It was my first game in that stadium. Talk about dreams. How many hundreds of times had my brother and I, as kids in the back alley in Fullerton, imagined playing there? That was the field of my heroes—Koufax, Wills, Parker, Drysdale, Davis. As long as I could remember, I'd wanted to play there someday—for the Dodgers, of course.

When I was in high school, Tom Lasorda, now the Dodgers' manager, was a coach for the team. His daughter went to my school, and she told him he ought to look at me. He never did see me, but he did send a scout, and the report wasn't too good. The Expos chased me pretty aggressively, though. Montreal sat at the end of

16

•

the earth, but the Expos were a new team, still struggling, and I figured my chances there were good.

Even after I'd begun playing in the Expos' minor-league system, I kept an eye on the fortunes of the Dodgers. The Expos were in the Eastern Division, the Dodgers in the Western, so I could root for them in a quiet sort of way. The old fondness persisted into 1975, until that first trip to Los Angeles.

Well, it seemed like half of Fullerton turned out to cheer the hometown boy. High-school pals, neighbors, friends of my father. There must have been 500 people from Fullerton in the stands. My father was there, of course. And Sandy. And Sandy's family. After the game, Sandy's parents were throwing a big party in honor of my homecoming.

Andy Messersmith was pitching for the Dodgers. He shut us out on three hits and fanned twelve. Four times he got me. He got me in the ninth for the last out of the game—a called strike three. I was catching, and in the sixth inning their catcher, Steve Yeager, had tried to score on a close play. He and the ball arrived at about the same time, and Yeager hit me. I went down, Yeager went down, and as I picked myself up, he gestured behind me, perhaps in anger, perhaps in apology; I never knew which. Whatever he meant by it, the crowd thought he was furious. The next thing I knew, I was being booed. Messersmith had been striking me out, I'd just been flattened, and the home crowd, Los Angeles, Fullerton, was smothering me in boos. And I was thinking, These are my hometown fans? These?

That was my first game in Dodger Stadium. Four strike-outs, boos, a dirty uniform, and a party in my honor. It was the end of something. From then on, the Dodgers were just another team. My hometown fans were in Montreal, period.

In that first game in Houston, Mike Scott made me look even worse than Messersmith had that day. I'd never felt so dominated by a pitcher. And I didn't remember ever feeling so tired. We all did. We'd played one game, a fast one at that, and we were exhausted. We were drained. There'd been this terrific intensity, as though the season rode on every pitch. The World Series was everything, but there wouldn't be any World Series if we didn't beat these Astros.

Sandy could see it. "Be yourself," she told me. "Stop pressuring yourself."

The trouble is, you go round and round. The harder you try not to press, the more you press. To think about pressing is to press. Round and round you go.

The Houston Marriott had saved us a room, a hospitality suite, for after the game. They'd laid out a buffet. There was a big-screen TV, so we could watch the coverage of the game on the late news. The team gathered, all of us with our wives and women friends, and we talked about the game, and about the next day, and watched ourselves on television. We did some drinking. It was nice, being together like that, commiserating, unwinding. Keith, who tends to be more boisterous off the field than on, went around promising everybody we'd beat Nolan Ryan the next day. Keith's nickname is Mex, though the only thing Mexican about him is his last name, and he is fond of referring to himself in the third person, as "The Mex." "The Mex," he announced that night, "says we're gonna get 'em tomorrow. The Mex says we can beat Nolan."

I would have been miserable going straight to bed. That hour with the team took away the mean taste of the game. It made all the difference. These guys, the 1986 Mets, were tied together not just by winning, but by the luck of chemistry. We liked each other; in a way, we loved each other.

I slept like a champ.

3

I love my wife and children, I love God, and I love playing baseball. Like any ballplayer, I love to hear the cheers. I'm thirty-three, and my teammates call me "Kid." It's been my nickname for years. It comes naturally to people; they see me that way. Kids are enthusiastic. They're happy.

They started calling me "Kid" during spring training in 1973, my first major-league spring-training camp, a couple of years before I jumped to the majors. I got into some hotel card games with some of the big guys, the stars. I remember Mike Torrez, the big right-handed pitcher, playing cards and saying, "Kid, why don't you run down and get us some ice cream?" I was a kid, all right, excited just playing cards with Mike Torrez, Ken Singleton, and Tim Foli. I'd charge out of there and fetch that ice cream. The nickname stuck.

I'm happy, and it's written all over me. As I've said, it crowds people a little. In Montreal, some of my teammates called me Teeth. For my smile. Always happy, they said. How can you be so happy? There's no *way* you can be that happy.

But there was.

I was playing baseball. I was making good money. In 1977, I signed a multi-year contract, and Sandy and I bought a house in Montreal. I enrolled in a Berlitz class and learned some French. After the

Expos finished second in 1979, endorsements started coming: Gillette, 7-Up, Chrysler Canada, Dominion Textile, and Warner Lambert. Some of my teammates, who weren't getting the calls, resented it.

I'd go into the clubhouse, and certain guys would glance at me and stop talking. Andre Dawson. Tim Raines. Steve Rogers. Warren Cromartie. Ellis Valentine. Complaints about me were in the air, spoken behind my back. Camera Carter, they said. Performs for the camera, the TV networks, Game of the Week. Put him on Game of the Week, and then he'll have a big game.

Many American ballplayers dislike playing in Canada. The dollar is weaker up there, and taxes are higher. The language difference causes confusion sometimes; the ballplayers feel the Canadians are being rude to them. And the weather—especially in the winter—can be brutal. About eighty percent of any crowd in Olympic Stadium is French-speaking; they yell in French, they even *cheer* in French. The newspapers are in French. Most of my teammates couldn't wait to go home. They wouldn't set foot back in Montreal till April. "Can you *believe* this country?" they'd say.

They'd ask me, "Do you like it here?"

I'd say, "Yeah. I think it's great."

They didn't like that. "Come *on*. You crazy?"

I got all the endorsements, they said, and I got all the attention. The endorsements were recent, but the attention went back to '75, the year I arrived. The Expos had been in existence only since 1969, and after the '74 season the front office decided the time had come to gather in the young ballplayers who had been developing in the Expos' minor-league system. Older guys who'd been drafted to form the original team were let go to make room for us kids. That year, 1975, the Expos went young. They called it Phase Two. Larry Parrish. Pepe Mangual. Pete Mackanin. Bombo Rivera. Me. Our manager was Gene Mauch, "The Little General." He was a disciplinarian, tough but fair, and I loved playing for him. Jim Fanning, the general manager, spoke glowingly of us. He predicted brilliant futures for us and the team. My name was often the first off his tongue.

Attention? Sure. If a reporter asks me a question, I answer him. It's his job, and cooperating with him goes with mine. If a kid asks me for an autograph, I give it to him. That, too, goes with the territory. My first two years with the Expos were played in an old minor-league ball park called Jarry Park. Our records those years were as dreary as the ball park: 75–87, 55–107. Then we moved to Olympic Stadium, site of the 1976 Olympics, and in this more glamorous setting, our fortunes improved. The locker assigned to me in Olympic Stadium was beside the clubhouse door; I was the first guy you saw when you walked in. I began to hear mutterings about this, as if I were a schoolboy choosing a desk at the front of the room, insisting on attention. Finally, before the 1984 season, I moved. I chose a locker in a far corner, invisible from the clubhouse door. If reporters wanted to talk to me, they had to find me. And they did.

Some of the guys, friends, told me they were sorry. They said it was unbelievable how hard some of the feelings were. They said some of those guys hated me.

I made other enemies. When I came to the Mets, some of the guys told me straight out they hadn't liked me. Bill Robinson, the first-base and hitting coach, broke it down in basic English: "I thought you were an asshole." "Uncle Bill," we call him. He and I are good friends now. Davey Johnson compared me to his Baltimore Orioles teammate Frank Robinson. Robinson played hard, he played aggressively, and he aroused a lot of dislike among opponents. He found ways and more ways to win. Davey said Robinson's teammates loved him.

I play hard. I love it. I'm grateful. I smile. That's how it is.

We won nothing during my years with the Expos except the one division championship, and a lot of the blame was thrown on my shoulders. I'd been called a "franchise player," and as the years without a pennant piled up, my detractors could say: "Carter's not a winner." All the envy could be expressed in that complaint: Carter's not a winner.

It was a bad rap, and I lived for the time when I could prove I was a winner. How many ways, for how many reasons, did I want to win this Championship Series with the Astros? Dozens. Hundreds. The reasons weighed on me; they sat heavy on my back. I felt them, and I pressed.

We had to win game two. We couldn't return to New York 0–2, especially with Mike Scott certain to pitch one of the three games in Shea. It was odd: we won the series in six games, and yet we were continually facing games we had to win. Mex, in his relaxed, postgame mood, had assured us we could beat Ryan. We knew we could. We also knew it wouldn't be easy.

Who wouldn't admire Nolan Ryan? Thirty-nine years old, and throwing the ball ninety-five miles an hour. Throwing like a strapping kid. The bullet fastball, and a good curve besides. I was first on a field with him in the 1979 All-Star game, when he was with the California Angels. He threw hard that day. Guys kept talking about how hard he was throwing. They say that his right elbow, his throwing elbow, is like a time bomb waiting to blow. They say that sometime, some pitch, it will give out.

The previous January, I'd gone to Honduras with Ryan. Vice President George Bush had invited us to promote baseball and good feeling between the two countries. We spent three days down there. We attended some official ceremonies, which included the inauguration of President Azcona, and taught some baseball clinics. There was a reception at the American ambassador's residence. Ryan was quite interested in the country's politics and economics. He owns a cattle ranch, and he inquired about selling cattle in Honduras. He's a nice man, a quiet man, who wears his fame easily.

We faced Ryan in the second game of the Championship Series, and got lucky. These days, you can hope he'll tire after seven innings or so. He's thirty-nine, after all. It was the opposite when he was young: he threw harder after seven. You beat him early or not at all. In game two, he left after five, losing 5–0.

Our pitcher was Bobby Ojeda. Bobby O. had been traded from

the Red Sox in the off-season, and surprised some folks, especially the Red Sox, by winning eighteen games, the most of anybody on our pitching staff. He's a lefty. He's a finesse pitcher: in, out, keep them guessing. Stick a fastball close when they're looking for the change of pace. On this night, Bobby O. was putting the ball exactly where he wanted.

We didn't score till the fourth. Twelve innings without a run. In the second inning, Ryan struck me out. Five at-bats, four strike-outs: it was like some crazy, sweaty dream. In my other Championship Series, '81, I'd hit over .400.

In the top of the fourth inning, Wally slapped a ground ball into center field—base hit. Mex swung and missed twice, then pushed a hit over second base off the thin end of his bat. My turn. Ryan threw me ball one, and I guessed fastball and got one. You have to guess some in this game. The fastball was away, and I stepped out to it, hit it hard. Home run, I thought. Good chance, at least. Then I saw Kevin Bass and Billy Hatcher, the outfielders, beelining toward the wall, and my heart fell. But the ball struck the wall in right center, high, caromed back as I pounded down to second base. Wally hesitated, then scored. Mex held up but made it to third. The ice was broken. All *right*, I thought. I'd broken out of it. I felt twenty pounds lighter. It's over, I thought.

It wasn't. Not for me.

Straw hit a fly ball deep enough to get Mex home. Next inning, Raffy, Lenny, and Wally sprayed singles, and Mex hit one over Hatcher's glove into Death Valley, a triple. I hit a fly ball to Hatcher, stranding Mex. 5–0.

Bobby O. took care of the rest. He allowed ten hits and was touched for a run in the seventh when Phil Garner hit an RBI single. We relaxed, became confident again: the game was ours. It was the only time in the series we were to feel in control. We never did in the World Series, even when we were winning big.

Mets 5, Astros 1.

And so back to New York.

◆   ◆   ◆

◆

THURSDAY, OCT. 9 at HOUSTON

METS (5)	ab	r	h	bi	HOUSTON (1)	ab	r	h	bi
Dykstra cf	5	1	2	0	Hatcher cf	5	1	1	0
Backman 2b	5	2	2	1	Doran 2b	4	0	1	0
Hernandez 1b	3	1	2	2	Garner 3b	3	0	1	1
Carter c	5	0	1	1	Davis 1b	4	0	1	0
Strawberry rf	3	0	0	1	Bass rf	3	0	2	0
Wilson lf	4	0	1	0	Cruz lf	4	0	1	0
Knight 3b	3	0	1	0	Ashby c	4	0	0	0
Santana ss	4	0	1	0	Thon ss	4	0	2	0
Ojeda p	4	1	0	0	Ryan p	1	0	0	0
					Pankovits ph	1	0	0	0
					Andersen p	0	0	0	0
					Puhl ph	1	0	1	0
					Lopez p	0	0	0	0
					Kerfeld p	0	0	0	0
					Lopes ph	1	0	0	0
	36	5	10	5		35	1	10	1

Mets	000 230 000	—	5	10	0
Houston	000 000 100	—	1	10	2

E—Hatcher, Davis. DP—Mets 2, Houston 1. LOB—Mets 8, Houston 9. 2B—Bass, Carter, Dykstra. 3B—Hernandez. SB—Wilson (1). SF—Strawberry. Game-Winning RBI—Carter (1).

	IP	H	R	ER	BB	SO
Mets						
Ojeda (W, 1-0)	9	10	1	1	2	5
Houston						
Ryan (L, 0-1)	5	7	5	5	0	5
Andersen	2	1	0	0	1	2
Lopez	1 1-3	2	0	0	2	1
Kerfeld	2-3	0	0	0	0	0

T—2:40. A—44,391.

Like any ballplayer, I love to hear the cheers. I love the feel of the noise in my blood. When you're deep in a game, concentrating, studying and studying a pitcher, then the noise recedes, but you still know it's there.

Shea Stadium, Opening Day, 1985. My first official game as a New York Met. Big, rambunctious crowd. With the score tied in the bottom of the tenth inning, I hit a home run, winning it for us, and about the time I danced across the plate, people began chanting my name. Ga-*ree*, Ga-*ree*. I'd never heard that before. In the dugout the guys slapped hands with me and pounded my back, while above, all around, the cheering continued. The crowd stood, insisting, and I bounced up into the April sunlight and waved. The air was thick with cheers. In my ten years with Montreal I'd had exactly one curtain call, and that was on a day I hit three home runs. Now, finally, the crowd began to melt down the runways, but I could still hear them— Ga-*ree*, Ga-*ree*—through the concrete tunnels of Shea.

That day, April 9, 1985, started something. From then on, whenever any of us hit one into the seats, the crowd would bring us back out of the dugout. They insisted: they wouldn't sit, wouldn't be quiet, till we showed ourselves. In more staid days, I used to acknowledge an ovation with a tip of the hat, but the Shea fans wanted more, and gave more. In time, I was answering the ovations with a raised fist. In time, I was bounding up out of the dugout, pumping the fist three times: toward left field, home plate, right field. Thank you, thank you, thank you.

As the 1986 season wore on, there was more and more talk about our curtain calls. Opposing players complained that we were rubbing it in, showing them up. They called us arrogant. It was said that we were the most hated team in the game. My name kept popping up. Some said that of all the Mets I was the worst offender, the biggest showboat, the most hated.

Toward the end of the season, *Sports Illustrated* conducted a poll among players as to who they thought was the league's most valuable player. Soon after we'd played the Giants in San Francisco, the magazine polled the Giants. One of them—they were anonymous— was asked about me. It was pointed out to him that I was leading the league in game-winning hits. His answer: "I wouldn't vote for Gary Carter for MVP if he had *162* game-winning hits."

It surprised me. I hadn't noticed any animosity toward me among the Giants. I don't try to insult anybody, but I can't help the way I play baseball. The raised fist, the smile, are sheer happiness. They're celebration. We won 108 games in 1986, and there was hardly a day when one of us didn't have something to celebrate.

After my double against Nolan Ryan in game two in Houston, I thought I'd broken the slump. I thought I'd thrown off all the pressure. I should have, I guess. But I couldn't help thinking that I had

had only one hit in six times at bat, and that a couple more quick hits would turn it respectable. One for six, I kept remembering, and I was still pressing. I might have been all right, even so, with a little more luck. After Mex hit his triple, I hit the ball pretty sharply, but to Hatcher in center field. I came up later with runners on first and second, a chance to do some big damage, and hit a fly ball to Hatcher. I hit that one pretty well, too. One for eight. *Again* I batted with runners on first and second, and this time Charlie Kerfeld got me to hit into a double play. One for nine. It went round and round in my head. And all those chances to drive in runs, to help, and I'd left them on the bases.

Saturday, October 11, was a bright, breezy day in New York. More good fall weather. Bob Knepper was pitching for the Astros, and Ron Darling, the handsome Yale man, was pitching for us. "R.J.," we call him. Shea was, of course, packed. By the usual reckoning, we were in an excellent position. We'd split with the Astros in their ball park and had come home to play three.

But it wasn't so simple. Over this game stretched the long shadow of Mike Scott. He was pitching the next day.

Mike Scott, Mike Scott. He'd been unbeatable in Houston. Maybe we could beat him here, maybe not. One thing we didn't want: we didn't want to *have* to beat him. We didn't want our survival to depend on it. And if we lost this game, we'd be behind, two games to one, and would *have* to win the next one.

The Astros drew first blood, quite a bit of it. Two in the first, two in the second. In that first inning, they didn't hit the ball hard, but they hit it often. The little base hits mounted up. Two runs. In their second, Craig Reynolds punched a single, and Billy Doran hit a home run. Score: 4–0.

We couldn't help wondering if we were about to get shelled in our own ball park. The immediate big question was whether to leave R.J. in the game. Davey did, and Ronnie started getting them out. Later, he said he'd been pumped way up, too high, in the beginning. After five, Davey took him out for a pinch hitter.

4–0: the game rode along like that till the sixth.

I was still having my troubles. First time up, I hacked a ground ball to shortstop, a low pitch, nice pitch by Knepper. I should have left it alone. One for ten. Then I hit one to right center, which Bass gloved on the gallop. One for eleven. It began to seem very possible that I wouldn't get another hit in this entire series. One for what? Twenty-five? Thirty?

Knepper was masterful through five. Then in our sixth, two out, Kevin Mitchell singled. Mex singled. I was up once more with men on base. This time I swung over Knepper's pitch and rolled one to Reynolds—under his glove, through his legs, error shortstop. One for twelve, but Kevin charged home, and it was 4 – 1.

Straw was up. Knepper still seemed in command, but he threw a fastball over the plate that Straw blasted for a home run. He glided around the bases, in no hurry, and the crowd threw down the usual deafening ovation. One pitch, and the game was tied.

The Astros grabbed the lead again in their seventh. Doran, a good, scrappy ballplayer, got another hit. Then Hatcher tapped a ground ball to Ray at third; Ray scooped it, dropped it, snatched and pegged it over Mex's head. Doran scored.

Astros 5, Mets 4.

Knepper pitched a runless seventh. Jesse Orosco took over for Rick Aguilera and pitched a runless eighth. Hal Lanier then summoned young Charles Kerfeld to the mound.

Kerfeld. He's a goofy-looking guy—wide, baby face behind glasses, cheek pushed way out with a big chaw. He's a big boy—six feet five, 245 pounds. On the mound he acts up, talking, frowning, squirting tobacco. Eccentric. He can throw hard, though.

Kerfeld blew us away in that eighth inning, one-two-three. While he was at it, he got me good and mad. I hit a ground ball behind him, one bounce, as he was following through. I hit it pretty well, actually, and Kerfeld, off balance, reached behind his big body, stabbed with the glove, and snared the ball—all in the sliver of a second. He was surprised, and so was I. I'd barely left the batter's box. With all the time in the world, he offered me a look at the ball before he tossed it to first. He held it out as if to say, "Here it is. See it?" Finally, he lobbed it to first. One for thirteen. *What do I have to do to get a base hit?* I thought.

27

•

The guys made sure I'd seen Kerfeld's stunt.

"You see that, Kid?"

"See it?"

"I saw it," I said.

Afterward, Kerfeld said he was only showing the ball to his catcher. He said he'd been so surprised he'd caught it, he thought he'd better show it to Ashby. Baloney.

J.O. set them down, no runs, in their ninth. And now Lanier pulled Kerfeld out and brought on Dave Smith. Odd decision, in a way. Smith had thirty-three saves and was their main guy in the bullpen. But Kerfeld had disposed of us easily in the eighth. Why not leave him in there, at least till he pitched into some trouble? We were surprised, but not at all sorry to be rid of Kerfeld.

No one was forgetting that Mike Scott was pitching the next day.

Wally, who had come into the game late, led off against Smith. He bunted. He nudged it down the first-base line; Davis took it, lunged to tag Wally, who flew by, twisting to avoid the tag. Safe. Dutch Rennert was working first base, and the Astros said he'd blown the call, said Wally had circled out of the base line. Lanier shot out of the dugout, hollering. Smith was furious. It had been a tough call: Wally had veered, but not by much. Rennert wouldn't budge, of course. It was a big play, a big call. In my opinion the whole series turned on that bunt by Wally Backman.

Now Davey sent Danny up to hit for Raffy. Wally ran with the pitch; Danny hit a ground ball. The play was to first. Tying run on second.

Lenny's turn. He had also entered the game late.

Little Lenny. Nails. Lenny bounced back and forth between Tidewater and New York early in 1985, and came up to stay July 1. Soon afterward a reporter was interviewing him for one of the New York papers. Lenny told him with a straight face that he, Lenny, was already pulling fans into Shea Stadium. Why? "I play this game tough as nails," he said. Nails: the nickname stuck, with a little help from Lenny. The guys like Lenny; so do a lot of women, though Lenny's happily married. At least one woman didn't know that or didn't care. She turned up at a game in Shea this year decked out in

28

•

a wedding dress and carrying an enormous sign: MARRY ME, LENNY. He receives a lot of mail from adoring young women. "Chicks," he says. "I get all these letters from chicks." He's cute is why. The curly yellow hair, the sunshine smile. Huckleberry Finn. To some, even his tobacco chaw is cute.

Little Lenny. He had a good swing at Smith's first pitch, and fouled it off. A good swing means a hard swing, in plenty of time; a good swing will spoil a pitcher's best pitch, if only by fouling it back. Sometimes a foul to the backstop is a hitter's victory. Lenny had a good swing.

Next pitch, he had a better one.

You don't expect Lenny to hit the long ball. He'd hit eight home runs all year. Now Smith laid it in there, and Nails whacked it—high and deep. There was a pause, then bedlam as the ball arced over the right-field fence and into the bullpen. Home run, and the game.

Wally Backman leaped about ten feet in the air, arms raised. Lenny did the same. The noise was deafening. We swarmed out to greet him at the plate, smothering him. One of the littlest guys on the team had just hit one of the season's very biggest home runs. Awesome.

Mets 6, Astros 5.

SATURDAY, OCT. 11 at SHEA

HOUSTON (5)	ab	r	h	bi
Doran 2b	4	2	2	2
Hatcher cf	3	1	2	0
Walling 3b	5	1	1	2
Davis 1b	3	0	1	0
Bass rf	3	0	0	0
Cruz lf	3	0	1	1
Ashby c	4	0	0	0
Reynolds ss	2	1	1	0
Lopes ph	1	0	0	0
Kerfeld p	0	0	0	0
Smith p	0	0	0	0
Knepper p	3	0	0	0
Thon ss	1	0	0	0
	32	5	8	5

METS (6)	ab	r	h	bi
Wilson cf	4	0	0	0
Mitchell lf	4	1	2	0
Orosco p	0	0	0	0
Hernandez 1b	4	1	2	0
Carter c	4	1	0	0
Strawberry rf	4	1	2	3
Knight 3b	4	0	1	0
Teufel 2b	3	0	0	0
Backman 2b	1	1	1	0
Santana ss	3	0	0	0
Heep ph	1	0	0	0
Darling p	1	0	0	0
Mazzilli ph	1	0	1	0
Aguilera p	0	0	0	0
Dykstra cf	2	1	1	2
	36	6	10	5

Houston	220 000 100	—	5 8 1
Mets	000 004 002	—	6 10 1

One out when winning run scored

E—Reynolds, Knight. DP—Mets 1. LOB—Houston 7, Mets 5. HR—Doran (1), Strawberry (1), Dykstra (1). SB—Hatcher 2 (3), Bass (2). S—Hatcher. Game-Winning RBI Dykstra (1).

	IP	H	R	ER	BB	SO
Houston						
Knepper	7	8	4	3	0	3
Kerfeld	1	0	0	0	0	1
Smith (L, 0-1)	1-3	2	2	2	0	0
Mets						
Darling	5	6	4	4	2	5
Aguilera	2	1	1	0	2	1
Orosco (W, 1-0)	2	1	0	0	1	2

HBP—Davis by Darling. WP—Darling. PB—Ashby 2. T—2:55. A—55,052.

29

♦

On Sunday night, October 12, Mike Scott beat us again in game four.

He struck out five, nine fewer than he had in Houston. We managed only three hits, but we did nick him for a run. He was tremendous, but not quite as dominant as he'd been in Houston. Not quite.

When a used or damaged ball comes out of a game, the home team holds on to it. That night we saved some of the balls Scott had been throwing. We had about twelve, and they all had round, half-dollar-sized scuffs. These little scratchy shadows were all alike. Davey gave the balls to Chub Feeney, the league president, and asked him to please inspect them. Feeney did, and said that the balls had all been bruised in normal play, skidding on dirt or striking the plate. He said he'd seen balls that looked like that.

Sid Fernandez pitched for us. He's from Hawaii. We call him "Duke" or "Dukey," after the great Hawaiian surfer Duke Kahanamoku. Duke, who's very young, seldom shakes off my signs. I call a pitch; Duke throws it, no questions asked. He was brilliant in the World Series, but on this night, in their second, Davis fisted a hit to right. Duke struck out Bass and Cruz. Ashby batted. He lifted a slow, high foul ball off third base. The ball club had extended the grandstand by a couple of rows for the postseason games, seats and a flimsy makeshift barrier encroaching on the playing field. Ray got over there and waited for Ashby's pop fly. Raffy was also following the ball. He yelled for it, Ray ducked, and Raffy stabbed and missed. The ball fell into the first row. Ray could have gloved it. Either could have if those new seats hadn't been there. I mention it because on the next pitch Ashby busted a home run. Duke was still in there in the fifth when Dickie Thon hit one over the fence in left, making it 3–0.

Our bottom of the order got us a run in the eighth. Mookie Wilson legged out an infield hit, took second *and* third on a ground-ball out, and scored when Danny hit a fly ball to Bass. Mookie's hustle got us that run, our only one against Scott. Roger McDowell threw a couple of perfect innings in relief. Doug Sisk added a runless inning.

Scott kept my personal nightmare going. My second time up, the quick Lenny was on second base, meaning just about any kind of hit would be a run. Scott struck me out. I also made the last out of the

30

•

game, a fly ball to Hatcher. Worrying about falling behind on the count, I hit the first pitch. Scott now owned the record for Championship Series strike-outs—nineteen. If there was a seventh game, he would pitch again.

I was now one for seventeen. I'd struck out five times. I'd made the last out in game three, and I hate making the last out, any time.

Astros 3, Mets 1.

SUNDAY, OCT. 12 at SHEA

HOUSTON (3)	ab	r	h	bi		METS (1)	ab	r	h	bi
Doran 2b	4	0	0	0		Dykstra cf	4	0	1	0
Hatcher cf	4	0	0	0		Backman 2b	4	0	0	0
Garner 3b	3	0	0	0		Hernandez 1b	4	0	0	0
Walling 3b	1	0	1	0		Carter c	4	0	0	0
Davis 1b	3	1	1	0		Strawberry rf	3	0	0	0
Bass rf	3	0	0	0		Wilson lf	3	1	1	0
Cruz lf	4	0	0	0		Knight 3b	3	0	1	0
Ashby c	3	1	1	2		Santana ss	2	0	0	0
Thon ss	3	1	1	1		Heep ph	0	0	0	1
Scott p	3	0	0	0		Sisk p	0	0	0	0
						Fernandez p	1	0	0	0
						Mazzilli ph	1	0	0	0
						McDowell p	0	0	0	0
						Johnson ph	1	0	0	0
						Elster ss	0	0	0	0
	31	3	4	3			30	1	3	1

Houston _____ 020 010 000 — 3 4 1
Mets _____ 000 000 010 — 1 3 0

E—Scott. LOB—Houston 3, Mets 3. 2B—Walling. HR—Ashby (1), Thon (1). SB—Backman (1). SF—Heep. Game-Winning RBI — Ashby (1).

	IP	H	R	ER	BB	SO
Houston						
Scott (W, 2-0)	9	3	1	1	0	5
Mets						
Fernandez (L, 0-1)	6	3	3	3	1	5
McDowell	2	0	0	0	0	1
Sisk	1	1	0	0	1	0

T—2:23. A—55,038.

Thinking about Mike Scott reminds me of Rick Rhoden, another guy with unusual pitches. Bill Robinson was Rhoden's teammate with the Pirates in his playing days. He told us Rhoden likes to use sandpaper. Now, when Rhoden pitched against us, Uncle Bill would needle him from his coach's box. He would rag him about cheating, try to break up his concentration. On June 6, in Pittsburgh, he accused Rhoden point-blank, and moments later the two teams were brawling.

Rhoden was beating us. We lost one game to the Pirates all year, and this was it. The year before, they'd finished last, and yet we were ten and eight against them. We were seven and five against the Giants, who finished last in the Western Division, and I can't help thinking we might have won a championship if we'd played better against the two cellar teams.

Here was our bad game against the Pirates, with Rhoden operating on the ball. I was at bat when the fuss broke out. Mex was at first. The game wasn't yet out of reach; I had a chance to get something rolling. Billy Williams was working the plate. Suddenly Uncle Bill let out a whistle through his teeth. We looked down there, and he was pointing at Rhoden.

"Check the ball," he said. He'd seen something.

I got out of the batter's box and asked Williams to look at the ball. Rhoden lobbed it in to his catcher, Tony Peña. The throw fell short. Williams picked it up out of the dust by my feet. Peña just waited. Williams stuck his mask under his arm and stared at the ball. You could see the half-dollar scuff.

"*Look* at it," I said to Williams. "You can *see* it, Billy."

The crowd started getting noisy. There weren't many people—there never are in Pittsburgh these days—but they were boisterous. It was me they were yelling at. I don't think they realized that Robinson had begun this whole thing. They were giving it to me. It was like that first championship game in Houston. I swear I'm going to keep my mouth shut from now on.

Jim Leland, the Pirates' manager, began to holler from the dugout. Davey was yelling too. Check the pitcher, Davey was saying. Check Rhoden. Leland jumped up and came scurrying toward Williams. Look at the ball, Williams told him. He showed it to Leland. Leland said he didn't see anything unusual about it. *Check Rhoden,* Davey was yelling.

Williams did. He marched out there, with Leland trailing behind.

The booing swelled. Rhoden, of course, played dumb. Williams inspected his glove and could find nothing. He dug a new ball out of his pocket and handed it to Rhoden. He should have bounced him out of the game. If he'd found anything, a tack, sandpaper, he would have been forced to.

But Rhoden stayed. Leland sat down, and Williams got the game rolling again. I was distracted and irritated, and Rhoden struck me out. The fans went crazy. It sounded like 50,000 people who couldn't have enjoyed anything more than seeing me strike out. The Pirates headed in. Rhoden strolled off the mound.

Uncle Bill had thrown the heat onto me, which was fine, except that this wasn't an ordinary year, or an ordinary team, and he isn't an ordinary first-base coach. So as Rhoden and he passed each other, Uncle Bill said: "Quit cheatin'."

Rhoden gave him a look.

"Quit cheatin'," said Uncle Bill. "We know you do."

Rhoden told Uncle Bill to screw himself.

Bill swung at him. Rhoden swung back. The dugouts poured Mets and Pirates, and the brawl was on, guys wrestling, swinging, piling on each other. In waded big Kevin Mitchell, who learned how to fight in the streets of San Diego and whose brother was killed in a street gang war. We call Kevin "World"—my idea, actually—because he can play any position, just about. Anywhere in the field, all over the world. World is our enforcer. I saw Sammy Khalifa whaling away at somebody, and suddenly World had locked an arm around Khalifa's neck. Khalifa could hardly breathe. I was in the middle of it, not fighting but trying to haul people away from each other. It's like trying to put out a brush fire: you stop it one place and right away it's burning someplace else.

The umpires did eventually talk everybody off the field. Uncle Bill was ejected and fined. Rhoden stayed, and beat us, 7–1. It was our second brawl in eleven days. There would be two more before the season was over. No, we weren't liked around the league, and I don't know why it kept surprising me. You'd think I'd have learned. This winter, Rhoden was traded to the New York Yankees. I didn't shed any tears. He's always given me trouble, with or without sand-paper.

While I'm on the subject, I should mention the Sarge, Gary Matthews.

Matthews is a good, good ballplayer. He's what is known as a "gamer," which means he gives his all, he plays with a certain courage.

I admired the man, and was puzzled when he tried to hurt me in a couple of collisions at home plate. These collisions are part of baseball; if I'm between you and the plate, you don't circle around me, you come through me. If I've got the ball, you try to jolt it loose. You hit me. But don't go extra to hurt me. I've slid hard into second base a million times. I've cut shortstops' legs out from under them. The idea is to prevent the double play. I've never tried to hurt anybody. Never.

Matthews was with the Phillies in 1981 when we won the second half of the strike-divided season and played them for the division championship. There was a play at the plate, Matthews running, me blocking, and he just blasted me. He cracked me on the temple with an elbow; my helmet went sailing. It took me an inning or so to shake the cobwebs out of my head.

A couple of years later, still with the Phillies, Matthews came home on another close play and hit me like a torpedo. He knocked me for a loop. I got up slowly and looked at him in disbelief, not anger. It made no sense. My helmet had flown in the direction of the Phillies' dugout, and as I trudged to fetch it, Matthews started hollering at me. "You want me? Come on, man. Come on." I didn't want him. I wanted my helmet. I believe he thought I was coming to fight him, and this seemed to be just what he wanted.

There were no apologies later. Most guys will speak to you after a home-plate collision, maybe give you a pat on the butt. "Hey, you okay?" they'll say. Or, "Way to be in there." I frequently say a word after I've taken a guy down at second base. You want to remind them it isn't personal.

Gary Matthews never mentioned these terrific crashes we'd had. I said hello a couple of times when he arrived to hit—I'll do that— but Matthews paid no attention. I stopped speaking to him. One time, I thought he started to apologize, when he was with the Cubs, but then he just said, "Aw, forget it."

Sports Illustrated spoke to Matthews when they were taking that MVP poll. He went on the record, unlike that guy with the Giants. "Gary and I have had our differences," he said. "We don't get along, but how can you not admire the guy? If I had to vote for MVP, yes, I'd vote for him." A pause, and then, as if he hadn't meant to go quite that far, he said: "Of course, Stevie Wonder could catch that pitching staff."

4

My mother, Inge, died of leukemia in the springtime of 1966, when I was twelve. She was thirty-seven. It was quick—six months. She was sick, was all I knew. Kids can understand illness, but death is something else again. "Mom, I love you and I'll see you soon," I said as she was leaving for the hospital for, as it turned out, the last time. I thought I *would* see her soon; I couldn't get my mind around the other idea. And then she was dead.

So it was me, Gordy, and our father alone in the house. We managed all right. I learned to wash the clothes and vacuum the floor. Gordy was four years older than I was, a fine athlete, and he got the admiration that comes with it in high school. He was no slouch at anything, as far as I could see, and I was an adoring kid brother. I was also a big kid brother, and advanced as an athlete; so Gordy let me play baseball with him and his pals. Sports bound us, kept us close. And close to our father, as well. He, too, lived and breathed sports, especially baseball. He was my Little League coach, then my Pony coach. Five, ten times a summer he took Gordy and me to Dodger Stadium. It was a good life in that house with its back alley full of dreams.

Later, our father remarried, and we moved. Gordy was at the University of Southern California by then, playing baseball for the

37

legendary Rod Dedeaux. I was in tenth grade. Our new stepmother had three daughters, and they all moved in. I got used to it, more or less. I had a small bedroom downstairs, apart from the women. I turned more and more to my games, my ambitions. That second marriage began happily, but lasted less than ten years.

For a time, I thought football might be my future. I was high-school All-American as a sophomore and as a junior. I loved the emotion of the game. That feeling of proving yourself. I couldn't play my senior year because of the knee injury, but more than a hundred big colleges offered me football scholarships. UCLA courted me hard, and I actually signed a letter of intent. The coach who courted me, Dick Tomey, is still a good friend. He's now the head football coach at the University of Hawaii and also a good friend of Sid Fernandez. Small world. But I signed with the Expos five days after graduation. I wanted to get away from home for a while.

All of this is leading to Gordy. Gordy was the baseball player in the family. I was a three-sport athlete and a hotshot football player; baseball was Gordy's turf. Because he was older, I was safely behind him—in baseball, at least.

I caught up with him in basketball when I was about twelve. Out in the alley. If we weren't playing baseball after school, we'd go straight out in the alley to shoot baskets. Often it was just me and Gordy, and we would go at it—one on one, alley ball, drive and shoot. Gordy always won. Then I turned twelve and was suddenly as tall as he was. I was a big boy. And I started beating him. Suddenly I was competition. I beat him a little too often, and he stopped playing basketball. They were angry games, but I never had a real fight, a punching fight, with my brother.

Gordy meanwhile was playing great baseball, and when he was a high-school senior, the California Angels drafted him in the second round. They offered him good money. But he thought he had plenty of time, and he went to USC to get educated and to play for the famous coach, Dedeaux. It was a marvelous team. Steve Busby pitched. Dave Kingman slugged home runs. They won two national championships. Gordy was their center fielder, but in his third year Fred Lynn arrived. From then on, Gordy shared center field with

38

◆

Lynn, platooning. Gordy didn't like it. USC left a bad taste in his mouth. After that season, he made the leap and signed with the San Francisco Giants.

The Giants assigned him to their class A team in Fresno in January 1972. I was drafted by the Expos in the June 1972 draft.

Now I'd always followed in my brother's footsteps. I admired him, and did what he did. The difference was, baseball was his sport, and football was mine. Gordy had gone to college to play his sport, and we both more or less assumed I would go to college to play mine. But the Expos' offer was good, and I wondered if my bad knee could hold up against the punishment of big-time college football. I took the plunge, and signed with the Expos. Gordy was with Fresno, and suddenly I was a professional baseball player too. I'd entered his territory, and for once I'd broken my pattern of following in his steps. It surprised him.

That year, in June '72, I played rookie-league ball for part of the season, and then the Expos sent me to West Palm Beach, class A, same level as Gordy. I hit .320 in twenty games with West Palm, and the following year the Expos pulled me up a level, Quebec City, double A.

In '73, I was invited to my first big-league spring-training camp; the reason was that I was a catcher. Gordy was an outfielder. And while I was in double A in '73, Gordy was still in class A in Fresno. I was called up to triple A later in the '73 season. Before the beginning of the '74 season, Gordy decided to leave baseball. The Giants refused to meet his salary request. He said at his age it didn't make sense to wait any longer. He felt overlooked, and he retired, just like that. He went into the restaurant business in Southern California.

It wasn't easy for Gordy. We'd been competing ever since we could throw a ball. Distance grew between us. By '75 I was in the major leagues, Gordy's little brother, and he was running a restaurant. We didn't see each other much, but when we did, Gordy would eventually start talking about ballplayers' salaries. Free agency had come in a couple of years after Gordy left baseball, and he couldn't get over how much ballplayers were making now. He'd go on and on about it. "I can't believe it," he'd say. "I can't believe the money these guys are making." He never mentioned *my* salary, but maybe it was my salary he was griping about. It was bitterness talking, and maybe plain bad luck, and I don't blame Gordy.

I've often wished he'd let his feelings out, talk about them rather than keep them inside. He could yell at me, he could scream; I wouldn't mind. Just let them out. I would like a closeness with my big brother. That doesn't change, even when you make the major leagues.

Back to Shea, game five. Jim Deshaies, who'd come over in a trade from the American League, was supposed to pitch that fifth game for the Astros. But it rained, and on the following day Lanier gave the ball to Ryan. Deshaies had won twelve games. I thought he was a good pitcher, and it says something about the quality of the Astros' staff that they never used him in the series.

I've said that the idea these days is to wait Ryan out. Late in a game, his fastball will lag, get a little fatter. Not this day, though. For nine innings, he threw like a kid with lightning in his arm. And those strong legs: drop, coil on the right leg, then push off hard, throwing with that momentum. Between hitters, he stalked the mound, anxious to get the ball again and go to work. His face was tight and hard with concentration. He'd talked about pitching the Astros into the World Series. He'd been there as a kid with the Mets in '69: one game, two and a third innings.

Dwight pitched for us, and was also brilliant. Doc stumbled in the World Series, and a lot was made of it. He was superb against the Astros, but unlucky, and people seemed to forget that. Scott beat him, 1–0, in game one. On this day, Doc pitched ten innings, surrendered a single run. This is not a pitcher who has lost his way.

Their run came in the fifth. Ashby clipped a right-field double. Reynolds singled; Ashby stopped at third. Ryan bounced one to Doc, who stared Ashby back to third, then forced Reynolds at second. Doran hit it on the ground to Wally at second. We missed the double play, and Ashby scored.

40

•

We got it right back in the bottom of the inning. We got it the opposite way, one swing. Strawberry. Straw pounced on the fastball, jerked it into the corner by the foul pole, straight and low, a home run. It would be a while before anyone scored again.

The Astros slapped the hits around, but couldn't score. We didn't either. There was Straw's home run and a single by Mex, period. Ryan struck out twelve. Fortunately, I wasn't one of them. I was, though, oh for three. One for twenty overall. In their tenth, Lanier sent Terry Puhl to hit for Ryan. Puhl singled, but the Astros couldn't score, and Ryan was gone, heroic and winless. The Astros' new pitcher was Kerfeld.

My friend Charlie. In the dugout, the guys teased me gently.

"Look who's pitching, Kid."

"Hey, Charlie's on the mound. Gonna show you the ball again, Kid."

"You bet," I said. "I'm waiting."

I got my chance right away. Tenth inning, one out. I wanted it, could taste it. Now was the time. *Now.* One for twenty, and big Charlie out there, squirting black juice, strutting, throwing that weight around.

He threw me ball one. And ball two. A hitter's count, my count. He heaved a giant sigh and pitched, and I was on it, I got it, a rocket just short of third base, a ricochet off the wettish dirt against Denny Walling's chest. Could have punched a hole in him—it was hit that hard. But the big-league third baseman was on it like a cat and threw true to first. And I was a ground-ball out, and one for twenty-one.

I may have been feeling sorry for myself earlier, but when Davis gloved Walling's throw, anger took over with a rush. I legged it to first, spiked the bag, and braked too hard, spinning furiously toward our dugout. That quick angry turn wrenched my left ankle. Flash of pain, and more anger. The ankle hurt from then on, though I never said anything.

Keith Hernandez was coming out of the clubhouse tunnel as I sat down and began buckling on the pads. He had been on the telephone with his older brother, Gary, out in San Francisco. This was nothing unusual. His older brother, like mine, is a former ballplayer. Gary

41

•

Hernandez was a second-team All-American at Cal Berkeley. Any-time we were on national TV, or playing the Giants, Mex might call Gary. Mostly, he'd call when he wasn't hitting, or when he had doubts about himself. "How's my swing?" he'd ask. "How do I look?" He always felt better after talking to his brother.

They'd been talking right after I hit that shot off Walling's breast-bone. Gary had been watching, and he told Mex, "By the way, tell Gary he looks good. He looks confident. He's swinging the bat *good.*"

Mex landed beside me on the bench—Kerfeld was shutting us down one-two-three—and told me what his brother had said. "Don't worry about it any more," Mex said. "You're swinging solid, Kid."

I looked at Mex. It was true. I was swinging solid.

Davey summoned Orosco, J.O., and he was perfect, three up, three down, in the eleventh. So was Kerfeld. So was J.O. again in the twelfth. The long afternoon turned darker. Lanier stayed with Kerfeld.

Lenny began our twelfth with a ground ball to Davis—easy out. Then Wally beat out a scribble of a hit down the third-base line. Speed. Mex's turn. Kerfeld, a right-hander, watched Wally over his shoulder. Watched him through his glasses. Wally dared a pretty good lead, till Kerfeld could not resist. He threw, bounced it wild, and Wally scooted to second base. Winning run on second, one out.

Lanier ordered Kerfeld to walk Mex. He had to. It was a baseball necessity: one out, first base empty, the run that ends the game at second base. You have to arrange for the double play or the force at third. Still, it always stings, if only a little, when they intentionally walk the guy ahead of you. Against all logic, it hurts. Mex bats left, Kerfeld throws right. I bat right, so it only made sense to let Kerfeld work on me. Righty to righty—percentages. Still, I didn't like it.

They'd intentionally walked Mex twice in game two. Larry Ander-son, then Aurelio Lopez. The first time, I'd cracked one pretty hard, but Hatcher had run it down. Then I'd hit into the double play, mak-ing them look like geniuses.

I was waiting by the on-deck circle with Straw, the two of us standing with the weighted bats while Kerfeld pitched around Mex, arcing the ball to Ashby, who jumped out of the catcher's box to grab it. We were standing there watching, and Straw said, "Don't let 'em do this to you, Kid. Don't let 'em do it."

That was all I had to hear. I was boiling.

"All you need is a little base hit, Kid," Straw said. "Don't worry about it."

Down at second base, Doran told Wally, "I don't like this. I don't like Carter when he's one for twenty-one."

Ball four. Mex chucked the bat and trotted to first. Kerfeld glowered and kicked dirt and rubbed up the ball. The crowd noise swelled. They expected us to do it now, they could taste it.

Briefly, Kerfeld lost the plate. He threw me three balls. I thought about the walk, thought about settling for it. I wanted to come through, get the big hit, but I couldn't help thinking, I'm one for twenty-one, and God knows, if I hit this ball, it might go right at somebody. Hatcher. Walling. I'll hit it right on the button, and they'll be there. In the box seats behind the plate, Sandy was so nervous she'd begun to cry. She was sitting with my father, our daughters, and her mother. Right then an ABC cameraman appeared in front of them, and put them on TV.

I looked down at Buddy at third base. He went through the motions, slapping, rubbing, touching: Take. I was glad to. Kerfeld poured it in there. Strike one. I stared at Buddy: Swing.

Kerfeld threw a good pitch, and I fouled it back. It was a short quick swing, to get a piece of the ball. Three and two. Kerfeld threw; I swung and sent it back foul. He threw, and *again* I fouled it back. These were good pitches. I was still alive, so already I'd had a good at-bat.

Kerfeld's next pitch was low and a little away, and I got it. I drove it, a one-hopper up the middle, just where I wanted to hit it, at big Charlie. Fat of the bat; I knew it was a hit, and the relief blew through me as I ran. *A hit, a hit.* First that relief, then: score, Wally. Score, score, score. I turned the corner at first, looked in, and Wally was sailing home, sliding, bouncing to his feet.

My teammates surrounded me. I looked over the heads of the

43

•

happy mob and found Sandy and the rest of my family in the stands. They were laughing, they were crying.

At last. It was one of the biggest, most welcome hits of my life. Kerfeld lowered his head and trudged off the field, thinking, I'm sure, about throwing the ball wild when he tried to pick off Wally. I don't dislike Kerfeld. He's a bouncy horse of a kid, his head stuffed with crazy young ideas. Just a kid. He's got a great arm.

We left them on the field. It's an awful way to lose, being left on the field. You go out there needing three outs to stay in the game, or to win it, and you never get them. The game's been grabbed away from you. You feel thoroughly beaten. We'd left them on the field in game three, when Lenny hit the stunning home run, and we'd just done it again.

While I was being interviewed by ABC, a crowd watched, pressing down around the dugout. They were hollering at me, cheering me, and after the interview I thanked them. I raised my arms in a V so wide and high my fists scraped the sky.

Mets 2, Astros 1.

Twelve innings. It was one of the very finest games in the history of these play-offs. The next day, Wednesday, we played the greatest ever.

MONDAY, OCT. 13 at SHEA

| Houston | 000 010 000 000 — 1 9 1 |
| Mets | 000 010 000 001 — 2 4 0 |

One out when winning run scored

HOUSTON (1)

	ab	r	h	bi
Doran 2b	4	0	1	1
Hatcher cf	3	0	1	0
Walling 3b	5	0	1	0
Davis 1b	5	0	0	0
Bass rf	5	0	2	0
Cruz lf	5	0	1	0
Ashby c	5	1	1	0
Reynolds ss	4	0	1	0
Thon ss	1	0	0	0
Ryan p	3	0	0	0
Puhl ph	1	0	1	0
Kerfeld p	0	0	0	0
	41	1	9	1

METS (2)

	ab	r	h	bi
Dykstra cf	5	0	0	0
Backman 2b	5	1	1	0
Hernandez 1b	4	0	1	0
Carter c	5	0	1	1
Strawberry rf	3	1	1	1
Wilson lf	4	0	0	0
Orosco p	0	0	0	0
Knight 3b	4	0	0	0
Santana ss	3	0	0	0
Mazzilli ph	1	0	0	0
Elster ss	0	0	0	0
Gooden p	3	0	0	0
Heep lf	1	0	0	0
	38	2	4	2

E—Kerfeld. DP—Mets 2. LOB—Houston 7, Mets 4. 2B—Ashby. HR—Strawberry (2). SB—Doran (1), Puhl (1). S—Hatcher. Game-Winning RBI—Carter (2).

Houston

	IP	H	R	ER	BB	SO
Ryan	9	2	1	1	1	12
Kerfeld (L, 0-1)	2 1-3	2	1	1	1	3

Mets

	IP	H	R	ER	BB	SO
Gooden	10	9	1	1	2	4
Orosco (W, 2-0)	2	0	0	0	0	2

T—3:45. A—54,986.

Moments after that fifth game, I was outside the pressroom, which was once the Jets' locker room, answering questions into microphones jabbing in from everywhere. Sandy and her mother were there, and my father. The press people were crowding me, throwing their questions at me. They all wanted to know about the base hit. I was talking when, over the tops of their heads, I saw Christy, my oldest, come flying around a corner. She came dashing at me, yelling, "Daddy. Daddy." The press guys melted back, I knelt, and Christy slammed into my arms. Then around the corner popped Kimmy, and *she* came charging. I pulled them both against me and told them how much I loved them, and so on. It was a nice moment. The hit, the win, and now this. Afterward a couple of the reporters told me it was like watching a scene in a play.

Our wives and women friends had flown with us to Houston on the first trip, but after Scott beat us in game four, which meant that we'd be going back, Frank Cashen appeared in the clubhouse to tell us we'd be flying alone this time. He came down as we were undressing. It's a large, comfortable room, carpeted wall to wall. Frank stood in the center and delivered a fifteen-minute speech. It was too bad we were going back to Houston, he said, but we were the best ball club, and we were simply going to have to finish them off in their ball park. We were the best. We'd shown it all year. We had a chance to win it all, everything. He went on like this, and finally worked around to this point: "As I say, we're going back to Houston, and the ball club has decided that the wives will make their own traveling arrangements."

Silence.

"Are there any questions?" Frank asked.

I popped my hand up immediately. If I hadn't, I think the thing would have died right there. "Frank," I said, "I really think the wives ought to be included. Sandy's part of my life, and I want her with me on the plane. I know I'm speaking for all of us."

Frank began explaining, but before he could say much, Keith jumped

45

•

into it. "I agree with Gary. I really want my wife to come with me."

Everyone stared at Mex. He and his wife had been separated for over a year. They were in the middle of getting a divorce. Mex wanted to bring someone on the plane, but she wasn't exactly his wife. Frank looked puzzled.

Then Mex grinned like a schoolboy. "Hell," he blurted, "that's not what I mean."

That broke us all up, including Frank.

Mex pushed on. He's our player representative, and it was up to him to fight this thing for us. It went back and forth, till Frank said Mex should sit down with him and they'd discuss it. Before that happened, I told Mex that if Sandy couldn't ride the plane *back* from Houston with the team, then I would wait and take a later flight with her. If there was a seventh game, it would be a night game. If I flew back with Sandy, I'd have to wait till morning. And I wouldn't have been the only one. Mex relayed all of this to Frank, who may have had visions of half the ball club boycotting the team charter. He told Mex the women could fly home with us. We'd won half the battle. The Mets' brass can be very particular about permitting our wives to travel with us. It does get irritating.

So we left New York, guys only, the evening of the long fifth game. I still had the wonderful taste of my winning hit. We all felt loose and good, but we also knew that we had to win tomorrow. This was what Mike Scott was doing to us. We were leading three games to two, and yet *we* were the team that had to win tomorrow.

On the plane I played hearts with Ray, Tim, and Mex. Mex may be the worst cardplayer in baseball history. He doesn't care; he plays for fun. On this night, too, he played for fun, drank some beer. As we played, he continued celebrating game five. Apropos of nothing he would reach over and slap me a high five. "Way to *go*, Kid. Way to come *through*" and "What about The Mex? The Mex came through, too." He also got going on the *Poltergeist* routine. "We're back. . . . We're gonna get you. . . ."

46

•

And he urged me to call his brother. "He'd love it, Kid. Gary'd love it."

"I want to call your brother," I said, and I did want to.

Mex and I walk through life in different ways, in different styles. But we get along fine, and I like and respect the man. He's the best-fielding first baseman I've ever seen, and one of the finest hitters. I often say to guys, "You're the best." It's my battle cry, my way of telling someone to hang tough. When I say it to Mex, I'm speaking the literal truth.

The plane hit the runway at 11:30 Houston time, which would be 12:30 by our body clocks. We were a weary bunch. Sandy, my father, and Mead were arriving an hour later. I rode the team bus to the hotel, settled in, and called Gary Hernandez in San Francisco. It was two hours earlier out there.

"I just wanted to thank you for the encouragement," I said. "It really helped. You helped me get that hit, Gary."

"You're swinging fine," he said. "You're there. Don't change a thing."

"Yeah?"

"You're there. And I'll tell you something. You're my pick for World Series MVP."

I had to laugh. We weren't even there yet. "Come on, Gary."

"You're my pick," he said. "World Series MVP."

It was about the sweetest music I'd ever heard. When you're slumping, it gets hard, in time, to believe in yourself. And a ballplayer has to believe in himself absolutely. When you're down, you need a lift, and this was a lift.

I wanted to give him something back. So I told him how Keith felt about him, and how special their friendship was. And I said, "Gary, you don't know how much I'd like to have a relationship like that with *my* brother. I've been starving for it for years."

I came on strong about it, which is my way, and Gary was moved.

"I'll talk to your brother," he said. "I'll talk to him during the World Series." His voice broke. "Don't change a thing," he repeated.

47

•

Meanwhile, Sandy, my father, and Mead were arriving. They were also learning that their luggage had been left in New York. Sandy reached the hotel at about one in the morning, minus her suitcase, and I couldn't help thinking about the ball club's refusal to let the wives fly with us. Sandy and I could have been asleep by now, and she'd have clothes to wear the next day.

We slept late and ate a room-service breakfast. The team bus left for the ball park at noon; usually I'll go earlier, but it had been a long night, and I waited and rode the bus. Sandy went shopping for a clean dress and other necessities. I took all my luggage on the bus. We all checked out of the hotel, even knowing that if we lost that afternoon, we'd have to go back and check in again. Naturally, no one wanted that. The Red Sox were in the same situation during the World Series. Before the sixth game, in New York, they checked out of their hotel. If they'd won, they'd have gone straight home. It's either that or check back into the hotel and try again the next day.

Mike Scott watched that sixth game from the Astros' dugout, and he haunted us. He stuck in the back of our minds. No, sir, we didn't want to face him the following day for all the marbles. Afterward the writers named him MVP for the play-off series, and it's hard to argue the choice. The man had a power over us even when he was spending a game on the bench.

Lefty Bob Knepper began the epic on the mound for the Astros. He's a good pitcher, but we didn't think he could beat us. After the day before's hit, I was feeling like my old self. I expected to hit the lefty. Bobby O. was pitching for us.

The game was out of Shakespeare. It was the game of games. I was privileged to take part in the most memorable postseason in baseball history, and in that postseason's most memorable game. "It ain't over till it's over," said Yogi Berra once. So true, and so easy to forget. The 1986 postseason surely set the record for premature celebrations. They were uncorking champagne in the clubhouse of the California Angels in the ninth inning of game five of their series with the Red Sox. Two out, a man on, and a second-string outfielder named Dave Henderson at the plate, two strikes. Already that inning, Don Baylor had hit a two-run homer. Now Henderson put one over the fence. That champagne never got drunk. Then, in the bottom of the tenth in game six of the World Series, Red Sox leading by two, two out, nobody on base, somebody began opening champagne in the Red Sox clubhouse. *That* champagne never got drunk.

There was no champagne in the Astros' clubhouse in that sixth game, but as our ninth began, Astros leading, 3 – 0, the crowd stood and roared, celebrating. They cheered Knepper, they cheered their team. They cheered a runless inning that never happened. I will admit, too, that we thought we'd won it in the fourteenth, and the Astros caught us. They almost caught us again in that crazy sixteenth. It ain't over till it's over.

Knepper disposed of us in order in the first inning, and in their half they knocked Bobby O. around for three runs, and should have gotten more. Doran hit. Hatcher forced him at second. Garner pulled a double to left field, and Hatcher scampered home. Davis shot one up the middle, and Garner scored. Bobby walked Bass. Jose Cruz jerked a hit to right; Davis scored. 3 – 0. A big inning was building, and Mike Scott was waiting for the next day. Ashby's turn, their catcher. Bass down at third. Lanier chose the suicide squeeze.

I'm glad he did. Ashby missed the ball. I ripped off the mask and, to my delight, found Bass dangling about halfway down the line. I chased him, boxed him in, and threw to Ray, who laid the tag on him. Cruz did get to second, but the momentum, the motion of the inning, had been checked. Ashby, trying to redeem himself for blowing the bunt, hit the ball hard, but to Raffy. Line-drive out. 3 – 0.

I led off our second, two for twenty-two. Knepper threw me the fastball. I swung just late, but hit it hard anyway, a long one to right center, Death Valley. Running catch by Bass. The drive might have found a wall in some ball parks, but not in the Dome. Two for twenty-three. Next time I lifted one to center—easy catch for Hatcher. Two for twenty-four. The old self-confidence was starting to shrivel again. The game flowed along, 3 – 0. I had one more crack at Knepper, and that time I really got it, a bullet, but straight at Hatcher. Two for twenty-five.

Two for twenty-five.

Knepper was sticking it to all of us. Both Mookie and Raffy rolled hits up the middle, and that was our total offense for eight innings. Knepper struck out six. Lee Mazzilli hit for Bobby O. in the sixth and fanned.

Bobby O. had done his job. He allowed only one more hit after that messy first. Aguilera picked up for him. He pitched three runless innings. What a bullpen!

And so we came to the ninth, our last chance to save ourselves from a seventh-game shootout with Mike Scott. In their dugout Scott paced, sleepy-looking as always. Haunting us. The crowd stood, waiting for Knepper to finish it. It was the pitcher's turn to hit, but Davey chose Lenny as pinch hitter for Aggie.

Lefty against lefty: the percentages favored Knepper. But we needed more than just any base hit; we needed excitement, sparks, something contagious. Nails was the guy. That was Davey's thinking, and it was good thinking, because Knepper put one a little high, and Lenny drove it into right center, Death Valley, a three-base hit. Knepper could kiss his shutout good-bye. Mookie, who'd been struggling at the plate all series—like most of us—punched a single to right field just out of Doran's reach, and we had our first run. The noise that had been bunching under the Dome began to subside. I noticed, too, gaps in the crowd, some of them sizable. People were heading home, perhaps congratulating themselves on getting out ahead of the thick traffic. It ain't over till it's over, folks. On that day hundreds of people drove away from eight of the most wonderful innings of baseball ever played.

The World man, Kevin Mitchell, was next. Knepper got World to hit one on the ground to Walling at third; Mookie had run with the pitch, so Walling had to throw to first to get the out. Mex's turn. Dave Smith was throwing hard in the bullpen. Knepper was about out of gas. He let another pitch escape high, and you don't throw to Mex's happy zone and get away with it, especially when he hasn't had a hit all day. He pounded it past Hatcher, a double, and Mookie frisked home. Astros 3, Mets 2. Tying run on second, one out. Lanier went out to get Knepper.

Another big moment for yours truly. Lanier brought in Smith, his bullpen ace, playing the percentages, righty against righty. I was two for twenty-five, hitting under .100, and this hitless afternoon had started me worrying again.

Smith threw ball one, and ball two. I had a good swing at the next pitch, but sent it back foul. Another good swing, another foul straight back. Smith threw me ball three. I fouled another back, and another. Every muscle in me, every fiber, seemed tight-strung. I felt as if I'd been battling Smith, fouling off his good pitches, for half an hour.

Ball four. Again a surge of relief: I hadn't made an out. Relief and, beyond it, disappointment. The tying run was at second; I could have brought Mex home. It isn't my nature, or my job, to settle for bases on balls. Still, when I'd trotted down to first, Uncle Bill gave me a pat on the butt.

"Great at-bat, Kid," he said. He held out a hand, palm down, at his belt level. "If he'd thrown you anything here, you'd have had him. You'd have crushed the sucker."

Good old Uncle Bill.

Smith had lost me, and now he had to pitch to a lefty, Darryl. The crowd had gotten very quiet. Straw looked at ball one and ball two. Smith had to throw the fastball, and Straw, of course, was primed for it. He let go with that huge, looping swing and nailed the ball—just a bit early. But he nailed it, a towering monster of a drive into the upper deck, the outer reaches of the Astrodome. The seats are purple up there. The ball climbed and climbed, and I'll never forget the sound of the crowd, a collective gasp, enormous and breathy, which was disappointment, and surprise, as well. Surprise: to see a ball hit that high, that far. Straw watched it, we all did, hoping, but you could see it curve, and it buried itself in the seats, just foul. Only three men—Bob Bailey, Andre Dawson, and Jimmy Wynn—had ever hit a fair ball into those purple seats.

The shot had its effect on Smith. He didn't want to give Straw another good swing, and he kept the ball away from him, and walked him. Bases full, one out, Ray Knight at the plate. A tough, tough hitter, but also a guy who can hit into the double play. Smith bore down and threw two strikes past Ray. Smith needed the strike-out, but Ray wouldn't give it to him. He kept fighting off pitches, foul ball, foul ball, foul ball. Finally he connected, just enough—fly ball to Bass in right center. Mex could have walked home. I tagged at second and sprinted, in a manner of speaking, to third. Straw took second.

I stood at third, the go-ahead run. It would have been nice, after the series I'd had, it would have been wonderful, to score the run that put us in the World Series. I thought of that as I took my lead off third. But, what a treasure of a ball game would have been lost if I'd scored. Wally batted for Teufel. (Tuff, a good righty hitter, had started at second against Knepper.) He was walked intentionally. Bases loaded. Raffy was due to hit, but Davey sent Danny to the plate, playing the percentages, lefty versus the right-handed Smith. Smith fell behind, three balls, no strikes. The Astrodome was as quiet as a funeral parlor. But Smith found the plate—three times, three strikes. Danny started to swing, held up, as the third strike zipped by. The crowd erupted, of course. Ashby flipped the ball toward the mound, and I saw Smith snatch it up angrily and slam it down on the turf. He was the ace, and he'd let us tie the game. The frustration was written on his face.

Off we went, into the bottom of the ninth, and way, way beyond.

Aguilera was gone, and Davey brought on McDowell. Roger is a superb athlete, smooth and graceful. Because of this, some of us call him "Skeets," after Renaldo "Skeets" Nehemiah, the great track star and former pro-football player. Skeets is a funny guy off the field, a hotfoot artist and collector of grotesque rubber masks. He gives a sort of shotgun hotfoot: matches wrapped with bubble gum around a cigarette that burns down and starts a spurting fire. He has all kinds of masks. You never know when you'll turn and discover the Wolf Man or King Kong in a Mets uniform sitting next to you on the bench. On the mound, he is another person. He won't joke, won't laugh, won't smile.

This day, he was tremendous.

My dad—my coach—with me as an 8-year-old

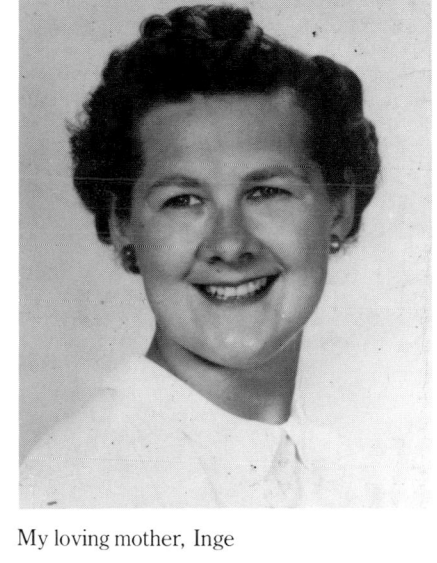

My loving mother, Inge

My prefootball days

My high-school football days

A special day for the family   SHAWNY LOREN

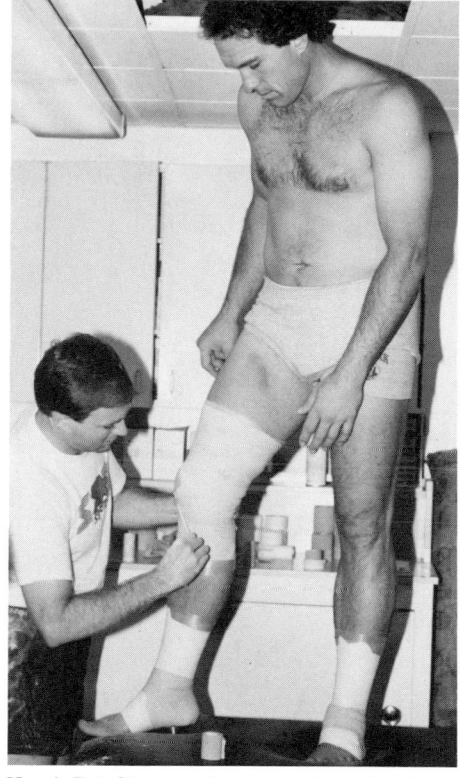

Here's Bob Sikes getting me ready for battle
© GEORGE KALINSKY, MAJOR LEAGUE GRAPHICS

In the heat of battle   IRA N. GOLDEN

Ready for a hanging curve
© GEORGE KALINSKY, MAJOR LEAGUE GRAPHICS

My armor—the tools of excellence
© GEORGE KALINSKY, MAJOR LEAGUE GRAPHICS

With Sandy and one of my childhood idols, the great Mickey Mantle
RICHARD COLLINS, PORT WASHINGTON, NY

Future Hall-of-Famer and good friend Johnny Bench   STEVE BABINEAU

Our skipper, Davey Johnson

Uncle Bill observing the hitters
IRA N. GOLDEN

The great Mike Schmidt and yours truly at the All-Star game
MEAD CHASKY

My big brother, Gordy

Yours truly giving a fist of congratulations

IRA N. GOLDEN

(LEFT TO RIGHT): Doc, Dukey, the legendary *Le Grande Orange,* honorary National League captain for the 1986 All-Star game in Houston wearing his uniform from his first team, the Colt .45s, Straw, and the Kid.   © GEORGE KALINSKY, MAJOR LEAGUE GRAPHICS

He was the unsung hero of that sixth game, and if he'd never pitched another out in the postseason, he would still have deserved to walk in glory. In the bottom of the ninth, he set them down in order. Understand the pressure he was under, the tension that now ruled in the always-heavy air of the Astrodome. Every play was pressurized. Every *pitch*. The entire series had been like that, and as we headed into extra innings, the knot was pulled even tighter. Roger entered game six at the most demanding moment of an incredibly demanding series, and pitched long and almost perfectly.

Five innings. One hit. No walks. He's a short-relief man, geared to pitch one, two, perhaps three innings. And there he was cruising through four, then five, like a starter. The Astros never threatened.

The Astros' pitchers, meanwhile, were matching him. Smith pitched an uneventful tenth. Puhl batted for him, did nothing, and Smith was lost for the game. Larry Anderson took over and threw three near-perfect innings, no hits, one walk. We were pretty deep into their bullpen now, which we'd been wanting all through the series.

In the thirteenth, Lanier removed Anderson for a pinch hitter. His replacement was Aurelio Lopez. He had acquired his nickname, "Smoke," in Detroit, where he had some good years throwing in relief for the Tigers. He had, in fact, pitched some decent innings in the '84 World Series. He was now thirty-eight, and his smoke had thinned somewhat, while he himself had done the opposite. I led off.

I've talked about the fatigue of these games. After just one game, we'd all felt wrung out. One game. The day before, we'd battled for twelve innings, flown halfway across the country, and gotten up for an afternoon game. And yet the fatigue would hit only afterward. Maybe my catcher's legs were tired, from the hours of stretching and squatting, but it was a distant tiredness, something I noticed only vaguely. At that point, the single feeling was intensity—as if we were playing in blazing white light, hard on the eyes. It would seem that way, too, in looking back; every memory, every play, seen in hard white light.

Lopez was careful, determined out there, but he hung one outside, and I cracked it into right field—base hit. He then walked Straw. Nobody in the ball park had forgotten Straw's foul ball into the upper deck. Ray bunted. Lopez jumped on it, remembered it was me lumbering to third, spun, and threw me out.

Wally was next. Lopez pitched inside, and Wally yanked it into right field—another base hit. Bass scooped the ball and threw home as Straw came around, gliding like a deer, but fast, running with everything he had. He wore a determined look: he was coming home no matter what. He was going to *score*. It would have been close, but Bass's throw sailed over Ashby's head. Ray took third; Wally scampered to second. Mets 4, Astros 3, runners at second and third. One out. The Astros, and the game, seemed to be unraveling.

It ain't over till it's over.

Howard Johnson, a Long Island neighbor, batted for Roger. Hojo and Lopez had been teammates in Detroit. Davey had let Skeets hit for himself in the tenth, the ultimate compliment, conceding the out to keep him in the game. Lopez now pitched tough; Hojo popped one straight up, and Ashby caught it near our dugout. Big out. Hojo came back muttering to himself; he knew Lopez and felt he could hit him. Lenny's turn. Lanier ordered Lopez to walk Lenny, who bats left and was hot. Quickly, Lopez got ahead of Mookie, two strikes. He threw Mookie his smoke. Mookie waved and missed, and our fourteenth was history.

We had a run, we had the lead. We were excited, pumped up, thinking pennant. Jesse was on his way to the mound, reliable J.O., and we knew, absolutely, that he would get the job done. He, though, was feeling the tension; you could see the nervousness scrawled on his round face. He is one of the those pitchers who needs the encouraging word now and then. Fernandez is another, and Sisk. A catcher has to know which guy to chew out when things go bad, which guy to praise. Some guys need to be told, over and over, that they're pitching like Cy Young. J.O. was nervous, and no wonder. After his warm-up pitches, I went out to pump him up.

Doran led off, and J.O. struck him out in superb fashion. The third strike was a hard, breaking slider. Hatcher was next. J.O. missed twice, and we were behind, 2–0. Decisions. Hatcher is a speed man, and we didn't want him on base. Give him first, he'll try to steal second. I wanted to make him swing, and I put one finger down, fastball. J.O. put it in there, and Hatcher launched it down the left-field line, a rocket, but foul. It had home-run distance, by plenty. The crowd woke, roared, sighed, and settled back. A home run, I thought; that's all we need. The count moved to 3–2. Again I asked for the fastball.

J.O. threw it inside, and Hatcher murdered it. It carried like a rifle shot, tracing the left-field chalk line, and struck the foul netting at a considerable height. Home run. It was instantaneous. The crowd reawoke, sent down a terrific ovation. I lifted off the mask and watched Hatcher trot the bases. What did we have to do to beat these guys?

I got the new ball and walked it out to J.O. His face had fallen noticeably; he looked pained. I put the ball in his glove. I felt wired, energized, and I yelled at him through the waves of noise from the suddenly wakened crowd.

"You can *do* it, J.O. You're still the *best*. You're gonna hold 'em." I was shouting, pumping my fist, insisting, pleading. "We're gonna get the run back; you're gonna hold 'em. You're the *best*."

J.O. nodded, and I slapped his butt and jogged back to the plate. It ain't over till it's over. Concentrate, Jesse, concentrate. He did. Walling pulled a ground ball to Mex. Out number two. Glenn Davis. Everyone in the ball park thought of the home run. Davis lifted a pop fly to Wally. The inning was over, but the game was not.

Astros 4, Mets 4.

In our fifteenth, Lopez got the rookie, Kevin Elster, who had replaced Raffy at shortstop. He got Mex. Then I banged my second hit of the day, my second off Lopez, a good line drive to right center. The slump was over, but I wasn't thinking about that. There was nothing in the world but this game, which had begun to feel unreal and endless—innings stretching out to infinity. Let's *end* this thing, I thought. When Lopez's pitch hit the dirt and bounced away from Ashby, I took off for second.

I've mentioned my speed—my lack of it, that is. I used to be able to run. I was a quarterback, and I could go. But the knee injury and repeated surgery left my leg weakened, and the years of kneeling and crouching built a heavy bulk of muscle.

The ball rolled away from Ashby, and I ran. Anything to end this game. The ball didn't roll far, obviously; Reynolds, and the ball, were waiting for me at second. It was a long walk back to the dugout. I probably should have stayed where I was, in any case. They would have walked Straw if I had taken second, and we wanted Straw to swing. I had seen a chance to put the winning run on second, and went for it. It was a split-second decision—a mistake, and I felt terrible.

J.O. held them in their fifteenth.

And then that incredible sixteenth.

Darryl began it with a fly ball to center, not deep. Hatcher apparently lost the ball against the dome; he faded back, found the ball, and sprinted in—too late. Straw cruised to second—Texas-league double. Excitement in our dugout, the guys on their feet, hollering. Ray, trying to hit to the right side to move the runner over, drove a single to right; Straw charged, and Bass let loose with another wild throw, wide and high, and Straw scored. Ray, meanwhile, took second.

We had the lead again.

Lanier went out and summoned Jeff Calhoun. Calhoun hadn't pitched a lot this year, particularly in tight situations. Wally was due up. He's a switch hitter, and I guess Lanier wanted to force Wally to bat righty, which is his weaker side.

The first thing Calhoun did was throw one wild past Ashby. Ray went to third. Calhoun walked Wally, then threw *another* wild pitch, and Ray bolted home. Two runs in, and big smiles and high fives up and down our bench. J.O. put down a bunt, a beauty down the third-base line, and Wally took third. Lenny lined one off Davis's glove into right field; Wally trotted home, and we led by three. We hardly noticed when Mookie hit into a double play. Many more fans went streaming out of the ball park.

Mets 7, Astros 4.

The guys shot out of the dugout with a yell. It was just a matter of getting three outs, just a matter of time. But as soon as Jesse began tossing his warm-up pitches, I knew it wouldn't be easy.

He was tired. He'd thrown a lot of pitches in this series, and even when he's rested, J.O.'s a one- or two-inning pitcher. He was pushing the ball at me, not snapping it. It was as if he hesitated in mid-motion to gather his strength. He'd broken off some hard, mean sliders, and there's only so much snap in the human arm. Still, Davey didn't start anyone throwing in our bullpen. It was going to be Jesse, period.

Reynolds was first, and J.O. struck him out. His pitches were drifting high, but Reynolds helped us out by trying to bunt on a 3–1 pitch. I was amazed. Reynolds swung and missed on the 3–2 pitch, which probably would have been ball four. Davey Lopes, a veteran and smart, batted for Calhoun. Lopes waited while J.O. threw four straight balls, all high.

I was calling for fastballs. Go with strength, was my thinking; give 'em your best stuff, tired or not. Doran, whom J.O. had fanned in the fourteenth, knocked the first pitch, a fastball up the middle— base hit. Lopes scored; Doran held at second. Tying run on first. Time to talk to Jesse.

He looked worried out there.

"I know you can hold 'em, J.O.," I said. He nodded like he didn't quite believe me. "You're still the best," I told him.

Walling. Long ago, years ago, it seemed, Phil Garner had been playing third for the Astros. Garner is a good right-handed hitter. Walling bats left, so we had the percentages with us. I had a feeling, and still do: Garner would have been trouble. The fastball strategy hadn't exactly worked, so I started asking J.O. for his breaking pitch, his slider. Walling pulled one on the ground; Mex went flat on the turf, positioned himself, and threw Hatcher out at second, by a hair. Beautiful play.

Davis. Lenny, in center, had to play the big man deep. The last thing we wanted was a home run; the next-to-last thing, an extra base hit. J.O. zipped the slider in at Davis's wrists, jamming him; Davis nubbed the ball off his bat handle into center, a huge swing producing a bloop single, fooling Lenny, who saw the swing and

57

•

started back. It had happened to Hatcher in the top of the inning. Lenny recovered, dashed in, too late. Doran had scored. Walling stopped at second—the tying run. Time to visit J.O. This time, Mex walked over too.

A story grew out of this conference. After the game, Mex, feeling good and talking in a loose, postgame sort of way, told reporters that he had instructed me to stay away from the fastball—no fast-balls to Bass, or we, Mex and I, would fight right there.

Mex would never say that to me, just as I would never tell him how to play first base. Later, Mex warned me that I'd read the story in the papers. He apologized. I let it go, but we'll set the record straight here.

J.O. was exhausted, and there wasn't much mustard left on his fastball. They'd been slapping it around pretty good. By now, Doug was warming up in the bullpen. Davis had punched the slider, but not hard. Bass would have loved to see a fastball at this point. He would have jumped on it. He was anxious. A base hit would have tied the game; a double in the gap would have won it. J.O.'s fastball was dragging, and we had to live or die by the slider. No one had to tell me that.

"You're the best, J.O."

I headed back to the plate. Bass dug in. He'd killed us all series, but I could see the anxiety in him now. Tired J.O. went to work. The crowd had risen and was going wild. I don't know how people can cheer that long, going on five hours at that point. J.O. threw his slider to Bass. Slider, slider slider. J.O. wasn't getting them over, but Bass was helping us, hacking at bad pitches. He's a switch hit-ter, so the slider was darting toward him. J.O. kept pouring in the sliders, and the count ran to 3–2.

One more pitch, J.O. One more slider.

It was a pretty good one, sinking down and in, probably ball four, but Bass chased it, swinging at air. Strike three.

We were going to the World Series!

I clutched the ball deep in the big mitt, and I didn't know whether to laugh or cry. We were going to the World Series. Jesse let out a whoop and whipped his glove a mile into the air. I threw my mask almost as high and charged him. He'd done it, and I wanted to tell him, thank him, hug him. *You're the best.*

A stack-up near the mound, guys hugging, the sweet smell of sweat and leather, a light-headed feeling of disbelief, ear-splitting yells, craziness everywhere. I remember Lenny launching himself like a glider, landing somewhere atop the pile. But Nails is too small to hurt anybody.

WEDNESDAY, OCT. 15 at HOUSTON

METS (7)   **HOUSTON (6)**

	ab	r	h	bi		ab	r	h	bi
Wilson cf	7	1	1	1	Doran 2b	7	1	2	0
Mitchell lf	4	0	0	0	Hatcher cf	7	2	3	2
Elster ss	3	0	0	0	Garner 3b	3	1	1	1
Hernandez 1b	7	1	1	1	Walling 3b	4	0	0	0
Carter c	5	0	2	0	Davis 1b	7	1	3	2
Strawberry rf	5	2	1	0	Bass rf	6	0	1	0
Knight 3b	6	1	1	2	Cruz lf	6	0	1	1
Teufel 2b	3	0	1	0	Ashby c	6	0	0	0
Backman 2b	2	1	1	1	Thon ss	3	0	0	0
Santana ss	3	0	1	0	Reynolds ss	3	0	0	0
Heep ph	1	0	0	0	Knepper p	2	0	0	0
McDowell p	1	0	0	0	Smith p	0	0	0	0
Johnson ph	1	0	0	0	Puhl ph	1	0	0	0
Orosco p	0	0	0	0	Andersen p	0	0	0	0
Ojeda p	1	0	0	0	Pankovits ph	1	0	0	0
Mazzilli ph	1	0	0	0	Lopez p	0	0	0	0
Aguilera p	0	0	0	0	Calhoun p	0	0	0	0
Dykstra cf	4	1	2	1	Lopes ph	0	1	0	0
	54	7	11	6		56	6	11	6

```
Mets      000 000 003 000 010 3 — 7 11 0
Houston   300 000 000 000 010 2 — 6 11 1
```

E—Bass. DP—Houston 2. LOB—Mets 9, Houston 5. 2B—Garner, Davis, Hernandez, Strawberry. 3B—Dykstra. HR—Hatcher (1). SB—Doran (2). S—Orosco. SF—Knight. Game-Winning RBI — Knight (1).

	IP	H	R	ER	BB	SO
Mets						
Ojeda	5	5	3	3	2	1
Aguilera	3	1	0	0	0	1
McDowell	5	1	0	0	0	2
Orosco (W, 3-0)	3	4	3	3	1	5
Houston						
Knepper	8 1-3	5	3	3	1	6
Smith	1 2-3	0	0	0	3	2
Andersen	3	0	0	0	1	1
Lopez L, 0-1	2	5	3	3	2	2
Calhoun	1	1	1	1	1	0

Lopez pitched to 2 batters in the 16th. WP—Calhoun 2. T—4:42. A—45,718.

Baseball, they say, is a boy's game. I am called "Kid," and certainly there's a lot of boy in me. Still, there's baseball and there's big-league baseball, and whereas baseball is a boy's game, big-league baseball is not. For one thing, a big-league fastball would crush a boy's skull. And boys don't play games with bone chips floating in their elbow, or cortisone deadening crippling pain in a knee.

Big-league baseball is a business. A big business. Boys don't receive money trickling down from television contracts. Baseball is my business, my life, my family's security, my kids' educations.

Maybe this is why, in the hours after that epic sixth game, I felt such deep emotion, such happiness. I kept thinking about my family. I got married young, maybe too young, and it was hard going for a while. Looking back, though, I see that it was beautiful, even on the stormiest days. It was the biggest event of my life, just ahead of the births of my children. I was present at all three births. I had no idea what it was like, what a miracle it was, and when Christy, our first, came, I cried when I saw her. On October 15, in Houston, Texas, I felt swamped with the same kind of awe and happiness. It was more than a boyhood dream. The World Series was the last piece in the puzzle of my career, the missing piece, an obsession. Call it "pride." All I know is, I had ached for this, and now that it had come, I couldn't stop thinking about Sandy, Christy, Kimmy, and D.J.

I was one of the last to reach our clubhouse, which was mobbed with reporters and misty with champagne. The writers surrounded me, shooting questions at me. Guys kept reaching over them and shaking champagne over my head, and I kept yelling, "We're going to the World Series!" Finally, someone passed me a cold bottle. I'm not a big drinker, but this was like nothing I'd ever tasted, a taste like diamonds, sweet and icy. The reporters kept asking me to comment. What could I say? What could anyone say? "The Astros are champions, too," I said into the microphones. I meant it. I felt for them—to fight so long, so well, then lose the thing.

After about an hour of interviews, bear hugs from teammates, and champagne dousings, I squeezed through the crowd and out into the corridor, where Sandy waited. Wet with champagne, I hugged her. We held each other for a long time. "I'm so happy for you," she said, and that was all. She understood. The alley in Fullerton, the hard times with the Expos, my pride, my obsession, all of it. Sandy knew.

Our chartered plane left Houston long after dark. The city glittered below us, tilted, and was gone. I saw Tuff gazing down, thinking, maybe, about the July night he'd spent in jail somewhere down there. Tuff, Aggie, R.J., and Bobby O. It had been a bad time for Tuff, and for all of us. Tuff had tried to walk out of the bar with a half-drunk beer, and a couple of off-duty cops had ordered him back inside. It turned ugly. Aggie, Bobby, and Ronnie were trying to protect Tuff, to steer him out of there. Whatever Tuff did to the cops, he'd gotten more than he'd given. They beat him up. He spent the night in a jail cell, bruised and cut. The guys had broken the midnight curfew, and Davey fined them. Davey is pretty lenient with his fines. All he asks is that you give a hundred percent on the field and don't embarrass him or the ball club off the field.

Roger got to the clubhouse early the day after. He got a roll of adhesive tape from the trainer's room, blackened the tape with a magic marker, and stuck it in vertical rows down the fronts of Tuff's, R.J.'s, and Bobby O.'s, and Aggie's dressing cubicles. Black bars, miniature jail cells. Tuff, with his swollen purple face, wasn't very amused. The other guys were able to laugh. "I should have known you'd do something," R.J. said. Of course: the clubhouse is our sanctuary, the place we can have our own fun. Anything goes in the clubhouse.

The plane climbed, leveled off. It was already noisy, a celebration cruising through the night. I remembered the ball. The game ball, the one J.O. had thrown past Bass for strike three and the final out. I'd held on to that ball, I'd saved it through all the wildness afterward. I remembered it then, in my jacket pocket.

I collect these things. I have the ball I caught in left field to end the 1975 All-Star game. Rod Carew hit it to me. I was a rookie, nervous as anything out there, and Carew hit a low arc that kept fading from me. I chased it, gloved it, and held on to it for dear life. In the clubhouse I got the guys to sign it.

61

And if that ball had been a big out, what was this? The out of my life.

Mex was in the seat behind Sandy and me.

"Hey, Mex," I said. "I got the last ball."

"Yeah?"

"I think I'll get it signed," I said.

"What you ought to do," Mex said, "is give it to Jesse."

He was right. J.O. had won three games. He could have been series MVP.

Mex said, "You give this one to Jesse, and you can keep the World Series ball."

J.O. was sitting a couple of rows in front of me. I yelled to him. He turned, grinning. I told him what I had and tossed him the baseball.

"Mex says I get the World Series ball," I said.

"You got it," J.O. said.

The party was getting lively. The beer and wine flowed. A tape deck played loud, loud music. The women got up and danced in the aisle. They sang, they danced, they shouted the rapid-fire chant that had rocked Shea all summer. *Let's go, Mets! Let's go, Mets!* I'll always remember that, the pretty women singing and dancing in the aisle, celebrating.

I guess it was a rowdier party than we realized. When we arrived in the clubhouse at Shea two days later to work out, we each found a note in our locker, an announcement. The note came from the front office. United Airlines had presented the ball club with a $7,500 bill for damage to the charter during the flight from Houston.

All I'd seen was some spilled beer and a lot of beer cans rolling around on the floor. We had, said United, ripped upholstery, broken seats, and generally drenched the place with beer. They said the plane had to be taken out of service to be cleaned and repaired. They said they weren't going to charter with us again.

Davey was ripping mad—not at us, but at the brass. He didn't like them reprimanding us without consulting him. He didn't like them reprimanding us, period.

One of the best cussers on our ball club is Wally Backman. Wally is an expert. The guys just laugh and say, "That's Wally." But Davey isn't too far behind Wally in the cussing department, and he let loose some choice nouns and adjectives to describe what he thought of the front office's note. He said we had a right to celebrate. He said what was $7,500 compared to what we were going to pull in for playing in the World Series. Davey's speech was short and, as I say, bristling. "The hell with them" was the politest thing he said.

"Let's forget it," he said, "and have a great World Series."

•

5

Davey Johnson had been predicting we'd win the division championship from the very first day of spring training. "We're not only going to win," he said, "we're going to win *big*. We're going to blow the rest of the division away." Davey would tell anyone who'd listen. His confidence, his *certainty*, was infectious. We believed it. The team had finished second two years in a row. Last year we'd won ninety-eight games. We were a young team. "We're going to win *big*," Davey kept saying, and pretty soon we'd all swallowed the conviction whole.

It had been a loose, pleasant spring training, with one ugly and terrifying moment: the injury to Mookie Wilson.

It wasn't the first of Mookie's troubles. The guy had been playing with awful luck for the last two seasons. Early in spring training in 1984—too early, maybe—a coach, Frank Howard, had the Mets' outfielders gunning long throws to the bases. Mookie threw, and tore some ligaments in his shoulder. He played hurt all season. He played hurt in 1985 till mid-season, when our team doctor, James C. Parkes, said enough was enough. Mookie went on the disabled list, and Dr. Parkes operated. This is no boy's game, folks: Mookie woke up from shoulder surgery and learned that the repairs had been partial, temporary, and that he'd have to undergo more extensive surgery at the end of the season. Mookie, God bless him, healed, more or less, and played out the season in pain. Then they operated on him again.

Rehabilitation was a slow process. I remember our trainer, Steve Garland, helping Mookie as he began throwing again under the Florida sun, lobbing the ball gingerly, as if his arm was as brittle as glass or china. Mookie began throwing a distance of about thirty feet, barely getting the ball there. Gradually he built the distance, throwing carefully under Steve's supervision. In time, he was winging the ball pretty well.

The ball club was pulling for him. Everybody loves Mookie. There isn't a sweeter guy in all of baseball than Mookie Wilson. He's a humanitarian. He cares. Also, it's a joy to watch him play baseball. The sight of Mookie running out a triple, or racing from first to third on a single, is a thing you don't forget. He runs like lightning and has the grace of a dancer.

Mookie had come back and back, strengthening the shoulder, lengthening his throws, till he looked ready to start for us in center field. Then he got hurt.

It was just before the start of the exhibition season. We were practicing the rundown. Mookie was the runner. I'd had knee surgery over the winter, and Davey, not wanting me to do much crouching on the still-creaky knee, had me playing first base. I was there, one end of the rundown, Raffy on the other side of Mookie. Mookie can be really slippery in a rundown. We chased him back and forth. Raffy had the ball, and Mookie faked toward first base, prompting Raffy to throw. But Mookie accelerated the other way— toward Raffy, toward the throw. It caught him dead in the eye. He had been hardly more than ten feet away, and Raffy had whipped the ball.

A crack of glass—Mookie wears protective glasses—and he dropped like he'd been shot. I was the first to reach him. I landed beside him and told him not to move, not to move. The guys all crowded around, shading Mookie. The lens had been crushed, although it was supposed to be unbreakable. An edge of the lens had cut him above the eye, and bits of it were *in* his eye, and I'll never forget the fright of wondering if this lovely guy, with all the bad luck dogging him, had now damaged an eye. There was swelling around the eye, and you could see blood inside it. Everyone got very quiet. We lifted Mookie, put him in a grounds keeper's cart. The rest of the practice was pretty dismal.

The injury wasn't as bad as it might have been, or as it looked, but Mookie couldn't do a thing for ten days. He couldn't throw, or run, or even do calisthenics. Naturally, this set him back. As it was, he'd been rebuilding the weakened shoulder. But back he came, till he got into several late exhibition games. And yet he wasn't a hundred percent, and the ball club decided to put him on the disabled list beginning Opening Day. Mookie stayed in Florida, strengthening himself, and joined us in the middle of April.

By then, there was no place for Mookie to play—at least, not full-time. George Foster was our left fielder, Lenny had begun to show his stuff, and right field was owned by Darryl. This was when Mookie showed his class. Becoming a part-time player is something I've never had to face. Maybe I won't have to, maybe I will. I don't know how I'd take it. I do know that when an injury put me on the bench for two weeks in August, it about drove me crazy. Mookie, suddenly, was a part-time player, and he took it uncomplainingly, with dignity.

He didn't sulk. He didn't ask to be traded. He didn't whine that he was better than guys who were playing while he sat. There was none of that stuff, and we were all aware of the bigness in Mookie, and it made us all closer, somehow. Mookie waited, played when he could, and contributed plenty before the long season was over.

Mookie brings to mind the opposite story, George Foster's. I'll get to George in a bit.

The Mets train in St. Petersburg, on the opposite coast from my home in West Palm Beach. My family was able to get to St. Petersburg only twice that spring, and I went home once. It was during

67

•

that spring training that the ball club announced it was going to shift its spring camp, starting in 1988, to Port St. Lucie. Port St. Lucie is a half-hour drive from West Palm Beach. Talk about dreams. Six more weeks at home. Six more weeks with my family.

I do wonder sometimes whether I'm doing right by my kids. Even in the off-season, I'm away from them a lot. Baseball is my business, and with good years comes more business—endorsements, advertising, consulting. I'm the national sports chairman for the Leukemia Society of America, and that has its obligations. My kids are growing so fast, shooting up before my eyes and also behind my back, because I'm missing some of it. It worries me.

Even when I'm with the kids, I worry. We built a swimming pool in back of our house on Long Island. In two seasons, two hot summers, I have been in that pool maybe three or four times. The girls are always wanting me to play with them in the pool, and I'm always begging off. I've been playing ball all afternoon, and my knees burn, and my legs are heavy as lead. Or I've got to play that night and must rest, must lie around in the shade saving all my energy for the game. Sandy understands. But when she thinks I'm missing time with the kids unnecessarily—talking on the phone too long, or going somewhere I don't absolutely have to—she puts her foot down.

Training in Port St. Lucie will make a big difference.

We left Florida on April 7 to play an exhibition game with our double A minor-league team in Jackson, Mississippi. It was a sentimental journey for some of us; Straw, Lenny, Aggie, Wally, and Mookie had all played there. Roger had met his Mississippi wife, Karen, right in Jackson. Memories, memories. The only problem was, the following day was Opening Day up in Pittsburgh. Most of us would have preferred to use the day working out on the artificial turf in Three Rivers Stadium. There's no artificial turf in Florida except the infield in Fort Myers, the Royals' spring-training site. It would have been nice to get reaccustomed. Also, you like to arrive in a city the day before Opening Day. It's a time to think, a time to prepare mentally. Your body is ready, but your mind might not be, not quite. But we played in Jackson, flew to Pittsburgh, and plunged right into the season.

We beat the Pirates that day. The afternoon was bright, the air soft. There were more than 48,000 people in the ball park, probably for the only time all season. Three Rivers Stadium is pretty empty these days. We scored twice in our first. Mex drove Lenny in with a double, and after a wild pitch, I drove Mex in with a sacrifice fly. An RBI in my first at bat, and even though I struck out twice and didn't get a hit, I was content with the beginning. As I said, I'm paid, mainly, to drive in runs. And it's nice to win that first game, get it rolling.

Dwight pitched, and made it look easy. Nine innings, a couple of runs, six hits, six strike-outs.

Mets 4, Pirates 2.

That night I talked to my business manager, Matt Merola, in New York. I told Matt I was going to win the MVP award this year. It was going to be that kind of season. And not just for me. For all of us.

It became a dream season early. Not right away, but early. Considering the year we had, it's hard to believe that any of us could have wondered, or doubted, but it took us about two weeks to see the writing on the wall. We were like a fire working up to igniting. No one, except maybe Davey, smelled the smoke.

April 9 was an off-day, and we worked out in Three Rivers Stadium, everyone eager to get into the cage and hit. In April and May, you can't get enough batting practice. You want to hit and hit and hit. You want to train your eye and toughen your hands. Good hitting is all liquid rhythm, and it takes practice and more practice to make it second nature. Late in the season, the joy goes out of batting practice. You've got it all down, the timing and rhythm, and you're tired. Some days you don't *want* to take batting practice. You want to stretch, get the arm loose, and play ball.

On April 10 it rained. Game postponed. On April 11 we went to Philadelphia. There, we lost two of three.

We won the first game, and I had myself a night. I love Veterans Stadium. The fences aren't close—330 down both lines, 408 in deepest center—but for some reason the ball flies in that big ball park. The background, black canvas above the outfield wall, highlights the ball. It rides. I've hit more home runs, twenty-three, than any other visiting player in the Vet. That Friday night, I hit one my first time up. It's always a relief, hitting that first home run. Thank God, you think, that's out of the way. You can quit wondering when it will happen.

It was a hitters' night. I hit two singles as well as the home run, driving in five in all. The game swayed back and forth. Ronnie got shelled. We hit Kevin Gross all over the place. Bobby O., who hadn't cracked the starting rotation yet, pitched some pretty good relief.

The final: Mets 9, Phillies 7. We were two and zero for the season, and sky-high.

The following day, the Phillies beat us in fourteen innings, 9–8. We broke on top with a run in our fourteenth, and the Phillies replied with two off Randy Niemann in their half. I got two hits. I'd begun a ten-game hitting streak. On Sunday they took us again, 4–2. Ray hit a home run. He'd hit one the day before, too.

On April 14, we opened the home season at Shea against—of all teams—the Cardinals.

The Cardinals don't like us, and we don't care for them. The feud, as far as I can tell, dates back only to the '85 season, when the two of us battled for the division championship. The race didn't end till the next-to-last day. It was a terrific race. We beat them two out of three in New York in September, and jumped into first place by a game. In that series, Danny Cox drilled George Foster with a pitch. George glared and pointed; Cox told him what to do with it; and the dugouts emptied. The pitch that clipped George happened to load the bases, and after peace was restored, Hojo hit a grand slam.

After we jumped ahead of them, it was a neck-and-neck race through most of the month. It seemed like every time we won, they won, too. When they lost, we did, too. We couldn't open any distance between us. They wore us out, caught us, beat us. We were eliminated by the Expos on the season's final Saturday in Shea. The

70
•

crowd, as I've mentioned, stood anyway, and cheered us handsomely.

Maybe Whitey Herzog, the Cardinals' manager, was thinking of this when he complained, "The Mets think they won the '85 pennant." (We didn't think we'd won; we know the difference.) Whitey is one of those who dislikes our style. The fists in the air, the celebrating. Ozzie Smith, their fabulous shortstop, has griped about our style. Some of us aren't crazy about his style, either—the handstands and cartwheels as he takes the field.

The Cardinals also objected to the attention we received while they were winning the pennant. They said we got too much media coverage. We got more than they did, they complained. Maybe we did, but, as my friend Mead says, "That's New York." It isn't my fault, or Keith's fault, or Dwight's fault, or Nelson Doubleday's fault that the *New York Daily News* has a bigger circulation than any other U.S. newspaper, or that the *New York Times* is read in every city in the country. That's New York. I never said I wasn't lucky to play there.

The Cards love to beat us. Ozzie Smith goes all out. He is spectacular with that glove, surer than usual. His manner is icy when he's playing us. When we were playing them later in '86—we'd buried them by then—Smith was batting once and missed a pitch. I came up out of the crouch and threw, and hit my thumb on his bat. I really whacked it: split the thumbnail. I winced and shook my hand. It was bleeding. He gazed at it a moment with those sleepy hooded eyes, then looked away, saying nothing. Say, Oz, I just about broke my hand on your bat, or didn't you notice? I was thinking.

The Cardinals were without Joaquin Andujar, the eccentric pitcher who had been traded to the Oakland As soon after the '85 World Series. He had been on the mound for a while in the seventh game of the Series. Things weren't going his way, and he'd thrown a tantrum and tried to push a couple of umpires. He and Herzog had been thrown out of the game, which the Cardinals had lost, 11–0.

I asked one of the guys, as he was getting ready to hit, how things were with Joaquin gone.

"Joaquin embarrassed the brewery," the player said. The brew-

71

•

ery is Anheuser Busch, owned by Gussie Busch, who also owns the Cardinals. "Don't ever embarrass the brewery. If you do, you won't be around long."

Opening Day in Shea, the Cardinals beat us. It was a cool and gorgeous April day. Sellout crowd, naturally. Doc started and pitched eight good innings. Their pitcher, Ricky Horton, was as good. Doc gave up two runs in eight innings. Roger pitched a runless ninth. After eight and a half, they led, 2–1. In our ninth we tied the game. They beat us in the thirteenth with four runs. I made the game's final out, hitting the ball pretty hard, but to the right fielder, Tito Landrum. As I said before, I always hate to make the last out. When I do, I take it home with me. I spend the night with it.

The Cardinals had now won five and lost none. We were two and three. The writers began wondering, in print, what was wrong with us. April 15 was an off-day, and then it rained in New York—hard, for two days. The Cards were supposed to play us two more, but left town still five and oh.

We didn't like it. The two games would be made up in August. They would be crammed in with four other games, six games in four days in the most grueling month of the season, the month when the aches have taken hold, and the season's end seems years away. It was tiring just thinking about it. No one mentioned our two-and-three start, but it was bothering us. There was a nervousness, something brittle, in the guys' faces. No one said a thing about it. But we were all thinking, Better get in gear. And fast.

Nobody smelled the smoke.

The Phillies came to town, the rain quit, and the fire began. We beat them on Friday night, April 18, 5–2. On Saturday, Doc beat them, 3–2. On Sunday, we shellacked them, 8–0.

Davey had me batting fifth in that game, instead of cleanup, where I almost always hit. He had Straw hitting cleanup. I wasn't crazy about the change. I take pride in hitting fourth. I brought it up, gently, with Davey, who said he wanted Darryl to get some good pitches to swing at. They wouldn't want to walk him with me up next, and would be less likely to tease him with bad pitches. They'd feed him pitches he could hit. Of course, the reverse was true: with

72

•

big Darryl following *me*, I got better pitches to swing at, too. It felt like a demotion, and we all hate demotions, but Davey insisted it wasn't. I think again of Mookie, and the dignity with which he accepted his part-time role. Batting fifth that day, I hit a single, a double, drove in a run, and scored one. Straw had two hits and drove in two.

We went to Pittsburgh. Davey lifted me back into the cleanup position, and I hit a home run. So did Ray. Mets 6, Pirates 5. Bobby O. beat them the next day, 7 – 1. Five in a row. We were seven and three, the Cardinals were seven and two. We went to St. Louis to play four games.

Before the weekend war began, Davey did something rash and gutsy. He announced that we were going to win three of the four in St. Louis. This, he said, would prove something. He said we were going to beat the Cardinals this year, and that we would begin that weekend in St. Louis.

We won all four games.

We beat them in ten innings Thursday night, and first place was ours. They led, 3 – 1, going into the eighth. We scored a run in our eighth; they answered with one in their half. In the top of the ninth, we tied the game. Roger was pitching now, the fifth pitcher Davey had used. He allowed a walk and nothing else for two innings. We got the run in the tenth off Todd Worrell, who had set a record for consecutive strike-outs in the '85 World Series. The win was our sixth in a row.

The next night we climbed all over them, 9 – 0. A shutout by Doc. Ray hit two home runs, his fifth and sixth. I was hot, but Ray was hotter.

I was glad for Ray. In spring training, the Mets had almost let him go. Ray had had two lean years, '84 and '85, and the ball club was running out of patience. He'd been in the league for ten years, and Frank Cashen was wondering if he had reached the end of the road. But Ray had been hurt. After the '84 season, he'd had bone chips taken out of his throwing elbow, and he'd also had shoulder surgery. He used to get his arm loaded up with cortisone to dull the pain enough to allow him to play. Ray's a tough cookie. He's a soft-spoken Christian, but don't make him mad. He was a Golden Gloves boxer when he was a kid, and he knows how to throw a punch. His Georgia Daddy, Ray says, taught him how to stand up and defend himself.

Ray is married to the great golfer Nancy Lopez. People are occasionally tempted to joke about this, but it isn't a good idea. Marty Noble, who writes for *Newsday*, once called Ray "Mr. Ray Lopez" in a story. Ray wasn't amused. Luckily for Noble, Ray is a gentleman as well as a good puncher.

Ray and I are close, and in the spring I did what I could to lift his confidence. Frank wasn't holding out a lot of hope, but Davey stood with Ray. "I want Ray Knight," Davey said, in that breezy yet stubborn way of his. Ray stayed. At first, Davey played him only against left-handed pitchers. On April 21, Ray was in the line-up against the Pirates when a righty, Cecilio Guante, entered the game. Eighth inning; we were down by two runs, man on base, Ray due to hit.

Ray, expecting to be lifted, was in the on-deck circle. He looked at Davey, the two of them trading a long look. Ray waited. Davey winked. Ray strode to the plate. It was the first time he'd faced a right-hander this season, and he hit one out of the park. He said afterward he was thinking home run all the way. From that moment, he was our everyday third baseman.

Ray became a free agent after the 1986 season. The Mets tried to keep him, but their offer was short of what he was asking. Neither side would budge and we lost him.

I keep hearing a comment around New York. I hear it wherever I go, from elevator operators, waitresses, TV sports reporters, a guard at Madison Square Garden. They all say the same thing, same words.

"Too bad about Ray," they say.

And it is.

On Saturday afternoon, April 26, in the third of the four-game series, we beat the Cardinals 4 – 3, on national television. We scored all our runs in the first, off Danny Cox. Lenny began the game with a home run. Cox got Wally, then Mex and Straw singled. I was batting fifth again. I must say, the strategy kept working. I hit a double, bringing Mex home. Danny singled, and Straw and I scored.

It was a frustrating afternoon for the Cardinals. It didn't help, either, that the game was on national television. Sid was our pitcher. They nicked him for a run in their first, then went scoreless until the last of the ninth. Then they got it going.

They knocked Duke out and hit Roger pretty hard. With two runs in, tying run at second, winning run at first, just one out, Lady Luck swooped down on our behalf. J.O. had come in to pitch. The hitter was Terry Pendleton. We hadn't scored since the first inning, and here was this ninth-inning uprising by the Cardinals; the tide was going the opposite way.

Pendleton rapped the ball hard up the middle. It hit the side of the mound, glanced off at an angle, and Wally dove and gloved it. Mike Heath was the runner at first. Wally scrambled up, flipped to Raffy, getting the sliding Heath; Raffy to Mex, *just* getting Pendleton, who went in sliding. Crazy, lucky, beautifully executed play. The Mex let out a yell, and came running in wearing the *biggest* smile.

On Sunday, we beat John Tudor, their brilliant lefty. Bobby O. went all the way for us. World, Kevin Mitchell, hit his first major-league home run. Mets 5, Cardinals 3. We'd won nine in a row. We were in first place, four and a half games in front of the Cardinals. I don't think they held the faintest hope of catching us. After Saturday's game, the fire had gone out of them. You could see it in their faces—something missing, a quiet look.

If an April series ever decided a division race, it was that one.

I was hitting a ton, but I wasn't throwing well. The reporters noticed this, and wrote about it. The Cardinals are a running team, and they stole some bases, whippets like Vince Coleman, Willie McGee, Pendleton, and Tommy Herr.

I'd had my third knee operation in the off-season, and, as I said, during spring training Davey had decided to save me from crouching

75
•

and played me at first and in the outfield. I didn't catch a game until about ten days before Opening Day. The knee still ached, and I was favoring it when I threw, not turning on it and pushing off. I was snapping my throws with my arm and upper body, and the runners were outracing the ball.

You hear a lot of discussion about whether a runner steals a base on the pitcher or on the catcher. It isn't all one or the other, of course, but most good base stealers will say they steal on the pitchers. Catchers, naturally, agree. On our staff, Ronnie and Roger hold runners very close and get the ball to the plate quickly; it's hard to steal on them—or me, if they're in there. The rest of our pitchers throw with a high kick of the leg, which can add a precious second to the time it takes to get the ball to me.

Catchers are a separate, distinct breed. We feel a certain brotherhood with each other. Joe Garagiola and Tim McCarver, the TV announcers, are both former catchers, and they don't try to hide their partiality for us guys behind the plate.

Any catcher will tell you a runner steals on the pitcher.

Our winning streak ran eleven games, stopping on May 1 in Atlanta. We then won the next seven. We led the league by five games, not an enormous lead, but a comfortable one. On May 23, we were three games on top. At the end of the month, we'd pulled ahead by six. Three games, five, or six: we were comfortable. We were like a long-distance runner who gets out ahead of the pack early, and who looks, at times, as if he can be caught, but who knows he won't be, because today is his day. His lead may not be enormous, but it is comfortable because he is equal to anyone trying to catch him. When this happens, self-confidence takes over, and it lifts and carries you like a wave.

On May 27, we had our first brawl. We were playing the Dodgers at home. We entered the bottom of the sixth tied, 1–1. Then their pitcher, Bob Welch, completely lost his stuff. We started knocking him all over the place. A couple of runs were in, the bases were loaded, and at last Tommy Lasorda pulled Welch out of the game. George Foster was the hitter. Lasorda brought in Tom Niedenfuer.

Niedenfuer, a good relief pitcher, had been having trouble with home runs. He'd given up a couple of beauties in the '85 Championship Series, and this year guys were continuing to take his pitches deep. So he was not enjoying the baseball season at that point.

He threw a fastball by George; George waved at it late and sloppily, and looked horrible. Niedenfuer decided to try it again, same pitch. George must have guessed that he would and been set for it, because he hit the ball a mile, a grand-slam home run.

George toured the bases in a slow home-run trot, and Niedenfuer seethed. He didn't know it, but they were showing his face on the instant-replay screen. The man was in agony. He looked sick. And angry.

Ray was up next, and you didn't need to be clairvoyant to know what was going to happen. Niedenfuer was boiling, and George had a lofty manner that didn't endear him to pitchers—especially after he'd hit one of their fastballs downtown. George, however, was safely on the bench, and Ray was in the batter's box. That's always the way. Niedenfuer bounced the first pitch off Ray's hip.

Ray had expected it, but he still didn't like it. He flung his bat away, his helmet, and went for Niedenfuer. Most baseball fights are fairly harmless: a lot of wrestling, grabbing, pulling, but not much violence. Ray, though, is a puncher. He popped Niedenfuer a couple of times before both teams swarmed out. Mike Scioscia, their catcher, was trying to get to Ray, but Uncle Bill got there first and held him back. I didn't see anybody else fighting. Ray was my buddy, so I talked to him, trying to soothe him and get him quieted down. I told him it was over, and he'd done the right thing, and he could forget it now. Everyone knew Niedenfuer was plain frustrated. I told Ray he was the best. Surprisingly, the umpires left Ray in the game. They left Niedenfuer in, too, but that was only temporary. A single by Raffy, base on balls to R.J., and Niedenfuer took the long walk to the dugout.

A brawl will usually leave a taste that will linger through the season. A grudge settles in. But this fight wasn't like that. Two and a half months later, the Dodgers were in New York, and Ray and Niedenfuer were invited to the same restaurant for dinner. I was there, and you would have thought the two of them were old friends. They never mentioned the fight. It was as if it had never happened.

The Mets brought Rick Anderson up from Tidewater early in June to pitch a game against the Phillies. Rick had caught Davey's attention when he'd thrown eight and a third perfect innings against Toledo on June 3. After the game he would be sent right back down; there wouldn't be room on our roster for him. Rick had been toiling in the minors for eight and a half years. A start in the majors was his dream. His father flew down from Alaska to watch him pitch. He threw seven superb innings, left the game, and did not figure in the decision. In mid-season Rick again came up from Tidewater. Davey used him both as a starter and in long relief. He pitched well. The guys liked him. Late in September, the club had a huge decision to make. We couldn't carry everybody on our roster into the postseason. Someone had to go. Rick was sent yet again to Tidewater. If anything upset the team that year, it was this demotion of Anderson. It didn't seem quite fair, or sensible. The ball club did reward him for his fine work by inviting him to the play-offs and the Series as our batting-practice pitcher.

Let's face it: nothing promotes harmony in a ball club like winning. But win or lose, the Mets were a congenial mix, even affectionate toward one another. It was so different from my years with the Expos—the cliques, the verbal sniping. There was always an uneasy feeling, like a bitter smell, in that clubhouse.

The '86 Mets were happy and loose, and when a team is that way, the funny guys act up, and the funniness spreads. There was Roger and his rubber masks, Roger and his hotfoot routines. There were the "rally hats" when we started building a big inning—the bill of the hat turned up and cradling a baseball, for good luck. A towel over the head was also supposed to be lucky; when the Mets were hitting, it sometimes looked like a convention of sheiks out in our dugout. Ballplayers are notorious pranksters, and that year, whenever it rained, whenever a field was muddy, somebody's hat would get wet and dirty.

The horseplay turned unfunny only once that I recall. We were in San Diego late in May. The field was very wet, and there were lakes of rain water in a couple of the low places. Before the game, Bobby O. and a couple of other jokers stole Kevin Mitchell's hat and began playing soccer with it. Stealing World's hat—stealing anything of World's—requires trickery. You have to distract him—tickle him or jab him in the ribs—while a partner whisks the hat away from another direction. They raced away with his hat and kicked it through the wet grass, through rain water, and across the muddy infield.

Naturally, World retaliated. He found Bobby O.'s glove, and when Bobby wasn't looking, he rinsed it thoroughly and then rubbed it in the dirt. The glove, as it happened, was Bobby's best. His game glove—his gamer, as we say.

Bobby O. didn't think this was funny.

And while World laughed his way through batting practice, Bobby O. went into the clubhouse, found a pair of scissors, and cut World's brand-new Fila running shoes to ribbons.

I was in the clubhouse when World came clattering in to put on his game jersey. His mouth dropped open. He was amazed as much as angry: Bobby O. had broken the rules. World stood there with his hands dripping Fila ribbons and spoke slowly, dangerously, to Bobby O.

"I can't *believe* you did this. Messin' with my *personal* stuff."

"You messed with my game glove," Bobby shot back.

"Yeah, but that's your *glove*. Get *my* glove. Get my baseball shoes, but don't mess with my personal stuff."

"My game glove's *my* personal stuff," Bobby said.

World started across toward Bobby. You could smell a fight brewing.

"Hold it," I said. "Let's just *settle* this thing now."

They continued eying each other.

79

•

"How much did the shoes cost, World?" I said.

"Ninety dollars."

I said, "You know that wasn't right, Bobby O. Why don't you buy him a new pair of shoes?"

"My grandmother bought me them shoes," World said.

"If your grandmother bought 'em," Bobby said, "how do you know they cost ninety dollars?"

"Because I do."

"Bobby," I said, "will you just give him ninety dollars?"

And Bobby O. did, and it was over.

These things can escalate. Up in Montreal one day I witnessed an unforgettable duel between Stan Bahnsen and Larry Parrish, retaliation upon retaliation upon retaliation, which might have ended with the incineration of Olympic Stadium. The Great Fire War, we'll call it.

Bahnsen was a hotfoot artist. Parrish was, and is, a rough customer. He was the Expos' enforcer, and the title was well earned. Bahnsen had been giving people the hotfoot. He'd given it to Parrish more than once, and one day Parrish said, "Don't do it to me anymore."

Parrish didn't usually have to warn anyone twice. And he wasn't used to having people disregard his warnings, which is exactly what Bahnsen did. Bahnsen gave him another hotfoot.

Parrish didn't do anything—right away. We played later that day. Bahnsen was watching the game from the bullpen; Parrish, of course, was in the dugout when he wasn't playing third base. But after the game began, Parrish went into the clubhouse to avenge the hotfoot.

Our dirty uniforms are sent out every day to be laundered. If they want to, ballplayers can use the same service for their own laundry and dry cleaning. We pay for it, but it's a convenience. Bahnsen had sent one of his wife's dresses to be dry-cleaned. A nice dress. A $300 dress. It had been returned that day and was hanging in Bahnsen's locker.

Parrish took Connie Bahnsen's dress, placed it on the concrete floor, wet it with rubbing alcohol, and put a match to it. Soon afterward, one of the guys came in, and noticed a charred tatter hanging in Bahnsen's locker. He called him on the bullpen phone.

Parrish had gone back out to the field. Bahnsen headed for the clubhouse. From Parrish's locker he removed underpants, undershirt, and socks. He laced them with rubbing alcohol and burned them. Somebody told Parrish.

Bahnsen was in the bullpen again. Parrish went storming into the clubhouse. Word had gotten around, and some of the guys who weren't playing slipped into the clubhouse to observe the proceedings. They watched him grab Bahnsen's street clothes, his shirt and slacks, and, of course, burn them.

The guys practically tripped over each other trying to get to the phone to tell Bahnsen. Bahnsen was furious. His street clothes!

He came in and incinerated Parrish's street clothes.

It wasn't entirely a fair exchange. Parrish favored a casual bluejeans look; Bahnsen was a snappy dresser. It could be said that Parrish was still ahead, though he didn't see it that way.

He was back in the clubhouse next inning, lighting up Bahnsen's shoes. This was reported to Bahnsen.

Bahnsen burned Parrish's shoes.

The Great Fire War finally ended when both lockers were empty. The two had to dig up old sweat shirts and sweat pants to wear home. Parrish did agree, finally, to pay for Connie Bahnsen's dress. After all, Connie hadn't given him the hotfoot.

6

Whenever catchers get together, they trade stories about the hard knocks that go with the position. They talk about collisions, knees bumping hard dirt a thousand times a summer, knee joints doubled down in a squat till they burn, foul tips pounding toes and fingers, bruises painting arms from wrists to biceps, hot pain filling throwing arms. Pitchers throw a lot? What about catchers?

I tell my fellow catchers about the time Tony Taylor hit me, low, as he tried to score, spraining ligaments in my knee. A sprain, not a clean tear: the ligaments remained attached by stretched-out threads, and the pain was fiercer than when I tore the ligaments in that right knee and needed surgery.

Old catchers will talk about the diminished circulation in the index finger of their catching hand. Baseballs pounding that finger over the years cause problems. Sometimes surgery is needed. Carlton Fisk, who has moved to the outfield in the twilight of his career, will talk about the concentration demanded of a catcher. On Fisk's busiest day in left field, he handled the ball no more than seven times. A catcher is part of every play.

I tell them how, when I go to the movies, I have to sit in an end seat with my right leg stretched out in the aisle. I tell them about a moment of such excruciating pain in my throwing arm that I leaned with my left arm against a wall and let the right arm dangle like a broken wing.

Catching hurts. It wears you down.

A big-league pitcher throws at a speed of eighty-five, ninety, maybe ninety-five miles per hour. A foul tip attacks a catcher at nearly twice the speed of the pitch, shooting off the moving bat faster than the eye can see. One of the first things a catcher learns is to keep his head thrust forward, and always, always, straight. Your instinct is to flinch away, to turn your head aside. If you do, a foul tip will catch you on the neck, or the ear. Take a foul tip against the ear, and you will hear bells ring. A catcher has to teach himself to expose his face to the ball, to take it on the mask, which is against human instinct. When the ball strikes the dirt in front of you, you have to stick your nose into the ricochet. You have to take it on the mask. Watch kids playing sandlot ball; watch what they do when a throw hits short and the ricochet attacks them. They turn their heads as far as they can. It's instinct. A catcher learns not to turn his head by days, weeks, and months of practice. He pays with many bruises, many headaches, along the way.

I began catching near the end of my final high-school season. I'd been an infielder and a pitcher. As long ago as Pony League, I'd been talked about as a big-league pitching prospect. But late in my final spring of high school, big-league scouts began telling my coach that I had the stuff to become a major-league catcher. What they saw was size, a strong arm, and the aggressive and enthusiastic way I played the game. I was avid, hungry, and loved being in the thick of things. The scouts passed their hunch on to my coach, Bob Barr, who obliged by sticking me behind the plate.

It was all right by me. The road to the big leagues is shorter for a catcher than anyone else except, perhaps, a pitcher. We're in shorter supply, and we wear out quicker. I was eighteen, and I wasn't worried about wearing out. I just wanted to make the big leagues. I strapped on the pads and went behind the plate. I caught about seven games that spring, getting by on raw, uneducated talent. I collected the bruises, but they weren't big-league bruises.

The big-league bruises began a month later, at the Expos rookie camp in Jamestown, New York. I arrived with no catcher's style, no technique. I didn't know how to shift my weight neatly to reach a wide pitch, or how to pounce sideways to block one away and in the dirt. I hadn't learned to take anything on the mask.

The coaches, a guy named Rick Summers and a former minor-league ballplayer named Bill MacKenzie, spent a month educating me. This guy Summers was tough, like a drill sergeant. He'd line us catchers up against the outfield fence and fire the ball at us low, skipping it five feet in front of us. I was the most inexperienced catcher in camp, and he and MacKenzie worked me and worked me. They'd set me up anywhere there was a screen—a backstop, a batting cage—and send those ricochets at me. Summers got me in the Adam's apple once. About squashed it. I had almost solid bruises up and down the insides of my thighs, but I learned.

Later, in the Instructional League, the coaches aimed a pitching machine at the dirt in front of me and let fly. The ball would hop off the hard dirt like a bullet, and always in a new direction.

Relax your muscles, the coaches taught me. You've got to make yourself as soft as you can, because if that muscle is taut, the ball will bounce off it and get away from you. Relax, be loose. The trouble is, when muscle is loose, the bruises are worse.

When a right-handed pitcher throws his breaking ball in the dirt, it will shoot back the other way, reversing direction. In other words, the righty's curve bends downward from my left to my right. When it hits the dirt, it grabs and spins up from my right to my left. I couldn't hope to block it if I weren't aware of the physics involved. You have to know the bounces. You anticipate: you don't go for the ball; you go to meet it. So you have to bear in mind, always, whether you've got a righty or a lefty throwing, because you'll never get to the breaking balls in the dirt if you have to stop and think.

You have to know a lot more about a pitcher than which arm he throws with. You learn, just by catching a guy, how and where his pitches travel. Catching, like hitting, requires a certain foreknowl-edge. A hitter has to guess, of course, but for whatever pitch he sees—fastball, breaking ball—he has to know, roughly, what the ball will do. I still can't figure out how Ashby was able to catch Mike Scott. I had no idea where his pitches would go. None. I couldn't look for the ball anywhere. A catcher has to know, exactly. This is why it's so dangerous to mix up signs. If I'm expecting the curve, I'm assuming movement, direction, and speed. Throw me the fastball—straighter, harder, different veer—and you could knock a hole in my chest.

Bruce Berenyi, who was injured early in '86 and sent to Tidewater in August, was difficult to catch. You never quite knew where his pitches were going. I didn't know, and neither did Bruce. His pitches—curve, slider, even his fastball—never behaved the same. I couldn't relax back there, couldn't slide to the ball. I was always lunging.

Bobby Ojeda is just the opposite. Bobby O. is a catcher's dream. He threads needles; the two of us almost always know where a pitch is heading. It might bite down, it might creep up, but I'm expecting it, and I'll be there.

Sid Fernandez is even easier to catch than Bobby O. He throws with a powerful thrust off his left leg, the arm coming not straight over the top but at three-quarters. His fastball climbs. It begins belt-high, then sails past the hitter at the letters on his chest. Duke's curve ball floats, and he will seldom bounce one in front of me. I relax when Dukey's out there.

Dwight Gooden throws hard, always. His breaking ball bites hard. His pitches are alive; they sail, they fly, which means they don't feel heavy hitting in the mitt.

Doug Sisk throws a heavy ball. He doesn't throw as hard as Doc, but he throws heavier. His pitches sink. They're burrowing down as they hit the glove, and they thud in there, heavy-feeling. Doug throws the heaviest ball on our staff.

Ron Darling is a little less easy than Duke, Doc, and Bobby O. R.J. often tries to be too fine with his pitches, too precise. He will aim for the tiniest corner of the plate, not relying on the natural movement of the ball to carry it there. This fine-tuning can crimp the flight of the ball, can make it erratic. Davey has a slogan: "Keep it simple, stupid." Don't try to be cute, he means. Don't get fancy. Set the target in the middle of the plate. Davey wrote it in my mitt: KISS.

As I get to know a pitcher, I get to know how his pitches will spin up out of the dirt. The general rule is that the breaking ball in the dirt will bounce the other way, but beyond that there are other rules, depending on the pitcher. You must always know the angle of the bounce: you've got to take it off your chest at a ninety-degree angle, so it will drop in front of you. You have to hunch your shoulders, make your chest as hollow as possible—anything to trap the ball as it shoots up out of the dirt. Anything to keep it in front of you.

You can't always know what a bounce will do. A hard clot of dirt, a pebble, will send a ball shooting off its predicted course. Then there's nothing you can do. You bounce sideways, on your knees, for a wide pitch in the dirt; you've got to block the gap between your thighs with the mitt. When the ball bounces crazy, you can only get in front of it, plug the hole between your legs, stick your head down, and hope that it hits you somewhere, anywhere.

You block a ball in the dirt on your knees, with the mitt down and palm out. This offers the underside of your wrist, the inside of your arm almost all the way up, to the ball. You get hit there, up and down the arm, a lot.

You try to keep your throwing hand out of harm's way. I'm a one-handed catcher; when there's no one on base, I tuck my right fist behind my back, where it's safe. With a runner on, you have to be readier to throw. Then, I clench my fist and hold it just behind the mitt, where the foul tips can't get it.

It may sound strange, after I've said I can't spare the fragment of a second it would take to whip my throwing hand from behind me to the glove, but I do use a split second to find the seams of the ball, and to grip it across the stitching. That way, the ball flies truer, straighter. A pitcher will let go with his index and second fingers wrapped along the seams, and this encourages the pitch to tail, which is the last thing I want, trying to gun a runner out at second. I don't think about hunting for that grip across the seams, but I try to hold the ball that way every time I throw. It has become instinct.

The foul pop-up is a catcher's special problem. For everyone else, a fly ball is an arc. It may rise almost straight up, like a finger, but even a finger tapers. The long fly ball sails, but eventually arcs down. The fly ball or infield pop, whatever its height, whatever its distance, is an arc from point A to point B.

The pop-up behind the plate obeys different laws. It is more a loop than an arc. The ball climbs almost straight up, arcs like any pop fly, then loops back. The problem is, you never know how severe the loop will be. An outfielder or infielder can figure out a routine fly ball instantaneously; he knows where it will come down, and can wait for it. Catchers can guess, but they can't be sure. We can look comical, wobbling around under a moving pop-up. My technique is to keep the loop well in front of me, and move into the ball as it falls. I don't want to have to back up frantically if the ball loops too far. You can never be sure where the ball is going to end up.

Outfielders and infielders don't lose sight of their fly balls. We do, obviously. We spin around—right or left, depending on where the bat scrapes the ball—whip off the mask, and hunt for the ball against the sky. In a cloudless sky—a high sky, as we call it—the ball is the hardest to find. We can educate ourselves as to where to look, but sometimes we figure wrong, and scan the sky in the wrong direction. We must look very foolish to fans.

One thing always to remember: throw the mask far away, so you don't trip over it.

I often flinch now on foul tips. I'll dip my head, just a little. I keep the glove right where it is, but my head will flinch. I didn't used to do this. But I've been hit so many times, been pounded and bruised so many places, that some deep instinct I can't fight has begun to work on me in that moment in which a pitch glances off a moving bat.

Maybe, finally, the body rebels against getting hit. The great Johnny Bench finally said, "Enough," and insisted on playing third base. Carlton Fisk has moved to the outfield. Catchers are used to hurting. We play in pain of one sort or another almost every day. There is almost nowhere I haven't been hit by a baseball. I've been hit in the shoulder, ear, wrist, foot, toe, nuts, and hand. I've been hit a thousand times in each of those places. I didn't used to mind. The pain didn't burrow as deep. It went away sooner.

The record for games caught in the big leagues is 1,918, set by Al Lopez. I've caught more than 1,500 games. I used to be able to catch more in a season than I can now. I caught 146 games in 1977, 152 in 1978, then 138, then 149, then 100 in the strike-shortened season, then 148. In each of those six years, I led the league in games caught, a National League record. For ten straight years I've caught at least a hundred games, three shy of the major-league record, held by Bench and Bill Dickey.

I can't catch more than 140 games a year anymore. I can't take as much punishment. I don't dive as hard or as far as I used to in spearing a runner as he slides in. I don't slide into second as aggressively as I once did. I still get my uniform plenty dirty, but I used to get it dirtier. If I catch 125 games in each of the next three seasons, I'll pass Lopez. But Bob Boone, the California Angels catcher, will own the record by then. He is about a hundred games short of Lopez. Bob is thirty-nine and still a regular catcher—an awesome achievement. Randy Hundley once caught 160 games for the Chicago Cubs, an achievement at any age.

And yet I don't want to give it up. If I were moved, permanently, to first base or the outfield, I'd miss catching. I'd miss handling the ball all the time, and being in the middle of things. Catching gives you a chance to help your team even when you're doing nothing with the bat. You can go hitless and save the game with a beautiful throw to second base, by blocking a pitch in the dirt with a runner at third, or by planting yourself in front of a runner barreling down the line like a fullback. You can go hitless and mastermind a rookie's shutout.

It's harder to brood after you've struck out or hit into a rally-killing double play; you're too busy catching. A pitcher can embarrass me again and again, but, every time, I have to buckle on the pads and start thinking about who's due up for his side and what pitches I'm going to call. This may be why I hate to make the last out in a game—there's no more catching to do, and I have plenty of time to think about it.

I can't talk about catching without paying respects to my friend and hero, Johnny Bench. John is everything a catcher should hope to be. From the time I arrived in the big leagues, he set the standard. He was the guy I emulated. John was what catching was about: intelligence, intensity, a rifle arm, and power at the plate. As a rookie, I couldn't wait to meet him.

My first chance to talk with him was at the 1975 All-Star game. We became friends right away. I was a catcher, after all. John liked my eagerness and hustle, and he must have sensed my admiration for him. From that day, he took an interest in me. Someone snapped a picture of us, and later John signed it for me: "In a few years, it's all yours." John's belief in me is one of the greatest compliments the game has ever given me.

Occasionally John would call me when we were in Cincinnati. Sandy took to him immediately. Sandy's mother keeps a photograph of John in her bedroom. "My boy friend," she calls him. I still run into John from time to time, and it's as much a pleasure as ever. I still feel that rush of awe when I see him.

I still emulate him. He's the man I want to be compared to. His records are the ones I'd like to break. Anytime anyone mentions me in the same breath with Johnny Bench, I'm being honored.

I'd hate to give up catching, and maybe it's as simple as this: I take pride in it. There's pride in the air when catchers get together and trade their stories. Baseball fans may or may not appreciate the pain and rigors of catching, but we catchers appreciate each other. When Bob Boone, at the age of forty, hunkers down in his crouch and looks out through the bars of his mask to begin a new, long season, there isn't a big-league catcher who won't feel his heart swell a little—in envy and, most of all, in admiration. Someone ought to send him roses. If I've landed a lot of times on the hard dirt on my knees, how many times has he? Eight more years of it. Eight more years of foul tips and fastballs in the dirt.

We look well protected in our chest protector and shin guards, but as the years go by, the protection feels less and less substantial to me. When a collision is looming, when a runner comes pounding around third and I'm looking out to right field, watching the throw, unable to look at this guy who's about to try to cut me in half, then I feel like I'm wearing tissue paper on my chest. I feel stripped and vulnerable. I'm waiting for the throw, waiting for the runner, knowing they might arrive at the same time and that I can't watch them both if that happens. Time seems to slow, and distantly, at the back of my mind, I'm thinking: these pads aren't enough.

They are nowhere near enough.

7

The World Series. I was going to play in the World Series. Me. I believed it after that Houston series. When we were running away with the division championship, Davey had told us that the League Championship Series would, in a sense, be our World Series. Our season would have been a bust if we'd lost it. There was more pressure to win, a feeling of fighting for survival. But, we'd beaten Houston: the worst was over. We'd been through fire. We'd earned our way into the World Series, and no one doubted we were there. When a dream comes that hard, you have no trouble believing in it. I was in the World Series, me, and until the end—until the sixth and seventh games—it was almost anticlimactic.

The press swarmed around like bees, thicker and nosier and more insistent than I'd ever known. I remembered talking to Johnny Bench about coverage of the World Series, the numbers of reporters and the excitement swirling around. He was trying to describe it, and I thought I was getting the idea. "Sort of like the All-Star game," I said. Johnny laughed. "Take the hype of the All-Star game," he said, "and magnify it a hundred times. Then you've got an idea."

I didn't believe it till it started. The reporters were from all over the country, and all over the world. Eighty million Americans watched us on television, and millions more in other lands. Japanese radio announcers called the play-by-play for listeners on the other side of the world. We worked out in Shea the day before the Series began, and the field was so full of reporters and cameramen that it was impossible to concentrate on hitting or fielding.

All of this, and still I felt easier in my mind, more relaxed, more hopeful, than I ever had during the Houston series. Whatever happened, I was going to get a ring: a League Championship ring or a World Series ring. I'd been saving the ring finger of my right hand for a World Series ring. A wedding ring and a World Series ring: awesome.

We were exhausted from the Houston series. Fatigue may have hurt us, and it may have helped us: in a strange sort of way, we were too tired to get terribly nervous. As the Series wore on, the fire rose in us, and then we started feeling the tension.

I had something else going for me, in a way. I'd performed so miserably against the Astros, I knew I couldn't do any worse. I could only be pleasantly surprised. I felt relaxed.

Our house on Long Island is spacious, but even Shea Stadium can get full. Sandy and I got home from Houston after that sixteen-inning finale—got home exhausted—and our loved ones began arriving the next day.

The cast included Kimmy and Christy, who had watched the middle three games against the Astros and were still there with Sandy's mother. (Her father and brother had gone home after the fifth game.) My friend from California Doug Jones and his wife, Debbie, had flown in. So had Gordy and his wife, Lindi.

Gordy had held off making plans; if the Angels had beaten the Red Sox, he would have stayed in California and watched the first two games on television, then the middle three in person in Anaheim. The Red Sox had won it, and that night, Thursday, Gordy had called.

"I'm coming, Gar."

I assumed he meant later, after the middle three games in Boston. "Great," I said. "I'll see you next week, then."

"I'm coming tomorrow," he said.

"You're kidding."

94

•

"No. We were just waiting for the outcome of the American League play-offs. We'll be there tomorrow."

So, after all these years, he was coming, *really* coming, to see me play ball. For years I'd been calling him whenever I was playing in Los Angeles, inviting him to come to Dodger Stadium. Come on, Big Brother. Want to come out to the game? I'll leave you tickets. Sometimes he came. Not often. His job kept him busy. When he did come, he was uninterested, almost as if I were imposing on him.

I told Gordy I was happy he was coming, and I was.

Sandy and I, Kimmy, Christy, Sandy's mother, Doug, Debbie, Gordy, Lindi, and my father.

My father. His back was bothering him. Arthritis? Who knew? It was killing him. He's sixty-eight and he's nagged and worried by all sorts of ailments. He doesn't suffer in silence. He's had arthritis for a couple of years.

Throughout the Series, I kept imagining all kinds of dire things in Dad's back. A disc, a vertebra. Gordy and I kept asking him, "Hey, Dad. You okay? Shall we get a doctor?" No doctor. He didn't want to see a doctor. Just before the Series moved to Boston, his back started *really* killing him, and Gordy thought about taking him to the hospital, against his wishes if necessary. It had been bothering Dad during the series with Houston. He was in his seat in the Astrodome during one game and was in such agony I had to send the clubhouse boy running up with a muscle relaxant and a pain killer.

Everyone in the house treated me like a king, staying quiet when I slept, protecting me from phone calls and neighbors banging on the door to ask a favor or wish me good luck. My mother-in-law performed a noble deed on the second day of the Series, when a policeman rang the doorbell and asked me for a favor.

This cop's name is Pete, and he keeps an eagle eye on the house when we're in Florida. He's very cordial, very helpful, and I'd hate to say no to him. I didn't have to.

He'd brought a new baseball. "I was wondering," he said, "if Gary could get the team to autograph this."

My mother-in-law stood her ground. "You and about 5,000 other people," she said.

The cop gave up. He's a nice guy and he probably realized that going around the clubhouse getting everybody to sign a ball is something of a chore during a World Series. But if he didn't see the light, he knew he'd run into an immovable object. He apologized and left.

I spent half of Friday, the day before the Series started, negotiating on the telephone for tickets and making driving arrangements. It was up to me to provide tickets for everyone, and to arrange transportation to the ball park. Sandy planned and cooked meals. The phone kept ringing. It was busy.

My father hung in there till the Series was over. Then he went home and saw a doctor. It turned out he had a muscle pull and a cracked vertebra. He'd hurt himself lifting a suitcase.

When I was in Little League, my father was my coach. When I advanced to Pony League, Dad moved with me. When my mother died and when Gordy went away to college, it was just me and Dad in the house. Scouts had begun noticing me, and my father and I suspected that I was going to make the major leagues someday. The knowledge bound us, made us partners. He was my first coach, in every sense. He had an investment in me. I depended on him, as if he were both parents rolled into one.

Which he was. He was as much a mother as I would ever have again. He helped me with my homework. He was very patient about that. He cooked for Gordy and me, and for me after Gordy left, always coming straight home from work and starting dinner. He worked for McDonnell Douglas as a parts inspector and purchasing agent. He knew the value of money. I had to earn mine—mowing lawns, baby-sitting, collecting bottles, delivering newspapers. I learned early not to take money for granted. Dad had certain values, and there was no arguing against them. Sandy and I spoil our kids by comparison, though we do try to teach them the values we learned as kids.

Dad left for the plant early in the morning, while I was still asleep.

96
•

I overslept sometimes. In the old days, my mother would come in and shake me awake, but I was on my own now, and I didn't always wake up. Then I was in trouble, because you needed a note when you showed up late for school. So I would go across the alley where we played ball to the apartment building where my grandmother, Dad's mother, lived. I'd try to talk her into giving me a note and then head for school.

My mother was an only child. When she died at age thirty-seven, her parents were stunned. I try to imagine this—one of my children dying before me. It would turn life upside down. My father, too, was stunned by our mother's death. It stunned me and Gordy. All of us.

We were churchgoing Presbyterians, and I had a question: How could a loving God allow my mother to die? She was young, she was good. I looked around and thought of people who weren't half as good as my mother and wondered, Why her?

I didn't have an answer, and I threw myself more than ever into sports. In the alley I played my games, dreamed my dreams, shot baskets till darkness hid the garage and my arm felt heavy as lead. I played sandlot baseball, then high-school sports—football, basketball, baseball—immersing myself, trying to forget about my mother, and coming home too tired to fret about the question: Why her?

My mother had been a gifted athlete. She'd been a fine swimmer, and I realize now that this ability of hers, which she valued and rejoiced in, inspired my mania for sports, especially after her death. She'd been cheated. I could get some of it back for her. I was playing for her, as well as for myself. I was her blood, her name. A kid doesn't consciously work all that out, but I believe it was going on.

I still feel it. I'm still getting it back for her. She died of leukemia, and that has landed me in the fight against the disease. Every time I sign a Gary Carter baseball card, a check goes to the Leukemia Society: money for research to fight this dread disease. For ten years I signed cards for nothing, but in 1984 I made a commitment: I would sign cards only in return for a twenty-five-dollar donation to the society. The donations are in memory of my mother. The big games, the home runs, a World Series, a dream season—all help in the fight. The more visible I am, the more I can do in the leukemia crusade.

I believe there's a reason for everything.

On Friday night, the night before the Series began, Sandy and I left our guests at home and went with Bobby Ojeda and his wife, Tammy, to hear Billy Joel sing in Madison Square Garden. We took a Mets jacket, white, with our logo, which we hoped to give to him.

The concert had started when we arrived. The Garden was dark, and we got in pretty much unnoticed. About halfway through the concert, Billy announced he was going to sing "New York State of Mind," and that he was dedicating the song to the Mets. This brought a big cheer. Indoor cheering is electric. You feel it in the Astrodome when it's full, and much more in a smaller arena like the Garden. Billy sang, changing some words, putting us in the song. The crowd loved it.

At our wives' urging, Bobby and I got up and moved down the aisle toward the stage. We didn't have far to go. The stage was ringed with security officers. One of the officers stopped us. He didn't recognize us right away. Then he realized who we were and invited us through. By this time Billy had seen us.

We climbed up into the white blaze of the stage lights, and a cheer filled the Garden. The whole band gathered around us. We gave Billy the jacket; he held it up. The cheering cascaded down, and it was like being loved by a million people.

As baseball fans know, the Boston Red Sox have a reputation for losing big games. People can get very dramatic, very fancy about this. They say that the team is cursed. They write about the tragedies of Shakespeare and the ancient Greeks, and so on.

I will admit I used to wonder why the Red Sox didn't win more. Looking across from the other league, I would marvel almost every year at the big names in their line-up. Freddie Lynn. George Scott. Carlton Fisk. Carl Yastrzemski, one of the most inspired and dedicated players of all time. Jim Rice. Dwight Evans. Good players kept coming. Tony Armas. Wade Boggs, with his astonishing batting averages. Marty Barrett, who turned out to be one of the smartest ballplayers and biggest pests I ever played against. I would look at these names, and the numbers they compiled, and wonder why this team didn't win more pennants.

Still, the Red Sox' reputation means nothing when it comes to playing baseball. It's like being told that a seventy-pound watchdog is going to shy away from you at the last minute. It's the last thing you count on if you're the one who must enter the premises.

The Red Sox had staged a miracle comeback in the ninth inning of their fifth game against the Angels. They'd shown a lot of spunk in that series, and all through the season. They'd seen some hard times, and had always risen to the occasion. We knew that, and respected it.

In at least one way, the two teams were alike. We were both thrilled to be in the World Series. We both had stars in our eyes. Dwight Evans had played in the World Series as a young man in 1975. Their first baseman, Bill Buckner, had been there as a Los Angeles Dodger in '74. No one else on the Red Sox had played in a World Series. Rice had been with the team in '75, but had missed the Series because of an injury. Those guys were all happy to be in it, and I couldn't help feeling a slight kinship with them. I remember little Spike Owen, their shortstop, smiling like a kid on his birthday as he went about his business in the infield, smiling on and on, as if he could never get over being there. I liked that.

I liked seeing new players in new uniforms, old-fashioned uniforms, especially after the Astros' gaudy jerseys, which look like advertisements for a Tequila Sunrise. It had felt as if we'd been playing the Astros for a month, and the change was nice.

At this point, scouting reports were important. On September 4, we'd played an exhibition game with the Red Sox in Fenway Park for the Jimmy Fund, and that helped a little. Still, exhibition games are not the real thing, and they don't teach you a lot about the opposition. The Red Sox had started a kid named Jeff Sellers; he'd pitched pretty well, but we knew we wouldn't see him in the Series.

We'd won the game with a big late rally, but we didn't draw any conclusions from that.

I did draw conclusions from the home-run contest that was held before the exhibition game. Three guys from each team took ten cuts apiece; the Mets designated Kevin Mitchell, Lee Mazzilli, and me. I was swinging for the famous wall, the Green Monster. It is an ordinary, dull green, with a rickety look, and it has been a baseball legend for most of this century. It is 315 feet down the left-field foul line, and angles deeper toward center field. To me it looked as tall and close as the apartment building in the alley in Fullerton as I charged into the batter's box when my turn came. I took big swings and hit five home runs. Ten swings, five shots over the famous wall. It was only batting practice, but sending those balls rocketing one after another into the slack screen above the wall, or over the screen and into the black sky, got me very excited.

We had one other source of information: Bobby O. Bobby had pitched for the Red Sox for five years, and his scouting reports were extensive. He fed us one bad report. He said that Bruce Hurst, the Mormon lefty pitcher, pitched too carefully, became timid when the pressure rose, that he had the stuff and should have won many more games than he had. Bobby advised us not to worry if Hurst began a game strong. He said sooner or later the runs would come.

I think Bobby O. would retract all that about Bruce Hurst now.

Bobby brought some resentment into the Series, not so much toward the Red Sox players as toward their management. He didn't like the way he'd been treated there. He'd often talked about it while driving to Shea with me and Hojo. He felt that John McNamara, the Sox' quiet-spoken manager, hadn't used him sensibly, or fairly. He said Mac kept switching him back and forth from the starting rotation to the bullpen, so that he was in the dark half the time and never did settle into any rhythm. He wanted to play the Red Sox in the World Series. He said the worst thing would be if the Sox got there and we didn't.

Naturally, Bobby O. wanted to beat his old team. He would have wanted to if he'd thought McNamara was a saint. You love to beat the team that trades you. I know about that.

100

•

I had one vivid, stray memory of Bill Buckner, against whom I'd played for nine seasons, before he was traded out of the National League. Buckner and I had had a bizarre run-in that left no scars and proved nothing, unless it was that neither of us can fight as well as we can play baseball.

Buckner was playing for the Cubs; I was still with Montreal. He was in a slump, angry at the world, when he lifted a pop-up behind the plate. I spun out, flung away the mask, and found the ball against the night sky. While I was waiting for it to come down, Buckner thought about how his slump was being extended by another bad at-bat, and the idea made him so mad he gave my mask a good whack with his bat. I was too busy chasing the pop-up to notice. I caught the ball, retrieved my mask, and discovered he'd clubbed the bars so hard they'd caved in. The mask was ruined.

He was in the Cubs' dugout by that time. I was upset at what he'd done, but I'm not one of those guys who will fly into a white rage and try to punch somebody's lights out. I brood and burn. So it didn't occur to me to do anything but get another mask and play ball. I didn't see Buckner, close up, again that night. After the game, the Cubs left town.

Our equipment is precious to us; we feel an affection for it, like a musician for his instrument. My teammates didn't let me forget this. They kept asking me what I was going to do about Buckner. They wouldn't let the incident die. They kept working on me, and I didn't say much, just told them I'd take care of it. A week later, we were in Chicago. The guys all waited, a little twinkle in their eyes, to see what I'd do. They were right, I thought, I probably should retaliate. And I did, the first time Buckner batted.

I didn't say anything to him. He didn't look at me. There was a runner down at first. Buckner cut under the ball and scooped a high, high infield pop-up. He dropped his bat and cussed and took off at a jog for first. Perfect. I picked up his bat, gripped it as far down the thin end as I could, and pounded it on the plate with everything I had. The bat snapped in two with a crack like a pistol shot. Not quite to first, Buckner spun around. His fly ball, meanwhile, had drifted into short left field. The shortstop dropped the ball, then threw to second, out, and on to first, double play, because Buckner was standing there gaping at me. Now he was embarrassed as well as angry. We were even. He stared a while, then headed for the dugout.

I batted next inning. I hit a fly ball, and was halfway to second base when the center fielder made the catch. The visitors' dugout is beyond the first-base line, so I had to pass Buckner on my way in. He was waiting for me. He stood in my way; I stopped.

"What'd you break my bat for?" he said.

What a question! "What about my mask?" I said.

He stood with his shoulders squared, chewing tobacco.

I said, "If you want me, throw a punch."

He did. He threw a big left-hand punch and whacked his knuckles on my batting helmet. It was a fight now, and I grabbed some of his shirt with my left hand and clipped him with my right somewhere below his left eye. He grabbed me back, and I got him again, and the clumsy waltz went on till we were yanked away from each other. It was your basic baseball fight. The first-base umpire was Harry Wendelstedt, big Harry, and he solved the mess in a funny way. Harry had been working the game in Montreal when Buckner smashed my mask, so he understood this feud. He told us to shake hands or he'd throw us out of the game. Fighting is supposed to bring automatic ejection. Buckner and I stood there like a couple of kids who'd been fighting on the playground, and Wendelstedt eyed us like a schoolteacher. The fans booed. Buckner sent me a dirty look—his face is lank, and he has a drooping black mustache, like the villain in an old Western—then sullenly stuck out his hand. I shook it.

It was over—truly. Neither of us ever mentioned it again, and by the time we met in the World Series, our fight was a stray and amusing memory. We play a man's game, but we do behave like children sometimes.

♦   ♦   ♦

Game one.

Here it was, at long last, and it seemed so strangely ordinary, so anticlimactic after the war with Houston.

It was a cold night in New York. Shea was full, of course, and it was a quiet crowd, as if they felt the way we did, as if the sixteen-inning struggle with the Astros had worn them out too. Then again, game one was a quiet sort of game.

One run, five hits for Boston. No runs, four hits, for us. We'd batted only .189 against the Astros, *one eighty-nine*, and we were still at it.

I got my first swing against Hurst in the second inning. I hit the ball on the ground, hard, past Hurst, but their second baseman, Marty Barrett, got to it and threw me out. Barrett had been playing me up the middle. I was an easy out, though I'd banged the ball pretty well, and jogging back to the dugout I thought: here we go again.

Ron Darling was pitching for us, and he was as good as Hurst. Barrett rapped a ground-ball single that Tim knocked down in the first inning, but R.J. got Buckner to hit into a double play. Buckner had hurt his ankle before the Series and could barely run. He wore Nike high-top shoes for support, and hobbled when he ran, pumping his elbows high in the air and leaning way forward, like an old man. The ankle was killing him. He won a lot of admiration for just getting out there, but he was their number-three hitter, and he couldn't run.

Barrett's first-inning single was a preview. He drove us crazy all through the Series. The game raced along, runless and quiet. In our dugout, Bobby O. kept promising us Hurst would eventually fall apart out there. We were beginning to wonder.

"The pressure'll get to him," Bobby said.

"He's made some good pitches," Mex said.

"It won't last," Bobby said. "Relax."

I conferred with Bobby a couple of times, to get some help with Hurst. Hitters love to get a general idea.

"First couple of pitches," Bobby said, "he likes to throw the change-up or fork ball. Every now and then, he'll bust the fastball inside, just to keep you honest. He won't throw the fastball out over the plate."

I was listening carefully. I was all ears.

"His out pitch," Bobby said, "is his curve ball."

The last nugget was the most important: the out pitch is a pitcher's best, his most trusted. It's what he throws when he has to have the out, or the strike.

With two outs in the third, I went up to hit with Lenny at first and Mookie at third. R.J. had struck out, then Mookie singled, stole second, and dashed on to third on a fly-ball out by Mex. Hurst had walked Lenny. The game was scoreless, a big chance for me.

Hurst threw me two balls, slipped a strike past me, and threw me the change-up, fat and slow but slippery, and I swung and got nothing. Two balls, two strikes. "His out pitch is his curve ball," Bobby O. had said. If a pitcher was ever going to throw his out pitch, it was now.

I looked for the curve.

And got the fastball.

It wasn't a scorching fastball, not overpowering, but it didn't have to be. He slipped it inside, and I fisted it on the ground to Barrett. Barrett tossed it to Owen, covering second, and the inning was over. And I'd left a run at third.

"He threw me the fastball," I told Bobby O.

"I know it."

"Good pitch," I said. "Good location."

"It won't last," he said.

Meanwhile, R.J. was mowing down the Red Sox. A single by Buckner in the fourth; then he went gimping down to second, elbows flying, on a wild pitch. A single by Henderson in the fifth. No runs.

In our sixth, Mex walked, and I got a good piece of Hurst's fastball and whacked it into center field—a base hit. I hauled down to first, turned the corner, and went back, to get the two-fingered slap of congratulations from Uncle Bill. And then it sank in. A smile rose from deep inside me and spread itself, wide, across my face.

"Hey, Uncle Bill," I said. *"I just got a hit in the World Series!"*

104

•

A catcher's view through the mask is squeezed by horizontal bars. And by crossbars just beyond the corners of his eyes. He can see straight ahead, but he doesn't have much lateral vision, and he can't always spot a ball, immediately, in the dirt at his feet. A catcher can lose sight of a ball and know, from experience, where it is. Then, he'll whip off the mask, look, and pounce on it. Sometimes, experience is no help; the ball isn't where it ought to be. He throws away the mask and stares at the dirt at nothing. The ball might be behind him. It might be anywhere.

In game one of the World Series I lost a ball—a wild pitch in the dirt by R.J.—behind the bars of my mask, which cost us the game. It was a wild pitch, without question; no one thought I should have gloved it. And yet I felt I might have if I had been able to see it.

We were in the seventh, still scoreless. R.J. walked Rice and, with Evans at the plate, a right-handed hitter, bounced the wild pitch. It was outside; I shot sideways, landed on my knees, jammed the glove down, but the ball was gone. Wild pitch. Rice cruised to second. Evans hit one back to R.J., who tossed to Mex. With Rice on first, it would have been a double play.

Rich Gedman, their catcher, came up. Gedman and Bobby O. had been roommates in Boston, and friends. They were still friends, real friends, and it was strange to see them battle each other when Bobby pitched against Boston.

Geddie sent a ground ball to Tuff at second, a lazy ground ball with no tricks or odd spin to it. Tuff leaned down, scooped at the ball, and missed it. It rolled on, not far, into right field. Rice came home.

Red Sox 1, Mets 0.

Hurst struck out for the third time. We weren't playing with the designated hitter in Shea. Up till this year, the DH had been used in alternating years in the World Series. This year, we played the National League's way in the National League park, the American League's way in their park. The DH is the American League's way of doing things. Hurst, at any rate, was not accustomed to hitting, to put it mildly. He looked hopeless up there.

Davey sent Kevin Mitchell up to hit for R.J. in the seventh. Hurst struck him out. Roger finished the game for us, and pitched decently, though they did load the bases in the ninth.

I got my final at-bat in the eighth. I still hadn't seen a curve ball and didn't see one this time. I hit what I think was the fork ball, driving it deep to left center field, where Henderson made a nice catch. Bobby O., I noticed, had stopped talking about Hurst collapsing.

Calvin Schiraldi pitched the ninth for the Red Sox. A big right-hander with a hard fastball, he had been our teammate the year before. He'd gone to Boston in the deal for Bobby O. After a miserable spring training, he had begun the season in their minor leagues. Later they'd brought him up, and he'd become their main man, their closer, in the bullpen. With the bases loaded and two out in the Red Sox' ninth, McNamara had removed Hurst for the pinch hitter, a kid named Mike Greenwell, who hit a fly ball to Lenny. With the DH, of course, Hurst would have pitched the ninth.

Schiraldi was a nice kid, but wasn't experienced in pressure situations. We'd said before the Series, as we'd said before the playoffs, that we wanted to test their bullpen. Schiraldi walked Straw, then pitched three quick outs. He struck out Danny, batting for Raffy, to end the game.

Red Sox 1, Mets 0.

SATURDAY, OCT. 18 at SHEA

BOSTON (1)

	ab	r	h	bi
Boggs 3b	4	0	0	0
Barrett 2b	4	0	1	0
Buckner 1b	4	0	1	0
Stapleton 1b	0	0	0	0
Rice lf	2	1	1	0
Evans rf	3	0	0	0
Gedman c	4	0	0	0
Henderson cf	4	0	2	0
Owen ss	2	0	0	0
Hurst p	3	0	0	0
Greenwell ph	1	0	0	0
Schiraldi p	0	0	0	0
	31	1	5	0

METS (0)

	ab	r	h	bi
Wilson lf	4	0	1	0
McDowell p	0	0	0	0
Dykstra cf	3	0	0	0
Hernandez 1b	3	0	0	0
Strawberry rf	2	0	0	0
Knight 3b	3	0	0	0
Teufel 2b	3	0	2	0
Backman 2b	1	0	0	0
Santana ss	2	0	0	0
Heep ph	1	0	0	0
Darling p	2	0	0	0
Mitchell lf	1	0	0	0
	29	0	4	0

Boston .... 000 000 100 — 1 5 0
Mets .... 000 000 000 — 0 4 1

E—Teufel. DP—Boston 1, Mets 1. LOB—Boston 8, Mets 8. SB—Wilson (1), Strawberry (1). S—Santana. Game-Winning RBI—None

Boston	IP	H	R	ER	BB	SO
Hurst (W, 1-0)	8	4	0	0	4	8
Schiraldi (S, 1)	1	0	0	0	1	1
Mets						
Darling (L, 0-1)	7	3	1	0	3	8
McDowell	2	2	0	0	2	0

WP—Darling 2. T—2:59. A—55,076.

106

•

Afterward, I was too tired to think hard about what had happened. We'd lost at home: that was worrisome. I'd realized my oldest, fondest dream, and yet I felt oddly flat. Certainly, I didn't feel tense and pressed, the way I'd felt all through the Houston series.

Mex sat thoughtfully on the stool in front of his locker, nursing a beer and pulling on a cigarette. The funny guys were quiet. Tuff stood up manfully to about fifty questions on the subject of his error. How deeply can you analyze a ground-ball error? The ball hopped lower and maybe quicker at the crucial moment; Tuff did not push his glove down low enough. Almost always in this game, a missed ball is glaring. As fielders, we have to be close to perfect; when we aren't, we usually pay a price.

The World Series games all began at 8:30 P.M., or a little later. Postseason games these days last longer than other games, because the TV networks cram in more ads between innings. Even the fast-paced pitchers' duels turn out quite long. With these late starts and lengthened games, we never got to bed before two in the morning. It was so tiring.

Sandy told me that night that a great change had come over Gordy. She said she'd never seen him enjoy a game so much—a game I was playing in—had never seen him give himself to it as he had tonight. Gordy had yelled when I came up to bat. When I'd hit the single, he'd cheered and applauded like the most far-gone Mets fan. He'd been withholding something, but was giving it now. I went to bed in the big blue master bedroom and slept like a champ.

8

I've never been benched for a big game: not in high school, not in the minor leagues, not in the majors. It's a hard thing for a ball-player. I've done a little sitting, and I hated every minute of it. Once, when I was with the Expos, Bill Virdon, the hard-nosed manager, sat me down for a game as punishment for loafing down to first on a ground-ball out. Virdon was right. He expected all of us to run the bases with everything we had, no matter what, and he was making an example of me. It hurt, but I didn't squawk about it. I sat for one game, played the following day, and ran the bases like I was being chased by dogs.

In 1977, after winning the starting catcher's job, I was benched. There was a reason. Barry Foote was the other catcher, and they wanted to trade him. They were showcasing him, and the only way to do this was to play him. No one explained this to me till I asked. I sat, fretting, aching to play baseball, while Foote caught. Dick Williams was the manager then. He was another tough cookie, but I sort of liked him, as I did Virdon. After a couple of games, I knocked on Williams's door and asked him why, if I was number-one catcher, I was watching from the dugout? Williams told me, and I waited, and pretty soon they traded Foote.

None of us is happy sitting on the bench. We can hate it but still understand it, the way Mookie did, when he accepted the necessity with so much largeness and dignity. I hated riding the bench in Montreal partly out of sheer restlessness, a hunger to be out there, to be *doing* instead of sitting. My two weeks on the disabled list in '86, two weeks on the bench, made me crazy, as I've said.

There's also your pride. Unless you're hurt, or getting a day's rest, you're sitting because you're not quite good enough. You can sweeten it a dozen ways: you're being platooned, or you don't hit well in a particular ball park, or you're in a slump and it's temporary, or they wanted to get more power in the line-up today, or more speed. A dozen ways, but it still boils down to this: on this day, you're not quite good enough. It gnaws at you; you bleed inside.

On Sunday night, October 19, Ray walked into the clubhouse and glanced at the line-up posted by the door. He looked, and his heart fell. Hojo was playing third base that night. Ray wasn't playing. He'd been our regular third baseman since May, and this was game two of the World Series, and he wasn't playing.

Ray didn't say anything. He went to his locker and sat down on his chair. Ordinarily, he will undress briskly and go to the trainer's room for a hot soak in the whirlpool. On this night, he didn't get in the whirlpool.

Davey had his reasons for playing Hojo. Davey had benched Mookie, too, for Danny. The Red Sox' young prodigy, Roger Clemens, was pitching. This had been his second full year in the majors. He'd won twenty-four games, lost four, and was a sure bet for the Cy Young Award. He was also a leading candidate for Most Valuable Player, which had inspired a lot of debate about whether a pitcher can really be more valuable than a guy who plays every day. Clemens is a big, good-looking Texas boy who throws right-handed and very hard. Hojo bats left-handed. He hits with power, and in his American League days had hit a long home run off Clemens. We had batted .189 against Houston and had been shut out in the first World Series game. Davey was looking for the long ball, the big inning.

Davey put Danny in there for a different reason. Danny would be one of our designated hitters when we got to Boston, so Davey

110
.

wanted to give him some playing time. You always have a feeling Danny might knock one out of the ball park; he has a weight lifter's arms and shoulders, all rolling muscle, and an incredibly thin hard waist. We call him "Arnold," after the body-building hero Arnold Schwarzenegger. Danny bats lefty, and it wasn't far-fetched to think he might knock one over the bullpen against Clemens. Anything, Davey was thinking, to raise some excitement.

Ray didn't see it that way. He thought he should be playing. He sat for a long time in front of his locker, trying to digest it. He dressed slowly, and no one could cheer him up.

"It's just one game, Ray-Ray."

"It's just an experiment, Ray-Ray. Shake it off, man."

Hojo, meanwhile, was a little hurt because Ray was acting like his, Hojo's, playing third base tonight was the end of the world. Hojo, like Ray, is a good friend of mine. I was happy for Hojo; he'd sat on the bench through the '84 Series, and here was his big night. Hojo's a team player, like Mookie. Ray and Hojo didn't speak to each other before the game. Ray didn't get much batting practice — the starters take more swings than the rest—and so he had plenty of time before the game to answer reporters' questions about being benched.

Ray didn't hold back. He said he didn't like it, and he said he thought Davey was wrong. Ray's a passionate guy; a tough and yet gentle man, who thinks deeply and feels deeply. Not playing is a hard thing. More than once, Davey himself had spelled this out. He knew how hard it is, and had told us it was all right to be selfish in wanting to play. You got to look out for number one, he'd said. He'd said it often.

I come back to Mookie Wilson, whose patience was gradually rewarded. Mookie was a valuable member of the team, and he had some big, big moments in this World Series. The opposite case was George Foster, who began the season as our starting left fielder and one of our big guns. It seemed like a long time ago, and it was hard to believe, in a way, that we were here and George wasn't.

◆   ◆   ◆

◆

George Foster was a mystery to most of us. I couldn't see inside the man very much, and I couldn't make out the moods and changes on the surface. He was a quiet guy, a loner, I think; he would sit by himself on a bus or plane and think his own thoughts, and I never really knew what they were. He seemed to have a chip on his shoulder; he had a hard stare. He could challenge you with that stare. He could make an opposing pitcher furious.

George was mostly silent, but he also had a sharp tongue. He would make remarks, kind of joking, kind of not; little barbs that he would flick at you across the clubhouse or around the batting cage. I heard some things like that from George when I first arrived to play with the Mets, in spring training of '85. Jokes, but with a sharpness to them. The sort of stuff I'd gotten in Montreal, except that it had been personal then, and had real poison in it. I knew George didn't mean to be nasty. He was the same way with the other guys. He looked at you from a distance, wouldn't let you come close. I never had a heart-to-heart talk with George Foster.

Ray had been George's teammate in Cincinnati. He talked about George's great pride, and said George had felt overlooked when he was with the Reds. Remember that George was, for a while, one of the game's most awesome hitters. He had hit .300 or better four times, with terrific power. In 1977, he'd hit fifty-two home runs. And yet, Ray said, he'd felt passed over. Ray said that Pete Rose, Johnny Bench, Joe Morgan, and Tony Perez had subtracted some of the glitter from George's achievements. It happens sometimes. Rose, Bench, Morgan, and Perez were *so* good. There are things to admire in George, besides his greatness as a player. He's a devoted family man and a devout Christian. I've never heard George swear. Never. He used to read his Bible on the planes. I'll always remember George sitting alone, reading the Bible.

George never quite came up to expectations in New York. His first two years, '82 and '83, were huge disappointments: .247 and thirteen home runs the first year, .241 and twenty-eight home runs the second. He was much more productive in '84 and '85, but he had left the great years behind him. He was in New York, where everybody notices, and his big years were behind him. It must have been hard for this proud man.

The way George played was also a mystery to us. He had a reputation for never getting his uniform dirty. It was said that he never dove for a ball in the outfield, and that he shied away from collisions with walls. Running into a wall is nobody's idea of fun, but an outfielder now and then has to if he's going to catch a ball. It was said that George wouldn't do it. There was some truth in it, as if George had disdain for crash landings, as if that was for lesser ballplayers. Was this pride? It should have had the opposite effect, we thought.

1986 was the final year of George's contract, and even before the season began, it was a good guess that he wouldn't be around the next season. The Mets were paying him for the kind of years he'd had in Cincinnati, and weren't getting them. And George was getting on, for a ballplayer. Still, we expected him to have a decent year, like the last two, and to help us win.

But George wasn't his old self. He got hot in May for about ten days, but other than that he wasn't much of a presence in our lineup. Every now and then he'd slug one of his mammoth home runs, but on the whole he was pretty quiet. Meanwhile, Kevin Mitchell and Danny were warming the bench, and so was Mookie, who'd lost his job to Lenny. Davey had three good, hungry ballplayers waiting in the wings. George was batting in the .220s.

After the All-Star break, Davey began using Mookie and World in left field, which meant benching George. And George was miserable. He turned more silent, withdrew deeper inside himself than ever. On July 22, we were in a big and wild brawl with the Reds in Cincinnati; both benches emptied, and it went on for a while. George, alone, did not leave our dugout. A battle on the field, guys getting pummeled, guys helping each other—and George sat in the shadows, watching. I don't mean he was supposed to come out and punch someone. It's a question of standing by each other. I don't enjoy fighting; I try to pull guys away from fights. But I'm there, right in the middle of it.

Around the end of July, the Pirates released Lee Mazzilli. Frank

Cashen signed him to a contract and sent him to our triple A team in Tidewater. Maz had been a first-class outfielder with the Mets in the middle and late 1970s, a local hero who had grown up in Brooklyn. He'd had a certain glamour about him, and had been very popular. After the Mets traded him, he'd spent a few years in the American League, then landed with the hopeless Pirates. His career was winding down, and it seemed like a nice idea to bring him back to New York for the glorious ride of 1986. However, there wasn't room for him right away.

From the beginning, George had been ungracious about being benched. He'd sulked. Almost within earshot, he'd talked disgustedly about Mookie's, Danny's, and World's abilities. He said right out that he was better. And I think he sealed his own doom.

My good friend and Florida neighbor Tommy Hutton was a fringe player with the Expos when I was there. He pinch-hit, played some defense in the late innings. He accepted his role, cooperated, was an enthusiastic member of the team. His attitude was marvelous, or they might have let him go. It made all the difference.

George was no fringe player, even now, but he wasn't playing every day, and it made him miserable, and bitter, and no fun to be around. He made Davey uneasy. He made all of us uneasy. And yet we felt for him, too, a man who not so long ago had hit fifty-two home runs, and been feared. About the time the Mets acquired Mazzilli, George started muttering about racism.

As I said, George sealed his own doom. He told a reporter that he was probably going to be released and replaced by Mazzilli, and that he smelled racial prejudice in the move. Next day, his statement was in the papers. Frank was furious. Two of George's replacements in the outfield were black, Mookie and World. Frank wanted Lee not because he was white, but because he was a kid from Brooklyn whom Mets fans still loved and who could still hit bigleague pitching.

On August 6, we had played the Cubs in Chicago, and before the game George was nowhere to be seen. He wasn't in the clubhouse, and he didn't take batting practice. The guys were wondering if he'd been let go. No one knew. The game began, and after a while George came out in his uniform. Strangely, on that afternoon Mookie had a game that summed up his year: he didn't start, came in late, and drove in the winning run with a single in the twelfth inning. George pinch-hit, his final act as a New York Met.

The next day, the papers carried more of George's talk about racism among the Mets. It was now inevitable: George was going.

He wasn't in the clubhouse that morning as the rest of us drifted in. There was a lot of talk in the air, though no one had heard anything. The guys were undressing, playing cards, passing the time, when George walked in, wearing his street clothes. Everyone was wondering. George called us together, and we gathered in the middle of the room. He cleared his throat and said he wanted to talk to us. He was gazing at the floor, face very long, very sad.

He said, "It looks like I won't be here much longer, and I just want to say that I'm sorry for any problems I might have caused. I don't know what all has been written, or what you guys have heard, but I want you to know I feel I've been misquoted. And I just want to say . . . if I've caused any problems, if I've *hurt* anybody, I'm sorry. I apologize."

He stood there gazing down at the floor, and no one knew what to say. He'd always held his emotions deep inside, and he held his feelings in then. I looked over at Lenny, who stared at George, looking worried and a bit puzzled. I wondered what he and World and the other young guys thought; they'd been kids when George had had his heroic years in Cincinnati, and I wondered if they knew what kind of ballplayer he'd been. George never paid much attention to the young guys. He didn't work with them much on the field, didn't take anyone under his wing. The reasons for this, like his reasons for not hitting the outfield grass to make a catch, were buried inside him.

"I'm sorry," George said again, and walked to his locker.

Ray followed him. He knew George better than the rest of us on account of his days with the Reds, and he's a good listener. He got George alone and, gently, confronted him with the accusations George had made. He challenged him. George became uneasy and struggled to answer. He admitted he'd said some of it, but that he hadn't meant it the way it had come out. He said he hadn't wanted to hurt anybody. And as he talked to Ray, he began to cry. His eyes filled up, and Ray saw tears run down his hard, proud face. George left the ball park, and I never saw him again.

Frank Cashen was flying in, to inform George he'd been released and replaced by Lee Mazzilli.

I've said that no ballplayer is happy sitting on the bench, but that isn't quite right, because Lee Mazzilli was. Maz was happy to be back. He was happy to play part time. He'd been knocking around the American League as a designated hitter, then playing not quite full time with the Pirates in front of crowds of 7,000. Now, he had come home. The big crowds loved him. He had a chance to help us win the pennant, the World Series.

His arrival made us all happy. He was like the last, missing piece in a jigsaw puzzle. You snap it into place, and you've got it. We were a unit. A team.

George Foster went home to Connecticut and waited. A couple of days later, Hawk Harrelson, the general manager of the Chicago White Sox, called Ray Knight. Hawk told Ray he was thinking about signing George. The White Sox needed help; they were having an awful summer. Hawk asked if Ray thought it was worth taking a chance on Foster. Ray said yes.

So the White Sox signed George, and of course we were all curious to see how he'd make out over there. In his very first game he hit a home run and a triple, and we were glad for him. Lord knows, we didn't wish him ill. A home run and a triple: George was on his way. He was going to do it, after all.

But George was barely heard from again. He managed something like two more hits, a couple of RBIs, and, with a sub-.200 batting average, was released.

It had happened so quickly. The year before, he'd still been one of the game's big names, and then he'd been released twice in a

116

Yours truly with World Series MVP Ray Knight
MEAD CHASKY

The great Doc PETER SIMON

Mookie, making things happen   IRA N. GOLDEN

Dukey just being himself   IRA N. GOLDEN

George Foster and I on a spring-training day
MEAD CHASKY

The World Man doing his thing   PETER SIMON

A high five for the Mex   IRA N. GOLDEN

Bobby O. letting one fly   IRA N. GOLDEN

My backup catcher, Ed "Ward" Hearn   PETER SIMON

Conference time with R. J., Raffy, and Wally. Let's get the signs straight!   IRA N. GOLDEN

Roger "Skeets" McDowell—all business
on the mound

Hojo, taking it all in   PETER SIMON

Nails getting dirty as usual IRA N. GOLDEN

My oldest daughter, Christy, hoping and praying for Daddy to get a hit in the World Series
NEW YORK DAILY NEWS

J. O. at the ultimate moment
© GEORGE KALINSKY, MAJOR LEAGUE GRAPHICS

Celebrating the dream   WIDE WORLD PHOTOS

season. *Twice.* I can only guess how he took it, and my guess is that he kept the pain buried deep inside him.

The day comes when you don't have it anymore. We get old soon in this game. Facing up to it is the problem. So many great ballplayers have overstayed. Willie Mays was playing when he could no longer count on those wonderful sprinter's legs. Mickey Mantle stayed about a year too long. It was a sad year. Pete Rose plays with all the fire inside him of a twenty-year-old, but his body, his quickness, aren't what they were.

Will I know when to get out, I wonder. Sure. Which is what every ballplayer says, before the time comes.

With Ray on the bench in game two of the World Series, the Red Sox shellacked us in our home ball park and took the lead, two games to none. So far, nothing was happening as expected. The pitchers were Clemens and Gooden, possibly the two best in the game, certainly two of the most exciting, if only because they were so young. Eighty million people tuned in expecting a nearly runless duel.

Well, Clemens lasted four and a third innings, and Doc lasted five. Both of them, Doc especially, got knocked all over the place.

The Sox scored three in the third. Owen walked. Clemens dropped a bunt on the grass in front of Mex, who grabbed it all right, but whirled and threw to second off the wrong foot, bouncing the ball in front of Raffy. Error, everybody safe. Barrett stung us with a single, which brought home Owen. Boggs got his first hit, a double pushed down the left-field line. Buckner singled. Three runs.

We answered with two in our third. Raffy singled. Doc pushed a bunt toward Buckner—perfect, base hit. The fans came alive. Lenny put the bunt down, advancing the runners. Wally whacked one up the middle—base hit—scoring Raffy. Doc stood at third now. Mex shot one off Clemens's leg; the ball skidded to Boggs, who took it with his bare hand and threw to first, in time to nip Mex. Nice play. Doc scored. My turn. My first time up I'd hit a fly ball to Henderson. This time I hit one hard, one bounce, near Boggs. I was pounding down the line and didn't see Boggs glove the ball, but the tape

117

•

shows him making a very sweet play. He threw me out.

Red Sox 3, Mets 2.

Then they went to work on us. Henderson began the fourth with a home run. He pulled Doc's fastball over the left-field fence; nothing cheap about the home run. He went bounding down the line, leaping and spinning in midair, and even running backward. In our fourth, Hojo came close to making Davey look like a wizard. He took an excellent swing at a fastball and was under it by the smallest fraction of an inch: a long fly ball to Evans in right. By a hair, he'd missed a home run.

In their fifth, Rice singled, and Evans hit a rocket of a home run over the fence in left. I mean, he *crushed* it. Another fastball. Evans pounced on it. Red Sox 6, Mets 2. Doc then fanned the side, but the horses, as they say, were out of the barn. Davey sent Mookie to hit for Doc in the bottom of the inning, and brought in Rick Aguilera.

Aggie got them all right in the sixth, and then came the nightmare seventh. The first five guys all hit singles, *cheap* singles, mostly; singles with eyes, accidents. Rice hit a clean one to left; then Evans just scraped the ball, a soft flare into center. Gedman got jammed, flicked his wrists and nudged a feeble hit into center. Henderson, who had done nothing but pull the ball to left, now popped one like a pool shot off the end of his bat the opposite way, right field. Owen, batting lefty, dribbled one to the left side, the ball rolling and rolling exactly where no one could touch it. Five hits, two runs. They were advancing a base at a time.

In the middle of all this, I walked out to talk to Aggie.

"Can't we get anybody out?" I said. "I can't believe this. When is it gonna stop?"

I wasn't mad at Aggie; it wasn't his fault. I was mad at the world, mad at their luck, mad at Henderson for making like a pogo stick when he hit his home run, mad at myself, mad at the unexpectedness of everything. Aggie was sweating hard in the chilly night.

But they kept nudging the ball through the infield, Henderson and Owen. And Davey went out and got Aggie. Jesse took over and put down the uprising.

Red Sox 8, Mets 3.

I haven't mentioned it, but we did manage a run in the fifth. The RBI was mine. Wally had walked, Mex had sent him to third with a ground-ball single. Clemens went in and took a shower. Steve Crawford came in to pitch to me. Crawford is a large right-hander. He hung a fastball, and I hit it on a line into left field—base hit, and my first World Series RBI.

They scored a final time off Sid in the ninth. Henderson singled, his third hit of the night. Talk about bench sitters: the man had begun the season, he and Owen, with the last-place Seattle Mariners, and he had been no more than a late-inning substitute from the time he joined the Red Sox. Then Armas had hurt himself in the play-offs with the Angels, and suddenly Henderson was the starting center fielder. Owen singled next, *his* third hit. Here was a guy who'd been advertised as a nearly automatic out. Boggs, who on this night looked like a .300 hitter, drove a double into right field, and Henderson flew home.

Red Sox 9, Mets 3.

We went down quickly in our ninth. Bob Stanley, another relief pitcher we thought we could handle, was pitching—his third scoreless inning. Stanley had struck me out looking, in the seventh. The game ended when Mex hit a fly ball to Henderson in center. I was in the on-deck circle.

Red Sox 9, Mets 3.

We were a worried bunch of guys, but it was their two-game lead, not the lopsided defeat, that troubled us. Getting slaughtered—if it doesn't happen often—is probably more upsetting to the fans than to a big-league ball club. The Sox had been plain tough knocking Dwight out—that was upsetting—but the barrage that came afterward was one of those hitting binges that has nothing to do with who is pitching, and has no meaning beyond the one game.

It happens: hitting becomes contagious up and down the line-up. A few guys hit, then a few more, and suddenly everyone is confident, relaxed, patient at the plate. You expect to hit, and you do. Confidence guides your bat; you meet the ball, and it's effortless, and the ball drops for a hit, or flies out of the ball park. It no longer matters who's pitching. Cy Young could be throwing bullets, and you'd put your bat on them, and it would be easy.

So we discounted the score, but not the fact that we'd lost. In Boston, they were talking sweep.

SUNDAY, OCT. 19 at SHEA

BOSTON (9)	ab	r	h	bi		METS (3)	ab	r	h	bi
Boggs 3b	5	1	2	2		Dykstra cf	3	0	1	0
Barrett 2b	5	0	2	1		Backman 2b	3	1	2	1
Buckner 1b	5	0	2	1		Hernandez 1b	4	0	1	1
Stapleton 1b	1	0	0	0		Carter c	4	0	1	1
Rice lf	6	2	3	0		Strawberry rf	4	0	0	0
Evans rf	4	2	2	2		Heep lf	2	0	0	0
Gedman c	5	0	1	0		Aguilera p	0	0	0	0
Henderson cf	5	2	3	2		Orosco p	0	0	0	0
Owen ss	4	1	3	1		Mazzilli ph	1	0	0	0
Romero ss	0	0	0	0		Fernandez p	0	0	0	0
Clemens p	1	1	0	0		Sisk p	0	0	0	0
Crawford p	1	0	0	0		Johnson 3b	4	0	0	0
Greenwell ph	1	0	0	0		Santana ss	4	1	2	0
Stanley p	1	0	0	0		Gooden p	2	1	1	0
						Wilson lf	2	0	0	0
	44	9	18	9			33	3	8	3

```
Boston _____  003 120 201 — 9 18 0
Mets   _____  002 010 000 — 3  8 1
```

E—Hernandez. DP—Mets 1. LOB—Boston 13, Mets 9. 2B—Boggs 2. HR—Henderson (1), Evans (1). S—Dykstra, Clemens. Game-Winning RBI—Boggs (1).

	IP	H	R	ER	BB	SO
Boston						
Clemens _____	4 1-3	5	3	3	4	3
Crawford (W, 1-0)	1 2-3	1	0	0	0	2
Stanley (S, 1) ___	3	2	0	0	1	3
Mets						
Gooden (L, 0-1) __	5	8	6	5	2	6
Aguilera _____	1	5	2	2	1	1
Orosco _____	2	2	0	0	0	3
Fernandez _____	1-3	3	1	1	0	1
Sisk _____	2-3	0	0	0	1	1

Aguilera pitched to 5 batters in the 7th.
T—3:36. A—55,063.

Our traveling arrangements were horrible. There's no other word for them. They seemed to have been designed to make tired men tireder.

The Red Sox left for Boston after the game. They probably didn't get to bed till five in the morning, but they'd arrived, they were through traveling and could sleep the next day. We, on the other hand, straggled home exhausted and sick with worry, fell into bed at four o'clock, and had to travel late that morning. The team was to gather at Shea at quarter to ten. I don't know how much sleep the other guys got, but I got about three hours. Before I left for Boston, I had things to do. Family things.

Kimmy and Christy had to go home. They had to go to school. Sandy's mother had to leave for California. We had to get up at seven and drive them to Kennedy Airport.

Gordy, God bless him, took care of our father. Dad's back was killing him. There was the big debate about whether to take him to the hospital. We got everything sorted out and everyone taken care of, and reached Shea on time for the bus ride to La Guardia, red-eyed and light-headed with fatigue.

It's a short ride from Shea to La Guardia. At the front of the bus, Davey was chatting with some of the reporters. He was telling them how tired he was. Today's program was to fly, check into the hotel, then work out in Fenway Park.

"If the guys are as tired as I am," Davey said, "I might give them the day off."

The writers didn't seem startled by this idea. But they were from New York. They were, more or less, our friends.

Davey got up, came back, and found Keith and me.

"I'm thinking of calling off the workout today," he said.

"Do it," Mex said.

"We need the rest," I agreed, "more than we need the workout."

"That's what I think," Davey said.

And he canceled the workout.

The press, especially in Boston, went crazy over this sensible, and trivial, decision. They concluded, first of all, that our not working out was one more example of our famous "arrogance." They had decided, I guess, that we didn't think we needed to get the feel of Fenway Park. We were down, two games to none, and we weren't bothering to take batting practice, or measure the famous wall. But we were not that cocky, believe me. We were in trouble, and we knew it. Arrogant? No: *tired.* Sleepless and muscle-weary.

Boston writers, particularly a couple of guys on the *Globe,* had another theory: we didn't show up in Fenway that afternoon because

121

•

we didn't want to face their questions. The assumption ran something like this: we hadn't known adversity all year, and were so startled by it we were tongue-tied, unable to admit we were as bad as people had begun to suspect.

It amazes me the way fans and baseball writers—especially the writers—leap to great judgments after a couple of games in a World Series. Did these people really think Keith Hernandez was a .143 hitter? Where did they think we'd won those 108 games—in an Industrial League? The Boston writers and fans picked out Darryl Strawberry as an object of special doubt, even ridicule. Darryl had struck out a lot against the Astros—he'd also hoisted a couple of long clutch home runs—and he'd already struck out four times against the Red Sox. But we all look bad sometimes. I'd looked miserable in the Houston series. It can last for one day or many. I don't know how a person can report on baseball day in and day out and lose sight of this. As a team, we'd batted .263 in 1986. Who did they think we'd gotten all those hits against?

No, we weren't afraid to face the music. We were tired.

We got to our hotel, Sandy and I, at about one in the afternoon, while the writers hung around Fenway waiting to pounce. Immediately we went to sleep. We slept for two and a half hours. We ordered from room service, watched some TV, and were asleep again at 11:30. We slept until noon the next day.

I woke up ready to play some baseball.

9

Our arrogance. There was that word again. We didn't work out in Fenway Park the day before the third game of the World Series, it was said, because we were *arrogant*. All year, we'd been called that.

We weren't arrogant. What, then? Cocky, maybe. There's a difference. We expected to win, loved winning, and celebrated it. I've talked about that. The fists in the air, the high fives. Arrogant means you think you're better than everyone else. We thought that only in a narrow, particular sense: that we could beat other teams on the ball field. We'd been winning big, we were in New York City, we were having fun.

We were disliked, it was said. Some said we were hated.

I was in Madison Square Garden recently at a basketball game between the Knicks and the Los Angeles Lakers. The Lakers were blowing them away, but that wasn't what interested me. What caught my attention was the way the Lakers all kept touching each other. Whenever a guy put one through the net, as many of his teammates as could reach him as they scattered back on defense slapped his hand. And they were warm hand slaps, firm, lingering. During the pauses for foul shots, the Lakers briefly clasped hands, or someone would wrap an arm around another's middle and maybe say something to him, congratulate him, or advise him. Magic Johnson, Kareem Abdul Jabbar, Kurt Rambis. If there was an instigator of all this touching, it was Magic, who is one of the classiest guys in American sports.

The idea of grown men, athletes, touching each other may bring some chuckles here and there. But it isn't sexual. Bill Robinson and I have a ritual, which we call our "good-luck hug." I go into the clubhouse every night and look for Uncle Bill. "Hey," I'll say, "where's my good-luck hug?" He'll give it to me. It would take a very brave man to suggest that Uncle Bill or I have a gay streak.

The Lakers touch a lot, and they're winners.

Watching them, I realized how the Mets had gotten into the habit of touching in the dream season of 1986. Ray and I, Uncle Bill and I. How many times had I charged one of our pitchers after a final out and nearly broken his ribs with a bear hug? How many times had I hugged Dwight Gooden and told him, "You're the best"? It comes from something, this touching. Closeness. Affection. Respect. Watch Keith Hernandez: he's a hugger. He and I are veterans, and for all the differences between us in style and even substance, we share something, a bond that is more than our ages. I love being his teammate, and I'll say it by grabbing his hand, or embracing him.

The Mets were close, and we touched, and the touching grew as the season went by. Touching is ritual, part of celebrating. I wonder now if it had something to do with the perception that we were arrogant—if our closeness made us seem as if we looked down on everyone else. People did love to beat us. And so there were bean balls, and hard words, and fights.

Our third fight occurred on July 11 in Shea Stadium, where we were playing the Atlanta Braves on national television. Their starting pitcher was David Palmer, who had been my teammate for many years in Montreal. Palmer had been, more or less, among the Dawson-Raines clique. Our wives were friends; they exchanged baby presents. But Palmer and I weren't close, and on that night in Shea, in front of 40,000 fans, I hit a first-inning three-run home run off him.

It was only the first inning, and Palmer was furious. Maybe it was me, maybe it was us. Straw was up next, and with his next pitch Palmer drilled Straw on the hip. Straw saw red. He took off after Palmer, who threw his glove at him. Straw almost had him when Mex came flying out of nowhere like a free safety and tackled Palmer. A moment later, the field was an unbelievable scene.

I hunted in the confusion for Darryl and tried to get him quiet. I felt bad: *I'd* hit the home run, and Straw had paid with a fastball off the hip. It's always the way. It took the umpires and other peace makers a long time to pull everybody apart and shove them off the field. Straw was left in the game, and when the inning finally did end, he was on third base. He and Palmer had to pass each other, and as they did, Palmer said: "You want some of me?"

"Yeah," Straw said, and if Buddy Harrelson hadn't rushed between them, they'd have really started slugging.

Sid was pitching for us; he got them out easily again in the second, and by the time I came to bat in our second, Palmer had loaded the bases. He probably would have loved to throw at me, but he couldn't do that with the bases loaded. He couldn't walk me, either, so I was going to see some pretty good pitches. I was coiled and ready and, sure enough, I got one I could hit. I drove it over the fence in left, grand-slam home run. Palmer was fit to be tied.

I'd hit two home runs and driven in seven runs in two innings. The fans brought me out for the curtain call. All of it was on national TV, remember. We'd fought with the Braves, and now we were piling up the runs. We were celebrating, touching, having the time of our lives.

To the Atlanta Braves, it was arrogance.

Palmer didn't throw at Straw again, for the simple reason that he left the game after my grand slam. The final score was 11–0. Lenny, Wally, and Ray all had two hits, and Duke, of all people, had three, including a double. The Mets' record for RBIs in a game is eight, owned by Dave Kingman, but I didn't get there. I hit a long fly ball to center my third time up, grounded into a double play, and drove another long fly ball my final time, just missing the home run.

Eleven days later, we had one of the year's most memorable games—and our fourth fight. It was a night game, in Cincinnati.

No one who plays in a game like that ever forgets it. For the rest of your life, the mention of the game will bring a smile, a little tug of affection. It wasn't a big game, a crucial game; we were twelve and a half games ahead of the rest of the division, and no one seemed to have a prayer of catching us. But the game became big; it took on a life of its own, stubborn and tricky, refusing to be taken in hand by either team. Winning this long, wild baseball game became a fierce desire—just because it was *there*, like Mt. Everest. The Reds felt the same way. The fight, which occurred in the ninth inning, naturally made everybody all the more keen to win the thing.

Because of our supposed arrogance, there was an aggressiveness, an edge, to the way people played us. Eric Davis, a rising young star, entered the game as pinch runner for Pete Rose, who had singled. He went out there bouncy and frisky, and I figured he'd try to steal, and he did. I didn't get him, either. Up he jumped, dusted himself off, and promptly stole third.

Ray was playing third. Davis slid, safe, and popped up out of his slide, shouldering Ray. Ray was sort of draped on him. They rubbed up against each other, and neither would budge.

Ray called Davis something. Davis called Ray something.

Ray let him have it, a short quick punch to the jaw. Davis's head snapped back. Eric Gregg, the third-base umpire, had been trying to interfere, reaching around Davis to pull him away. He still had his arms around Davis when Ray belted Davis, who stumbled back in Gregg's embrace, then lunged to get at Ray. By then, of course, both teams were spilling out over the field.

Chaos. I saw Gregg heave Davis aside, and Davis scramble for Ray. I tackled Davis. We both went down. I had him wrapped tight around the middle, and we stayed sprawled on the turf, Davis squirming and writhing and trying to yank himself free to get to Ray, who was now fighting with Tom Browning. Davis lunged and twisted, wiry and powerful underneath me, but I kept him pinned. He called me a couple of names, but it was Ray he was interested in. There was fighting going on all around us.

126

•

Bruce Kimm, the Reds' bullpen catcher and a coach, began shoving me, trying to roll me off Davis.

"Let the guy go," he hollered.

I held on, and told Kimm up over my shoulder, "I'll let him go if you take him to the dugout and get him out of this."

"Just let him go," Kimm said.

The umpires were running around hauling guys away from each other. They'd break up one fight, and another would begin. Browning and Ray were still going at it. John Denny, a pitcher, was trying to charge through a wall of bodies to get to World.

I decided I'd held on to Davis long enough, figured he was more or less in command of himself, so I let go of him and burrowed into the pack to help separate Denny from World; they were in a tangle on the ground, trying to kill each other. As soon as I got up, Davis dove right into the thick of things again. I saw Doug Harvey trying to drag him away. I was eye to eye with Denny. His eyes bulged; his face was pale with fury. He looked like he was having a seizure. I kept pushing him away.

"John," I said, "settle down. Settle down, John."

It was a big fight, and Davey was worrying that one of us was going to get injured. He was trying to get us to stop fighting. He might have been worrying, too, about keeping guys around to finish this ball game. You could assume Ray would be ejected, which was bad enough. Davey had already used quite a few players.

Gradually, the brawl broke apart. Harvey, the Lord, sent everyone to the benches, and the umps conferred and decided to toss Ray, World, and Davis out of the game.

We were in a jam. We'd lost our third baseman. Hojo, the only other genuine third baseman on the team, had batted for Raffy and was playing shortstop. *Someone* had to go down there, and I was nominated. It was the second time I'd played third base in my big-league career. The last time I'd done it had been in my rookie year, 1975. I'm now listed in the record books as the eightieth Met to play third base.

Not that I objected. Are you kidding? This was going to be fun. Ed Hearn came in to catch. I threw off the pads, the mask, grabbed my fielder's glove, and frisked out to third like a kid on a sandlot. This was when the game turned into a lark, loose and fun, but still with that fierce incentive to win. Davey had another trick up his sleeve, stranger even than me playing third. He sent Roger in to play right field. He told Jesse to warm up.

Doug Sisk was pitching at that point. The game was tied, 3–3. If he could keep the game alive—Davis had stolen third with two out—Davey was going to bring in J.O. We didn't have another outfielder on the bench. That's why he used Roger, and since he was in the game, and since he's a righty and J.O.'s a lefty, why not let him pitch to the right-handed hitters, and let J.O. pitch to the left-handed hitters? Why not?

Doug got the third out. We didn't score in our half of the tenth. J.O. came in, and the fun began.

Every time a guy came up who batted the opposite way from the previous hitter, time was called, and the pitchers swapped places. Mookie had been playing left field, and if a left-handed hitter came up, Mookie moved to right field, while Roger played left. Davey placed the pitchers where he thought they would do the least damage in the outfield. Even so, Jesse caught a fly ball.

Pete Rose wasn't amused. He went out and talked to Harvey about it. A relief pitcher is permitted eight warm-up pitches when he enters a game, and Skeets and J.O. were exercising this right almost every time they returned to pitch. Rose complained, but Harvey said there was nothing he could do about it. Rose protested the game, and lost.

As for me, I was a kid again, rediscovering the fun of playing baseball. I couldn't wait for them to hit the ball to me. Every play was a triumph. I was used to the outfield, and to first base, but this was third, the hot corner, Brooks Robinson's position. There's a feeling of freedom, too, after you've been doing a lot of catching, to get out there without a mask on.

Luck was with me; I had all sorts of chances. There was a double play with runners on first and second. The hitter bunted; Mex was on top of him as soon as he laid it down. Mex whipped the ball to me—out—and I threw to Tuff, covering first—double play. Buddy Bell hit a line drive that skidded to my left; I dove, stabbed it, and although the ball did slither out of my glove—a base hit—I thought it was a great play.

Meanwhile, neither side could score. Mets 3, Reds 3. The difference was, we were having more fun. Rose was mad at the umpires for letting Roger and Jesse warm up every time they returned to the mound. No one in the fight had been hit as hard as Davis had been popped by Ray. The Reds were seething, and we were playing an improvised, sandlot game and loving every minute of it. Neither side could push across a run—until our fourteenth. Then, with Hearn and J.O. on base, Hojo hit one out of the ball park, his sixth home run, and we had the lead, 6–3. Roger finished off the Reds in the bottom of the inning. Afterward, the league warned Ray that if he fought again, he'd be suspended.

The game took five hours. Winning it inspired us. It seemed one more proof that we were 1986's team of destiny. The game was offbeat, wacky, and we'd won it; it was like a trick pitch you don't expect and hit anyway. We'd had tricks of our own, and they'd all worked. I went oh for six, and didn't mind a bit.

Arrogance in a successful big-league ballplayer shouldn't be surprising. However, the supposed arrogance of the '86 Mets was collective, a team attitude. From it came our closeness. Together, we were disliked. Separate us, take us one by one, and you'd find that the New York Mets were, and are, no more, and no less, arrogant than any group of excellent professional athletes. It shouldn't come as news to anybody that there isn't a lot of humility running around in big-league sports.

When we won the World Series, my biggest dream, I felt I had just about everything I wanted. I was thirty-two years old, and had climbed the mountain. I was there. Jubilation swirled through Shea; the champagne ran. Outside the clubhouse, Sandy waited for me, my wife, my best friend. My three healthy children were sleeping safely or watching this on television half-asleep. This was everything, every heart's desire, it seemed. And when Bob Costas of NBC pushed a microphone at me and asked me to comment, I gave thanks, there on national TV, to the Lord, Jesus Christ.

I suppose some people, in their living rooms across America, winced to hear it. I've seen interviewers go blank for a split second when I've invoked Christ's name—a brief frozen look, as if I'd sprung something on them. If it's a TV interview, I always know they'll never rerun this portion. They'd rather forget about it.

But I look at it this way: Christianity is a major force in my life. I'm a lucky man. I've been showered with good luck. To be lucky is to be blessed, and I have my own beliefs as to where the blessings flow from. A blessing is a gift—whether it's your child or the ability to hit a baseball. And I feel grateful for these gifts and I like to give thanks for them.

In 1973, when I went to my first major-league spring-training camp, the roommate assigned to me was a thirty-four-year-old catcher named John Boccabella. The Expos hoped he would teach me some of the finer points of catching. He taught me more than that.

He was a devout Roman Catholic, and it didn't embarrass him to talk about it. We became friends, and I told him about my mother.

John talked to me about Christianity. He gave me Scriptures to read. He took me to Mass with him. He helped me to come to terms with things, even the death of my mother. I needed that then. I needed to be more than a hard-nosed kid playing baseball. In church with John, I felt my life widen. I was clearer about things.

I realized what was missing in my life, and I accepted Jesus Christ into my heart and soul as my Lord and Saviour. This gave me peace, and for the first time I could understand my mother's death. It gave me a brightness in my life that I could share with other people.

Maybe some people feel crowded by my Christianity and maybe it has isolated me in some ways, but I don't push it on others. I know that the Lord directs me and that He's with me always, at home, in church, and on the ball field.

I'm not saying I'm perfect—not by any means. I don't have the answers to everything. I don't always know what's right and what's wrong. I do, however, try to set an example, especially for kids.

If you *do* think a team is arrogant, as the people of Boston did about us because we didn't work out in Fenway that weary Monday, then don't, in the next breath, talk about sweeping the team four games. Sweep! The word jumped off the pages of the Boston papers. Did they think it was going to be that easy? Nothing could have lit a quicker, hotter fire in us than that word.

And if that wasn't enough to rouse us, there was the skinny, nervous right-handed pitcher Dennis "Oil Can" Boyd. Boyd would be on the mound that night. He would be pitching against his old teammate Bobby O.

Everyone who follows baseball knows about Oil Can. He's very young, very talkative, and his emotions zoom up and down like a Yo-Yo. He's done a lot of unusual things in his brief career. His latest surprise was walking out of the Red Sox clubhouse when he discovered he hadn't been chosen for the '86 All-Star team, and holing up in his apartment for a week. Oil Can may be cordial and cooperative with the reporters or he may spit curses at them. It depends how he's going. On the mound, he struts and glares and hollers to himself. He's one nonstop twitch out there.

Oil Can had been in a serious but friendly mood when the Sox returned from New York. He spoke at a press conference and said he was going to "master" us. He said Bobby O. had always had trouble pitching in Fenway because of the wall, and would be unnerved when he got out there. This talk by Oil Can made us as mad as the predictions of a sweep.

It surprised us some that Bobby O. himself didn't get riled at what Oil Can said about him. He liked the Can. He said Boyd acted crazy sometimes, obeying any wild impulse that popped into his head, but that there was no meanness in him. He said Oil Can was a nice kid.

Sandy and I had lunch that afternoon with Gordy, his wife, and our father. We ate out of sight, in peace, in a corner of the hotel

131
•

dining room. I felt more rested than I had in weeks. My body felt good. The Houston series seemed long ago. Against the Red Sox I'd been putting my bat on the ball, getting some hits. After a slump, it's a pleasure to find that you're still a big-league hitter, a good hitter and that there's no telling what you might hit on this night, or the next night, or the next. You've wakened from a bad dream.

Lunch was pleasant. We took our time over it. Then Gordy drove me to the ball park. He said Dad's back was still killing him. What else is new? I said. Gordy dropped me off a block from Fenway. It was long before the game, and anticipation was in the air.

"Good luck, Gar," he said.

I liked it. I sent him a grin and a wave, and walked up an old narrow street past the brick arches of Fenway. There were groups of kids loitering under the archways, and the vendors were setting up. It wasn't New York, and I sneaked up the street almost unnoticed and entered Fenway Park.

The clubhouse in Fenway looks its age. It is tiny, and when it fills up with ballplayers, it looks like a roomful of giants. Some of the guys had arrived. Wally and Raffy were playing cards.

They asked me if I'd read the stuff Boyd had been saying.

Just looking at Wally and Raffy, you knew Boyd had made a big mistake talking like that.

I found my locker and began, slowly, to undress. I looked around the drab little cellar of a room and thought of the men who had pulled on uniforms here and gone out onto that ball field, which is full of juts and angles, with the crowd wrapped around so close. Ty Cobb, Babe Ruth, Lou Gehrig. And Mickey Mantle, one of my all-time favorites. How many times had I been Mickey Mantle in the alley in Fullerton? Now I was in the procession.

The left-field wall waited for me, the Green Monster. I remembered the home-run contest in September—ten swings, five home runs. I remembered the ball jumping into the night sky, clearing the wall with plenty to spare. What a place to play baseball, even without its ghosts and its history. I remembered from the exhibition game how well you can see the ball there—distinct as a pearl against the green background.

I was excited, I couldn't wait to jump onto that ball field. It hit me then what a dull place the Astrodome is. That quiet, echoing, new-fangled place with its controlled air and plastic grass. It's tough playing there; you have a feeling beforehand that recalls trudging off to work on a Monday morning.

It was pure joy playing in Fenway.

Bobby O. must have had some mixed feelings. He resented the way John McNamara had used him the year before, but still, Bobby had put in six years here and had some fond memories. Rich Gedman was his best friend. He liked Al Nipper and Bruce Hurst, who stole up behind him while he was doing an interview before the September 4 exhibition game and squashed a shaving-cream pie in his face. The prank was all fun and friendship. Bobby O. swore he was going to get even; he was going to sneak into the Red Sox clubhouse and cut their clothes to ribbons. Bobby never found a way into their clubhouse, but he got even on the pitcher's mound.

He knows how to pitch, Bobby Ojeda. He puts his pitches here, there, everywhere, and knows exactly where they're going. He's a finesse pitcher, like Hurst. And yet, good as he is, he'd won as many as twelve games only once for the Red Sox, and his earned-run average had always been so-so. Oil Can wasn't imagining things when he predicted they'd hit Bobby tonight. A lot of good lefty pitchers have suffered in Fenway, gone someplace else and won big. John Tudor was a Cy Young Award candidate in our league after leaving Boston. That wall can seem awfully close.

Bobby's scouting report on Oil Can was more helpful than what he'd told us about Hurst. The Can has a decent curve ball, but it's a roundhouse; it doesn't bite down. He throws the change-up all the time, and his fastball, which he likes to talk about, isn't particularly fast. His strength is that one fastball is never the same as another.

133

•

It is always traveling at a different speed. Oil Can will fool you, but he won't overpower you.

I don't think any pitcher could have denied us that night. We were a good team, an explosive team, and we were in a corner, fighting for our lives. That will wake anybody up.

The game's first hitter, Lenny, exploded one into the right-field seats, a high, arcing home run. Boyd, always emotional, talked to himself. You could see him mouthing words, bobbing his head. Wally shot a single to right. Mex singled to center. My turn.

Oil Can did an odd thing with me. He threw me two pretty good change-ups, slow pitches I couldn't stride into and hit. Both were strikes, and he had me in the hole. I didn't expect to see anything good for at least two pitches. I expected to be teased. Then what does he do but slice the plate almost in two—fastball, and not too low. It was up there, and I got it, clubbed it. The ball sailed to the deep part of Fenway and hit the wall where it angles to the bleachers in faraway center.

Wally stepped home, Mex stopped at third, and I had a double. That doused the fire of Oil Can. He wasn't stamping around the mound, wasn't slamming the ball into his glove. He'd talked so positively about beating us, and the boast was getting shot full of holes in the first inning.

He struck Darryl out. It wasn't going to be an easy three days for Straw.

A slapstick comedy followed. Ray bounced one to Boggs. Mex was chugging home; Boggs threw to Gedman, so far ahead of Mex that Mex braked and waited for Gedman to chase him back to third. I hustled from second as close to third as I could sneak, so after they tagged Mex, I would be at third, at least.

Gedman worked Mex back toward third, waiting to throw to Boggs at the last split second. He chased him and chased him, then threw— too late. Mex was past Boggs. He dove, and had third base.

Then they had me.

Boggs tossed to Owen, who chased me back to second. We were almost there when Owen glanced over his shoulder to see what Mex

134

•

was up to. He was just standing on third. While Owen looked, I belly-flopped into second—safe. The bases were loaded. You don't commit mistakes like those in the World Series without paying. Danny lined one into center—base hit—bringing home Mex and me.

Mets 4, Red Sox 0.

That was all for a while. Boyd found a rhythm and kept his pitches low. We didn't rough him up again until the seventh.

Meanwhile, Bobby O. was the pitcher doing the mastering. The Sox scored in the third, when that little pest Marty Barrett punched a single into right, bringing home Henderson. (Barrett punched two singles again that night.) That was their offense. Bobby struck out his buddy Gedman, twice. He pitched seven strong innings, tired a bit, and Davey summoned Roger. Skeets was perfect: six up, six down. He had them mashing the ball on the ground; five ground-ball outs, and a fly ball by Evans.

We ended Oil Can's season in the seventh. Raffy and Lenny singled, and, with two out, the Can walked Mex. Big chance for yours truly. Again Boyd slipped two strikes past me. With two strikes, he tried the change-up; I swung just early and fouled it back. Another change-up, another foul, straight back. Then he let the ball hang high enough and over the plate. Just make contact, I was thinking, just make contact, and I reached for it and pulled a soft line drive between Boggs and Owen, into left field. Base hit. With two out, the runners went flying; Raffy and Lenny scored.

Mets 6, Red Sox 1.

In the entire Houston series, six games, two of them long ones, I'd had four hits, two RBIs. Here, in eight at bats, I'd equaled it.

They tried to get Lenny at the plate on my single, and I rounded first, the old gazelle, and went churning into no man's land. Gedman threw to Barrett, and I was caught, a mile from either base. Barrett and Owen ran me back and forth. Owen put the tag on me.

Exit Oil Can Boyd.

They brought in Joe Sambito to pitch the eighth. Joe had been with us for a while the year before. He's a lefty and used to throw very hard, but he'd had arm surgery and those days were behind

135
•

him. Straw led off with a single, and Ray hit one off the Green Monster, bringing home Straw. Joe took the long walk to the dugout.

Mets 7, Red Sox 1.

So much for the sweep. When will people learn?

TUESDAY, OCT. 21 at BOSTON

METS (7)					BOSTON (1)				
	ab	r	h	bi		ab	r	h	bi
Dykstra cf	5	2	4	1	Boggs 3b	3	0	1	0
Backman 2b	5	1	1	0	Barrett 2b	4	0	2	1
Hernandez 1b	4	1	2	0	Buckner 1b	4	0	0	0
Carter c	5	1	2	3	Rice lf	3	0	0	0
Strawberry rf	4	1	1	0	Baylor dh	4	0	1	0
Knight 3b	4	0	1	1	Evans rf	4	0	0	0
Heep dh	3	0	1	2	Gedman c	4	0	0	0
Mitchell ph	0	0	0	0	Henderson cf	2	1	1	0
Mazzilli ph	1	0	0	0	Owen ss	3	0	0	0
Wilson lf	4	0	0	0					
Santana ss	4	1	1	0					
	39	7	13	7		31	1	5	1

```
Mets _____  400 000 210 — 7 13 0
Boston _____  001 000 000 — 1  5 0
```

DP—Mets 1, Boston 1. LOB—Mets 6, Boston 6. 2B—Carter, Baylor, Knight. HR—Dykstra (1). Game-Winning RBI—Dykstra (1).

	IP	H	R	ER	BB	SO
Mets						
Ojeda (W, 1-0)	7	5	1	1	3	6
McDowell	2	0	0	0	0	0
Boston						
Boyd (L, 0-1)	7	9	6	6	1	3
Sambito	0	2	1	1	0	0
Stanley	2	2	0	0	0	1

Sambito pitched to 2 batters in the 8th. WP—Ojeda, Sambito. PB—Gedman. T—2:58. A—33,595.

10

I had read in the papers, and had even heard from a few players, that the Red Sox had some guys who were more concerned with personal statistics than winning, and I was reminded that I'd been accused of playing selfishly during my years with the Expos. The only way, really, to get out from under this label is to help your team go all the way. In Montreal, I kept hearing I wasn't a team player, and therefore not a winner. More than any other player, I was blamed for the Expos' failure to bring home a pennant. When I think of the cliques on that ball club, of the nastiness in the clubhouse, of Cromartie's needling and instigating trouble, I wonder: What more did they want from me?

I wanted the Mets to win it all, and I wanted to be part of it, in the thick of things. I can't imagine any ballplayer not wanting that. We dream of glory from the time we can throw a baseball and read the back of a bubble-gum card. *Seventh game of the World Series. Ninth inning. Two down. Here comes Mickey Mantle.* No kid in our alley in Fullerton, no kid in any alley anywhere, imagines he is watching the big moment from the dugout or the on-deck circle. No: he wants to be in the thick of it.

Which is why, when I left the game in Shea Stadium on August 16, my thumb swollen and throbbing, I felt a chill that was as near to panic as I have ever known. It's broken, I thought. It's broken, broken, broken. I was through for the season. It wasn't possible. Yes, it was. Yes.

It was a Saturday, a day game with the Cardinals, on national TV. We were in first place by sixteen games. Mex was resting. I was playing first base. Sandy was at the ball park.

In the second inning, with a runner on first, their catcher, Mike LaValliere, pulled a ground ball my way. I thought he'd really cracked it, and I spun to my right, dove, and found I'd reacted too quickly, that the ball hadn't been hit so hard. I landed on my knees, hesitated, gloved the ball on the hop, and then, instead of rolling, instead of tucking my hands safely against me and rolling on my shoulder, I stuck both hands down to break the fall. My left thumb caught, jammed, folded. There was a spasm of terrific pain, but I was too busy to worry about it—rearing to my knees and whipping the ball to second to wipe out the lead runner.

I got up, strolled back to my position. It was broken; I knew it. Oh, God, no, don't let it be broken, I thought. Red-hot pain. I didn't say anything. I had a wild hope that if I ignored it, it would go away.

What an inning! The thumb throbbed inside the first-baseman's mitt and the tight leather batting glove I wear under it. Greg Matthews, their pitcher, batted next. He squared to bunt, got only a piece of the ball, and squirted it foul toward our dugout. I went hard after it, dove, took it one-handed on my side. Met Play of the Month, according to Metropolitan Life, which makes an award after studying each month's replays. The crowd cheered me.

God, don't let it be broken. The thought kept going through my head. I slid the mitt off, gingerly unpeeled the batting glove. The thumb was very swollen. It looked broken. Or torn. I worked the gloves back over it. Ozzie Smith was the next hitter.

LaValliere was still on first, so I was close to the bag. Smith hit one hard on the ground, again to my right; again I crashed to my knees and backhanded the ball. *Nice* play. I dove the other way, tagged the base, and Smith was out. Some inning.

As I came off the field, the guys were all yelling how awesome

I'd been out there. But the pain was settling in, taking hold, and I knew I couldn't wish it away. The trainers, Steve Garland and Bob Sikes, were both in the dugout, and I told them I wanted to see them. We went inside, down the runway to the clubhouse. I stripped off the batting glove. The trainers leaned in and peered at the thumb. Steve worked it gently back and forth.

"Better get an x-ray."

"I don't want to come out of the game," I said. That was crazy, and I knew it.

"You're gonna have to."

"I'll be all right, you guys. Really."

"Get Dr. Parkes down here," Steve told Bob.

James Parkes III, our team doctor, is an orthopedic surgeon. He was at the game, watching from his own box seat.

"Take your shower," Steve said, making it final, and real.

Bob went out to tell Davey. The third inning began, and the PA announcer told the crowd that Lee Mazzilli was playing first base. Sandy jumped right up and headed for the clubhouse. She knew I was hurt. She'd seen me play baseball with every kind of ache and pain. She'd seen me play with a temperature of 104°.

Dr. Parkes turned my thumb over in his long surgeon's hands, and said he wanted an x-ray. Alone in the clubhouse, I unwound the tape from my knee and peeled it from my ankles. I took a shower. I'd broken this thumb before, and I thought about that, but it hadn't mattered then the way it mattered now. It had been in 1976. I was playing right field for the Expos. The bases were loaded. Darrell Chaney was hitting for the Braves. You never forget these details. Chaney banged one between me and Pepe Mangual. I yelled I had it. I didn't hear Pepe. I was running full tilt, Pepe was out of sight and out of mind, and, as I gloved the line drive, we collided with a bone-loosening jolt that flung us both to the ground. I felt hurt all over and dazed, as if I'd fallen off a building. I realized I'd held on to the ball. Pepe was lying still. He'd been knocked out cold. I scrambled up, pegged the ball in, and felt a roar of pain in my left thumb. I pulled off the glove. It was broken, all right. I started walking.

It was the only time I'd ever been on the disabled list. It was different then, more acceptable. It hadn't been the year of my baseball life, the year of years.

Dr. Parkes drove to Roosevelt Hospital with Sandy and me.

"I can't believe this is happening," I said. I remembered I was leading the league in RBIs. I felt, though, that it *was* happening. My thumb was broken. Ligaments all torn up. Something. I was through.

Dr. Parkes looked at it as we drove. He moved it around some more and said it wasn't broken. He said he thought I'd torn some ligaments. He said I hadn't severed them, because he could bend the thumb to a stopping point. I guess if I'd torn the ligaments completely, the thumb would have flopped all over.

I still believed the worst. Surgery. They're gonna tell me I need surgery, I thought. Dr. Parkes reassured me over and over. I thought of all the times I'd been injured.

Somebody—Dr. Parkes, I suppose—had called an orthopedic surgeon who specialized in hands. We found his office and were led right in. They got some x-rays and then the doc jabbed the thumb full of Novocain. He bent it this way and that. He read the x-rays. No broken bones. A partially torn ligament.

"You won't need surgery," he said, "but I'm going to put the thumb in a cast for a week. Then you can play."

Elation. Gratitude. "Are you sure, Doc?" I said. "Are you *sure*?" He was. The thumb felt better already.

"Do you *have* to cast me?" I said.

"I think it's best."

"Let me play," I said.

"Listen to the doctor," Sandy said.

"I can play with it," I said.

Sandy said, "Listen to the doctor."

"They'll put me on the DL," I said. "I'll miss two weeks."

"Honey, will you *please* do what he says?"

Did I have a choice?

⋄   ⋄   ⋄

⋄

Those fifteen days were the longest, itchiest, most boring of my life. The worst week was the first one, when I was wearing that cast. Saturday till Friday: an eternity. Monday night we were to begin a series with the Dodgers in Los Angeles, and I insisted on making the trip. The ball club said okay, but I sensed they wouldn't have minded letting me heal at home, where I wouldn't be costing them a hotel room and meals. But I wouldn't have it. I wanted to be at the edge of the games, if I couldn't be in the middle of them. I wanted to pull on the uniform each day. Thank God for my buddy Doug Jones. Doug, who lives in Fullerton, took on the job of distracting me on that West Coast trip. I saw him every day while we were in Los Angeles. On an off-day, we took a bike ride on the boardwalk in Newport. That night I had a home-cooked meal at Sandy's parents' house.

On the bench I fidgeted, paced, kept moving. Every nerve in me was a live wire. My hands itched to grip a bat; I'd grab mine, number eight, out of the rack and find Davey.

"Hey, Skip. Can I take some batting practice? Lemme try it, Skip."

"You're driving me crazy," he said.

I'd sit next to somebody, talk a while, get up and find somebody else. Back and forth, back and forth. I wanted to be *doing*, I wanted action. The only action in the dugout is horseplay. I leaned on guys, shoved them, put head locks on them, knocked off their caps.

"Will you go *play*?" they said.

"God, do something, *anything*."

"Will somebody take his cast off and let him play?"

"He's driving me crazy," Davey told the reporters.

One thing I knew: I was coming off the disabled list on August 31, and I was going to play. Swelling, pain, weren't going to stop me. I was going to play baseball.

On Friday, I followed the team to San Francisco, and my cast came off. The thumb was pretty sore, but I wanted to play. And if we'd been fighting for first place, I would have. If the race had been close, I wouldn't have let them put a cast on me. I would have taken a few days off and jumped back in. Before the game, I threw. I ran

141

•

up and down the outfield. Lord, I wanted to play. I felt like I was being punished. The days dragged on.

The team kept winning. Without me, they won, won, won. Young John Gibbons had replaced me on the roster. He and Ed Hearn were sharing the catching, and playing marvelous baseball. Ed is a conservative guy whom we call "Ward," after the father in the old TV series *Leave It to Beaver*. Ward was my understudy, but he was as big a supporter as I had on the team. The ball club rewarded Gibbons for his play those weeks by inviting him to the play-offs and World Series as our bullpen catcher. The team won eleven, lost three, with me on the bench. Mike Schmidt, meanwhile, drove in some runs and jumped ahead of me to lead the league in RBIs.

From San Francisco we moved down to San Diego. On Tuesday, with Dr. Parkes's permission, I ran into the cage with the thumb taped and took batting practice. The thumb hurt, but so what? I hacked and swung like a maniac. It felt wonderful.

On August 27, I left San Diego ahead of the rest of the ball club and flew home to West Palm Beach to spend a day with my family. Sandy had moved the kids down there because the girls had to start school. I hadn't seen her or the kids since the day after I'd hurt the thumb. That weekend in New York was to be my last with the kids for a long time, and the injury had sort of soured it. I'd planned to take Christy and Kimmy to dinner and a movie, but my thumb hurt and I was in a black mood, and I begged off. The girls were upset but they understood. The game keeps pulling me away from my family, one way or another. I was beginning to wish I hadn't agreed to go to Japan with Davey's American team. The nearer November got, the more I wished I weren't going.

That night, late, I watched us play the Padres on TV. It was a magnificent game, a magnificent win—the kind that summed up our season. Eleven hard-fought innings. We'd led, 5–1; the Padres caught us in the eighth. In the top of the eleventh, Mex hit a sacrifice fly to get us the lead. In the bottom of the inning, with Garry Templeton on first and one out, Tim Flannery drove a ball up the middle for a base hit. Lenny charged the ball, and threw home as Templeton came flying down the line. Gibbons was catching. He took the

142
•

throw, put the tag on Templeton for the out as Templeton crashed against him, knocking him flat. Flannery, meanwhile, thought he could sneak to third. Gibbons jumped up, pegged the ball to Hojo as Flannery slid. Out, and the ball game was over. The guys were celebrating like it was the World Series, slapping hands, hugging, the whole bit. We were twenty games in front of the Phillies. The guys romped off the field, and I felt far, far away from them, separate in a way I never had been.

It was as if time had sped on without me. I felt like I was living in the past; I felt forgotten. Life goes on, I thought. Time doesn't stop because Gary Carter can't play baseball. The ball park fills; the guys play ball—with or without me. Life goes on.

Next day, I flew to New York.

I had three more days to wait. I took a lot of batting practice. I counted the hours, the minutes. The Giants came to town, and on Labor Day, September 1, I was in the line-up, and I was batting cleanup. Sandy flew up for the game. It was a day game, and the September sun shone down out of a cloudless sky.

I see by the box score that the attendance was 44,272. I was aware of the fans before the game began, I could hear them as I swung in the cage and stretched in the outfield.

Ga-ree, Ga-ree.

Aw-right, aw-rahhht . . .

I smiled. The starting line-ups drifted out over the PA system. *Batting fourth, the catcher, number eight . . .* The crowd welcomed me back with a cheer that drenched me like rain. Sometimes you can *feel* the noise on your skin. I was like a race horse in the starting gate in the moments before we took the field. I was leaning, poised, and I shot out of there and sprinted for home plate like my life depended on it. A new roar.

Ga-ree!

Ga-ree!

I was back, almost. Duke got the Giants out, and in our half of the first Wally singled and stole second, and was still there when I batted. Kelly Downs was on the mound, a pitcher I'd never seen. I pushed the noise away, distanced myself, and concentrated. Downs threw me the breaking ball, trying to keep it away from me, and I swatted it over Kutcher's head, the third baseman—a base hit. Wally flew home. I'd gotten the ball toward the end of the bat, soft line drive, but a hit is a hit. I stood at first and waved to 44,272 good friends. I was back.

I had another hit in that game, and almost had three. My second time up I drove one hard into left center field between Candy Maldonado and Dan Gladden. Gladden got his glove on the ball and lost it, and the scorer gave him an error. I went to second sliding—feet first, saving my thumb. I bounced up to my feet. The cheers flowed. I was a kid, and it felt like my first game in the major leagues.

Mets 5, Giants 2.

We were surprised, and not sorry, when John McNamara announced that Al Nipper was pitching game four of the Series. McNamara came out with this in New York, after the Sox had beat us up in game two; his idea was to take a chance with Nipper, and let his two aces, Hurst and Clemens, rest another day. It was fine with us.

I don't mean to disparage Nipper. Hurst, Clemens, and Boyd were their three best pitchers; there's no arguing that. Nipper had been badly hurt early in the season when my old teammate the Enforcer, Larry Parrish, had nearly sliced him in half in a home-plate collision. Nipper's knee had been mangled, and it had taken him a long time to heal. Bobby O. said we could beat him.

He can't fire the fastball by you, Bobby said. Look for a lot of clever breaking balls, a lot of junk. Bobby O. liked Nipper. He liked Hurst, Boyd, Nipper, and Gedman. It was a strange time for Bobby O.

Ronnie was our pitcher. Our second nickname for him, after R.J., is Mr. P., for Mr. Perfect. He is a cover boy. He has that quiet, Ivy League style and dark good looks, and carries everything off with a certain elegance. He spends almost as much time primping in front of the mirror as Aggie does, whose long wavy hair is patted into place even more perfectly than the dark hair of Mr. Perfect himself. Ask Ronnie if he wants to go out for dinner and take in a movie, and he'll answer, if the idea appeals to him, "It sounds like the perfect evening." Mr. P.

Nipper pitched us very tough for three innings. In fact, I was beginning to wonder if Bobby O. had fed us another bad scouting report. Slow junk? In the first inning, with a count on me of three and two, I got what was probably the cleverest, nastiest pitch I saw all Series. It was a slider, a beauty. It skidded on air, surprising me with its movement, and I just stared; strike three called. I went back to the dugout talking to myself.

Barrett—who else?—hit a double in their half of the first. R.J. briefly lost the plate, walking Rice and the designated hitter, Don Baylor. It wasn't a game we could afford to lose, with Hurst pitching the next day. (How many of these games had we played in the post-season? How many times had we known we had to win to stay alive?) Bases loaded, two out, Evans the hitter. Give him the curve ball, we figured. It's those fastballs he kills. R.J. got two strikes, and broke off the curve nice and low. Evans chopped it into the ground, couple of easy hops to Wally. We were out of the inning.

Nipper cruised through the second and third, and we busted loose in the fourth. Wally singled. Mex hit a ground ball to Owen, who had to get the out at first, because Wally was running with the pitch. My turn.

It was the first time in the game Nipper had pitched with a runner on second. This creates a nuisance; the runner can see the catcher's signs, the fingers stuck down between his thighs. Signs are more or less universal: one finger is the fastball, two is the curve, three the slider, four the change-up. Sometimes a wiggle of the hand is the change. The big question for the hitter is whether the pitch coming is the fastball: a big-league hitter, if he knows it's coming, can hit almost anybody's fastball. As I said, a runner at second base will read the catcher's sign, if he can, and relay the information to the batter. How? It's all been worked out beforehand, the improvised sign language of baseball. Watch the runner at second. He'll touch his hat or tug at his belt, informing the batter: I've got the signs, I've broken the code. Keep watching me. He might stand straight up if the pitch is a fastball, lean with his hands on his knees if it's the breaking ball. He'll glance to his left if the pitch is supposed to be thrown on that edge of the plate, to his right if the pitch is to be thrown that way.

To prevent this, the pitcher and catcher must complicate the signs. Scramble them, use code. What the runner sees is a series of signs— maybe four flicks of the hand, four sets of fingers. The second one may be the sign. Or the third. Any of them. Or we might use an indicator; one, two, or three fingers meaning the sign is the first, second, or third one coming. You can't make it regular, or they'll figure it out. I change the code with every pitcher. I change it, sometimes, from game to game. I like to make it easy for the pitcher. Pitchers have enough to think about without having to remember complicated sign systems. Often when a catcher jogs out to talk to his pitcher, the subject is signs. I seldom go out to chew a pitcher out. Most big-league pitchers don't need that. The topic is usually dry and undramatic: signs.

So when I was up in that fourth inning, and Gedman held two lengthy conferences with Nipper, the subject could only have been signs. Geddie's two visits checked the flow of the game, and might have broken Nipper's rhythm. As I was getting into the box, Geddie asked for time and went hustling out there. Maybe they were discussing how to pitch me. Maybe it wasn't signs the first time. Maybe Nipper disagreed with Geddie's strategy, and they were straightening it out between them, though they should have straightened it out earlier.

They talked. Gedman came back behind the plate, Nipper stared in, and Geddie raced out to see him again. They looked worried. The home-plate umpire was an American League ump, Joe Brinkman, and I asked him if Nipper had trouble seeing signs. Brinkman said he didn't think so. The nervous powwow ended, and Gedman trotted in. Nipper still hadn't pitched to me.

I thought, Fastball. He'd struck me out with a slider on the outside corner, and I figured he was thinking he'd planted it in my mind, and I'd be looking for it again, leaning out for it. And so he would zip the fastball inside, taking me by surprise, strike one. Then he could begin teasing me again with the junk. Fastball, inside. I figured right.

It was a fastball, it was inside, and I hit it. It climbed, and as I ran I watched Rice, the left fielder. He was fading, looking up; I saw him go slack, giving up, and I looked for the ball. It fell against the screen, home run, and the crowd went quiet. I was light as a feather, running on air. Bill Robinson gave me a high five and a big grin. I didn't have to say it; he knew. *I just hit a home run in the World Series. Hey, Uncle Bill. Hey, Sandy. Hey, Dad. Hey, Gordy.*

Joy. And relief. Big guys are expected to hit a home run or two in the World Series; we expect it of ourselves. I'd done it, and could relax. Darryl, as big a guy as there is, didn't get his home run until the seventh game, and I think it troubled him, I think he pressed, trying to find that first home run.

Mets 2, Red Sox 0.

Straw kept it going with a double pushed to the opposite field. Ray lined one into center field—base hit—and Straw glided home.

Mets 3, Red Sox 0.

Leading off in the sixth, I hit a double to right field. Straw lifted a fly ball to Evans, deep enough to let me get over to third. Then Ray lined a ball to left field; Rice made the catch. I tagged up, and when Rice seemed to be having trouble digging the ball out of his glove, I ran. Gedman was waiting for me with the ball; I was out by ten feet. I hadn't exactly been brilliant on the base paths in the Series.

Crawford came in to pitch to us in the seventh. He had shut us out for a couple of innings in game two, but game two was now a long time ago. Mookie singled and stole second. With two out, Lenny drove one to the Red Sox bullpen. Evans got there, reached, and touched the ball, barely, as it fell into the bullpen. Home run.

Mets 5, Red Sox 0.

A hanging curve ball is a curve ball in your happy zone. Every hitter has his own happy zone; mine is near the middle of the plate, maybe a shade inside, and high. No pitcher in his right mind intends to put the ball in a hitter's happy zone.

When I see a hanging curve, my eyes light up. They widen. In the tiniest fraction of a second, I feel surprise, delight, and a terrific rush of energy. You don't hit a hanging curve; you attack it. You pound the sucker.

In the eighth inning of game four, Crawford threw me a hanging curve.

There were two strikes on me. He'd been throwing me some pretty good pitches. Still, I'd hit a home run and a double, and when you do that, you relax. You're confident, you're patient. It helped, too, that I'd gotten a hit against Crawford in game two. The two strikes didn't worry me. I'd find a pitch I could hit. He threw me a good, tough pitch on the outside edge, and I fouled it back. Then came the hanging curve.

I knew it was gone the instant I hit it. Maybe I knew it was gone *before* I hit it. It flashed through my mind that I ought to stand still and watch it disappear above the city, but I tossed the bat away and broke into my trot, watching as I went. It was over the wall, over the screen, long gone before I reached first base. Uncle Bill gave me another high five.

What's better than hitting a home run in the World Series?

Answer: hitting two.

Mets 6, Red Sox 0.

R.J., meanwhile, was pitching superbly. No runs, four hits after seven. He was a little tired, the game was ours, and Davey figured he'd need Mr. P. again in this Series. So he pulled him out and gave the ball to Roger.

They hit Roger. With two outs and a couple of runs in, Jesse took over to pitch to Boggs. Boggs slapped a ground ball to Raffy, and the inning was history. Mookie singled in our ninth, his second hit of the night. J.O. put them down neatly in the bottom of the ninth. He fanned the superstar, Rice, to finish the game.

Mets 6, Red Sox 2.

It had come down to a best-of-three series.

Nipper's and Gedman's trouble with signs just before I hit my first home run reminded me of the Expos' pitcher known to his team-mates as Lights—as in, the lights are on but nobody's home. Lights was not the brightest ballplayer I've ever known. A runner on second base was an enormous problem when Lights was pitching, because we couldn't complicate the signs too much or Lights would be just as confused as the base runner. The only possibility, really, was the first-sign indicator: I'd put down one finger, meaning that the first sign in the sequence—the next sign I flashed—was the pitch I wanted. We could only hope the opposition didn't catch on. I would put fingers down four times when Lights was pitching with a man on second, beginning always with one; the next one was the live sign, and the last two were decoys.

149

One night, with us winning big, Lights was in there, and some-body hit a double, so we had to go to the indicator. Chris Speier was playing shortstop. I asked for time and jogged out to refresh Lights's memory, and Speier asked for time and walked in and joined us. As I was turning back toward the plate, Speier said, "Give him the third-sign indicator, Kid." Speier was an instigator, always stir-ring up mischief.

I went back, sank into my crouch, and—I couldn't resist—stuck down three fingers, meaning the third sign was the live one. You don't pause after the indicator; it's all very rapid. Three, one, two, one, and I offered the mitt, the target for Lights to pitch to.

He was leaning forward, peering in the way pitchers do, and he kept staring, his face beginning to fog up. I ran through the series again: three, one, two, one. Lights's mouth fell open. He removed his foot from the pitching rubber and yelled for time. I sneaked a glance at Speier. He had buried his face in his glove and was laugh-ing. I jogged out to talk to Lights.

"Hey, Kid," Lights said, "what kind of signs are those?"

"Third-sign indicator," I explained.

Speier's face was still inside his glove.

"Huh?" said Lights.

"Tell you what," I said. "We'll go back to the first-sign indicator. You remember how that works, don't you, Lights?"

"Sure," he said.

How dim was Lights?

There's an old and elaborate gag used on rookies that requires the participation of most of the ball club. It's called "man in the middle," and you want to get the kid in his game uniform, minutes before he's to take the field. The Expos got me when I was a rookie. They got somebody just about every year. Lights was always in on the joke, but he could never get his part straight.

Ozzie Virgil, a coach, was excellent at masterminding the gag, which goes like this:

Raines, let's say, begins it. "Ozzie Virgil can lift three guys," he says.

"Three guys?" someone says. "At once?"

150

.

"Yup."

"Get outta here," Dawson says. "No one can lift three guys."

"I can," Ozzie says. "There's a certain technique about it."

"Bull," someone says.

"I've done it," Ozzie says.

"If he says he can do it," Raines says, "I got to believe him."

"I'm tellin' you, I've done it," Ozzie says.

"It's not possible," I say.

"It's all in the technique," Ozzie says. "You got to line the three guys up, lift them level. That's the whole trick: keep 'em level."

"I'll bet you twenty bucks you can't lift three guys," Dawson says.

"I'd just be takin' your money, Hawk," Ozzie says.

"Twenty bucks," says Dawson.

"All right," Ozzie agrees, reluctant. "It's your money."

"I'd bet with you, Kid," says Raines. "I'll bet on Ozzie."

"Anybody else?" Ozzie says.

A couple more guys say, yeah, they'll take the bet. When the bets are arranged, Ozzie looks around the room.

"It's very important," he says, "that the three guys are the same size. I got to keep 'em *level*, see." Ozzie's gaze sets on Dawson. "Hawk, you'll be good. Lemme see, now, who's about your size?" Ozzie notices me. "Kid, you're about right. Hawk, Kid, and . . ." The victim is, let's say, the rookie pitcher, Charlie Lea. Ozzie finds him sitting by his locker, taking it all in.

"Charlie," he says. "How much you weigh?"

"Two-oh-five," Charlie says.

"Perfect," Ozzie says. "I'll lift Hawk, Kid, and Charlie."

Dawson and I put on faces like we haven't got the vaguest idea what's expected of us.

"You guys lie down," Ozzie says. "Come here, Charlie. I want you in the middle."

"What difference does it make?" asks Dawson, as though he suddenly smelled a rat.

"Balance," Ozzie says. "Lie down, you guys."

So the three of us stretch out on the floor, on our backs. Ozzie hovers over us, supervising.

"Close together. That's it. Now, what you do is, you lock arms and legs. You got to be *rigid,* understand?"

Dawson and I wrap our inside legs around Charlie's legs. We tie our arms to his. The kid is tied down. Pinned. Helpless.

Out comes the mustard, the ketchup, and the shaving cream. The two end guys hold tight. The mustard, the ketchup, the shaving cream are applied liberally up and down the victim's clean uniform. The others unbutton his shirt, unbelt his pants, smear him up and down. The prank ends and the victim is released when he is as coated with condiments as a giant ball-park hotdog. Welcome to the big leagues, kid!

How dim was Lights?

When the victim was tied down and ready for the treatment, Lights would rush to the mustard, bring it, cackling with pleasure, scoop out a big gob—and smear it on one of the guys on the end.

The gag seldom worked when Lights was with the ball club.

Lights was so dim that you could pull the same trick the next week, and he'd end up in the middle. We never tried it, but that's how dim he was.

11

I thought Dwight was going to be fine in game five. The Red Sox had knocked him out of game two, and I didn't think it would happen again. After he'd lost that second game, a question was repeated: What's wrong with Doc? The question had been raised many times over the summer. Apparently every time Dwight went to the mound, people expected brilliance, magic, and if he pitched no more than a fair game—sometimes even when he pitched a good game—the question rang out: *What's wrong with Doc?*

He was, of course, being measured against his first two years in the majors, especially his second. In 1984, he won seventeen games, lost nine, and had an earned-run average of 2.60. He was nineteen. In 1985, he won twenty-four, lost four, and allowed an average of 1.53 runs per game.

In 1986, he won seventeen and lost six. His earned-run average was 2.84. He struck out 200 batters. The idea that something is wrong with a guy who wins seventeen games, strikes out 200 guys, and holds his ERA below 3.00 is very strange.

If anything *was* wrong with Dwight Gooden in 1986, I ought to know. My answer to the question boils down to this: not much. I'll put it another way: nothing serious.

He was throwing his fastball as hard as ever. It was my hand the ball was pounding, my index finger. The fastball was sailing in as furious as ever, but it wasn't quite the same. It had lost some precious bit of movement, and I believe that somewhere in the beautiful ballet of Doc's pitching motion a little mechanical foul-up developed, invisible to the untrained eye. It was tiny, whatever it was; just enough to cause this slight alteration in the veer of his fastball. The soreness in my left hand tells me he throws as hard as ever.

New York should understand, and I think does, that Dwight Gooden is a franchise player, a pitcher of perhaps unlimited potential. He is wise about his profession at an incredibly young age. In spring training, he knows how to take his time, knows how to break in his arm, knows patience. It sounds easy, but I've seen many a cocky kid who thought he could go out under the Florida sun the first day and throw a baseball through a brick wall. I've seen a lot of kids damage their arms throwing hard early. Not Doc. It's lovely to watch him toss the ball lightly, gently, waiting with all the savvy of a veteran for the right time to come around to rear back and cut loose.

This maturity as a pitcher is all the more surprising considering how easy success had come to him. He was Rookie of the Year in '84, and won the Cy Young Award in '85. In '85 his fastball was so alive, so blazing, that I used to think he could throw nothing but the fastball for nine innings and win. It seemed so effortless, pitching seemed so natural, that Davey backed away, left him alone, as if any interference would be meddling with perfection. "That's the Doctor," Davey would say. "Let him do his thing."

His success in '85 was so phenomenal, and he was so young, that the Mets worried about the publicity chasing him. He was twenty, and he was being photographed, interviewed, followed, and gossiped about. He didn't seem to mind, but the ball club decided to insulate him from some of it. The rule was laid down that he could be interviewed only on the days he pitched. He went along with this, not out of any arrogance or conceit, but because he worked for the Mets, and it was what they wanted.

Doc is young. He's not immature, but he's young. There's a lot to cope with in this business, at any age. The attention can be wearing. It can be stifling. On a city street, in a restaurant, or at a sporting event, autograph seekers can come at you in sudden mobs. Some of the people are polite, some are pushy, but either way you can feel hemmed in, even bullied. And then there are reporters. Generally, I like talking to them. I enjoy the give and take. Still, an interview is tiring. Shaping answers and parrying the hard questions can be demanding. But fans can sometimes be particularly troublesome.

Early this season, I found a message in my locker at Shea saying Joe had called from Florida and wanted me to call him back, collect, that it was urgent. I wouldn't have paid any attention except for the invitation to call collect. And only a first name on the message, as if I should know him. I figured I must have made some promise I'd forgotten, or that this was an endorsement opportunity that had slipped my mind. Anyway, I didn't see any harm in calling collect. My mistake was calling from home.

Joe sounded like a kid about eighteen. He was a fan of mine and a ballplayer himself who had just broken his arm. He was feeling very down about this and wanted to talk. I tried to be nice. We chatted for a few minutes; I told him to hang in there and so forth, and finally got rid of him. I forgot all about him until, one month later, he called me. Of course: when his phone bill had come, with the collect call itemized, he had my number. I wasn't as nice this time, but Joe wasn't to be discouraged. He kept calling. He called and called and called, at all hours. Every year we have to change our phone numbers. The numbers are unlisted, but people get hold of them, I don't know how.

Such aggravations and pressures come with being a visible big-league ballplayer. We all have to learn to cope. It can take a little while—I know it did for me. Dwight, a superstar at nineteen, has had to learn fast.

I didn't rely on his fastball as much in '86 as I had the year before. We went more to his curve, which is no doubt why people kept insisting he wasn't throwing as hard as he used to. To repeat: Dwight won seventeen games and struck out 200 major-league hitters. His fastball couldn't have been too shabby, and his curve must have been more than decent. He's a proud, confident kid. He's a competitor, full of fire.

He'd thrown the fastball often in game two of the Series, and I planned to mix in more breaking pitches this time. The Red Sox hit the fastball well. As much as anything, I thought our strategy had been our failure in game two. Take Dwight Evans. He could look awful when we bent the curve ball by him, but he'd spring at the fastball with a hard, perfect swing. His home run in game two had been a tremendous shot.

For once, it was a game *they* had to win. The Sox couldn't return to Shea trailing three games to two. Hurst was their pitcher. Even though the Sox had lost the night before, this was what McNamara wanted: a rested Hurst, and a rested Clemens Saturday night in Shea. McNamara had been willing to swallow a loss to set the stage this way. Clemens would finish it for him in New York. Clemens was their glamour pitcher, their Gooden, but Hurst impressed me more. Clemens had thrown a lot of innings, he'd won a lot of big games, and he may have been a bit burned out by the time we saw him.

This was the game, game five of the 1986 World Series, that was put off for about ten minutes so that NBC could air *The Cosby Show*, as usual. Future generations will probably remember the '86 Series better than they'll remember that episode of *The Cosby Show*, but the show was enormously popular, and so, ten more minutes of waiting around. Ten minutes deeper into the early hours of morning before we piled into the plane to fly home to New York.

You won't hear big-league ballplayers, including me, complain much about the impositions of television. I'm not going to bite the hand that feeds me. Still, I would like to suggest to the networks and to major-league baseball that they think about scheduling at least a few World Series games in the daytime. For the kids.

Keith brought this up in a couple of interviews. He said that the World Series had excited him when he was a kid, had driven him. He watched the Series, he dreamed, he made plans. We all did. I remember listening to the Series on transistor radios I'd sneak into school. I'd listen through an earplug. Sometimes we were able to coax a teacher into hauling a television set into the classroom and giving the day over to the ball game. After school, Gordy and I would run home to catch the end of the game.

The way it is now, the games begin at 8:30 in the east, 5:30 on the West Coast. Postseason games are always long, remember. A kid on the West Coast can watch the whole game, but a kid at the other end of the country is out of luck. The networks like to point out that the late start enables working people to see the games. True, but some working people don't like staying up past midnight. And children can't. The World Series has been taken away from young kids.

And so at 8:40, after America had digested *The Cosby Show,* Bruce Hurst took a deep breath, looked for his sign, and pitched to Lenny Dykstra. Right there, inning number one, we knew it wouldn't be easy. This guy Hurst can pitch. Lenny hit a ground ball to Barrett. Easy out.

Tim Teufel was playing, as he had in game one against Hurst. Davey likes Tuff's right-handed swing against lefties. As it turned out, Tuff and Mookie were our offense on this night. Tuff banged one off the wall, a double. But Mex pulled one on the ground to Barrett, and I hit *another* ground ball to little Marty.

I did what Hurst wanted: I swung at his pitch. It was a change-up that looked like it was in the strike zone and was not—at least, not by the time I hit it. A change-up with movement, dipping as I swung, and I clipped it off the end of the bat, sending a ground ball to Barrett. Davey complains sometimes that I try to pull the ball too much. As a kid, after I'd advanced from the alley to the sandlots, I played a game called "over the line," in which any ball hit to the opposite field—right field for a right-handed hitter, left field for a lefty—was an out. The game was designed for days when only a few kids turned out to play, not enough to cover an entire ball field. I played "over the line" for quite a few years, and I wonder sometimes if it put an instinct in me to try to pull everything to left field. Whatever I was

157

•

doing on this night, I was chopping ground balls. Hurst threw me some beautiful dipping curves, and that dancing change-up. I was swinging at his pitches, not mine.

The Red Sox came straight at Doc in the first inning, and just missed scoring. Boggs grounded out, and that pest Barrett walked. With Buckner at bat, Doc spun and picked Barrett off first. A good thing, because Buckner singled, and Rice hit a ground ball that Tuff knocked down. Base hit. Baylor was next, the designated hitter. We got two strikes on him, using mostly breaking balls, and then, with the count one and two, Doc hit him in the shoulder. Baylor holds the major-league record for getting hit by pitches; he hangs his big body way out over the plate and isn't afraid of letting a pitch drill him. Bases loaded. Evans lifted a fly ball to Mookie in left, and we'd escaped.

They went to work on Doc in the second. It was slow work, over four innings. I thought he was throwing well in the early going. Looking back, I wish we'd used more curve balls. With one out in that second, Henderson drove one, low, into right center. Straw loped over, tried to snare the bounce backhanded, but the ball skidded under his glove. It clattered up against the bullpen, and as Lenny took the carom, his feet slipped out from under him, and he sat down, hard. Henderson is fast, and legged to third easily. It wasn't the most awesome triple I'd ever seen. Little Owen was next, and he hit a fly ball to Mookie, deep enough to bring in Henderson. Bad luck for Doc.

More bad luck in the third. Raffy, one of the game's slickest shortstops, muffed an easy ground ball by Buckner. Rice walked. Doc fanned Baylor, the second out. Evans up: curve-ball time. We'd thrown him a lot of curves, and he'd looked bad, hacking and missing, or chopping little ground balls. It seemed, with Doc pitching, that Evans was always geared for the fastball. It was as if he knew he'd get it sooner or later, and might just as well be expecting it every time. And yet you have to vary your pitches. So in that third, we let Evans see a fastball, and he whacked it into center field. Base hit and a run.

Red Sox 2, Mets 0.

In their fourth, Boggs and Barrett singled with two out. Buckner pulled a ground ball to Mex, and we were out of it. Hurst, meanwhile, was making pitching look easy. He struck me out in the fourth. He'd thrown me two change-ups, and I was looking for another, or maybe the curve—change or curve for sure—and he laid a fastball down the middle of the plate. I could only watch it go by—strike three called. It was my third strike-out in the Series, and the third time I'd struck out with the bat on my shoulder. Straw then singled, but Ray grounded into a double play.

Rice started their fifth with a line drive against the bullpen in right center; it missed going in for the home run by a few inches and popped back between Lenny and Darryl, a triple for Rice. Baylor then looped the ball in slow motion into short right, the tiniest base hit you could imagine from such a big man. It hit the grass and died. Rice trotted home. From the dugout, Rice yelled out at Baylor, kidding him about the puny base hit. The Red Sox had begun to enjoy themselves. Evans shot a base hit into left field, and the season was over for Dwight Gooden.

What I remember, as Davey went out to get him, was how surprised Doc looked. He looked like he simply could not absorb what was happening. He was getting lifted for the second time in the World Series, and it bewildered him. It was the wrong ending.

He hadn't pitched that badly. Luck had run against him. He'd pitched two long and beautiful games in the Houston series. There will be a lot of next years for the Doc.

Davey called Sid, the unsung hero of this World Series. Duke struck Gedman out. Henderson, who never stopped surprising us, knocked a double off the wall, bringing Baylor across the plate.

Red Sox 4, Mets 0.

In our sixth, Mex grounded out, I grounded out, and Straw watched a third strike zip past his knees. Straw didn't like the call, and he stood for a long moment, fixing the home-plate umpire, Ed Montague, with a dirty look. It was about this time that Straw and the Boston crowd struck up a relationship that was a long way from friendly. They began booing him. They really let him have it.

They'd never seen Darryl, but they'd heard about him. My guess is they'd heard he was loaded with talent, could see it in the size and grace of the man, and they'd been waiting all along for him to erupt. They'd been expecting it: home runs, tremendous throws from the outfield. It hadn't really happened, although Straw had chipped in with some hits. Tonight, Henderson's triple had bounced under his glove. Then he'd watched strike three go by, and I think it suddenly hit these fans that Straw didn't scare them anymore. They'd been afraid of him all Series, and in that moment the fear passed, and they let him have it.

The spotlight was on Hurst: Could he hold the lead? Ray singled to begin the eighth, but Hurst fanned World, who was our DH, and easily disposed of Mookie and Raffy. Meanwhile, almost unnoticed, Duke was dominating the Red Sox. After Henderson's double, the only other hits off Duke were an eighth-inning infield single by Boggs, and a double by—guess who?—Barrett. Neither scored. Duke struck out Gedman twice, Rice, Baylor, and Owen. They couldn't get his fastball. It would shoot up by them as they swung. Here was a weapon—Fernandez—we hadn't really used yet.

In the eighth inning, Tuff got us on the scoreboard with a bases-empty home run. He punched an outside pitch down the right-field line—*on* the line, low, the ball traveling to the foul pole and into the seats. Mex singled. Still swinging over those falling curve balls, I hit another ground ball to Barrett. Then Straw hoisted a high, high pop-up near the third-base dugout. Boggs waited, gloved it, and the crowd let loose a river of boos for Darryl. The little ball park was full of the noise.

Straw threw away his helmet, grabbed his glove, and trotted gloomily to right field. The booing continued, and then some genius, or maybe a group of geniuses, started calling his name, slowly, mockingly, the way you might tease a bad-humored little boy. *Da-rulll . . . Da-rulll . . .* It was loud on the ball field; the chant hung in the air. It sounded as if the entire crowd was chiming in. Finally Straw lifted his hat to them. He held it a moment high over his head. "I hear you," the gesture said. We all felt for him, but it probably wasn't as painful for him as a lot of fans and writers seemed to think.

160

*

Straw's been in the big leagues a while, and a big-league ballplayer expects to be razzed and booed at times in opponents' ball parks. Straw had heard worse. We all had. The bleacher bums in Wrigley Field can be merciless. The Shea fans aren't exactly angels. A ballplayer expects to hear all kinds of things playing away from home. We didn't make any dramatic vows to punish the fans of Boston for taunting Darryl. He, of course, wanted to redeem himself, but these fans in Fenway were no more than an irritation. It's part of baseball. He knew that.

Getting booed at home is what hurts. In August, Straw was in a ferocious slump; in Shea that month, he didn't get a hit in forty-seven at-bats. In that dry stretch, the crowds began to boo him. It comes as a surprise in your own ball park. I know it affected Straw. He began putting pressure on himself, which never helps a hitter. The fans, I guess, expect big things of him. He's had some good years, but the press, and our noisy city, have built him up as a potential Mays or DiMaggio, a kid of such breathtaking talent that he ought to hit forty home runs and bat .300 as a matter of course. Straw may yet have years like that, but until he does, people may feel cheated. I've even heard it said that he has the talent to hit fifty home runs. Maybe he does, but the expectation is a heavy burden to carry.

Da-rulll . . . Da-rulll . . . It floated over the ball field. Darryl put on his hat and forgot about it. It's part of baseball.

The fact that the fans felt comfortable enough to tease him told me that they figured their team had the Series won. When will people learn?

We entered the ninth trailing, 4–1. Ray hit a ground ball to Barrett. One down. World lifted a pop-up to Barrett. Two down. The crowd stood and urged Hurst on, hollering his name in unison: *Bruce, Bruce, Bruce.* All quiet in our dugout. Mookie got hold of one and banged a double to left. Raffy pushed a single to right, and Mookie sped home. Lenny's turn, lefty against lefty. Hurst had been throwing a long time and had to be tired. He summoned everything he had left and gave it all to Lenny, the beautiful curves fading down and away, the surprise fastballs. Nails is never an easy out, especially when his back is to the wall, but Hurst struck him out, and the game was history.

Baseball can be so humbling. I'd had two good games, six runs batted in, including two home runs the night before. I'd been whacking the ball all over the place. And yet on this night I couldn't hit the ball out of the infield. When you're going strong, a game like that always makes you stop and think.

Red Sox 4, Mets 2.

THURSDAY, OCT. 23 at BOSTON

METS (2)	ab r h bi	BOSTON (4)	ab r h bi
Dykstra cf	5 0 1 0	Boggs 3b	5 0 2 0
Teufel 2b	4 1 2 1	Barrett 2b	4 0 2 0
Hernandez 1b	4 0 1 0	Buckner 1b	5 1 1 0
Carter c	4 0 0 0	Stapleton 1b	0 0 0 0
Strawberry rf	4 0 1 0	Rice lf	3 1 2 0
Knight 3b	4 0 1 0	Baylor dh	3 1 1 1
Mitchell dh	4 0 1 0	Evans rf	4 0 2 1
Wilson lf	4 1 2 0	Gedman c	4 0 0 0
Santana ss	2 0 1 1	Henderson cf	4 1 2 1
		Owen ss	3 0 0 1
	35 2 10 2		35 4 12 4

```
Mets          000 000 011 — 2 10 1
Boston        011 020 00x — 4 12 0
```

E—Santana. DP—Boston 1. LOB—Mets 8, Boston 11. 2B—Teufel, Henderson, Barrett, Wilson. 3B—Henderson, Rice. HR—Teufel (1). S—Santana. SF—Owen. Game-Winning RBI—Owen (1).

	IP	H	R	ER	BB	SO
Mets						
Gooden (L, 0-2)	4	9	4	3	2	3
Fernandez	4	3	0	0	0	5
Boston						
Hurst (W, 2-0)	9	10	2	2	1	6

Gooden pitched to 3 batters in the 5th. HBP—Baylor by Gooden. T—3:09. A—34,010.

So it was back to New York—to live or die in front of the home crowd. The team was down when the fifth game ended, no question about it, even though we'd accomplished what we'd had to in Fenway, which was to win two of three. It had seemed like an awesome task four days ago, but winning the first two had given us a shot of hope that we could sweep in Fenway. The pressure was on: we had to beat the Red Sox two in a row.

On the plane ride from Boston, Mex got talking about his other World Series, 1982, when he was with the Cardinals. The Brewers had led, three games to two, and the Cardinals had to face Don Sutton and then Pete Vucovich, who had won the Cy Young Award in the American League that year. It had looked pretty desperate, but the Cardinals had taken both games. The moral was: anything can happen in a World Series. Players forget this, just like fans and writers.

It was Lenny, though, who erased the gloom in the airplane. We'd just settled in our seats. The plane was taxiing, and Lenny, in that funny, piping way of his, said, "It's over. We're gonna win it. It's *over*, man. We're gonna go home and win two in a row. It's over."

I laughed, everyone laughed. Little Nails. It was cute, it was funny, it was Lenny being Lenny. But it was bigger than that. We'd all come to feel that we were 1986's team of destiny, chosen by fate to win it all. Certain teams, in certain years, are like that. It may be self-fulfilling prophecy: by believing it, you make it so. *It's over, man.* Lenny was reminding us that this was our year. It was our World Series.

Everyone on the plane relaxed, and we began feeling good again. Friday, there would be no workout. The rest had done wonders for us before.

We'd clinched the division championship, but not the pennant, in Shea Stadium. On September 12, we'd gone into Philadelphia for a three-game series. Our magic number was two: any combination of Mets' wins and Phillies' losses adding up to two would end the race. In other words, all we had to do was beat them once. From Philadelphia we were to travel to St. Louis for two games, so it didn't seem likely we'd be clinching in Shea.

Huge crowds filled Veterans Stadium for every one of those three games. Thousands came from New York to be there when we wrapped it up. They came streaming down the New Jersey Turnpike every day—in cars, in buses. They made a lot of noise. It was almost like playing at home.

We were twenty-two games in front of the Phillies. They weren't going to catch us. But that weekend they summoned up all their pride and stubbornness, and played us as if their whole season had boiled down to these three games. In a way, maybe it had. Denying us our biggest win of the season, if only temporarily, would be a message: wait till next year.

We'd brought champagne. That champagne went a lot of places: Philadelphia, St. Louis, and back to New York. It was the year of the postponed champagne. The Phillies whipped us three straight.

The Phillies' third baseman, the great Mike Schmidt, had a brilliant series. In the first game, he hit his 493rd career home run, a three-run shot in the fifth inning. The final score was 6–3. In those three games, Schmidt drove in six runs. In an odd sort of way, it was a big series, closely watched, and he came through.

Schmidt came through, and Carter flopped. I managed one hit and one RBI. There was another race going on, individual: for the Most Valuable Player Award. Schmitty was having that kind of year, and some people thought I had a chance of winning the award. Schmitty had won it in 1980, and I'd finished second. It was going to be close between us again this year, and he helped himself that weekend; I didn't. I finished third, as it turned out, behind Schmitty and Glenn Davis. The World Series is the dream of dreams, but I'd be lying if I said I didn't want to be MVP someday. Schmitty talks about retiring soon, and I kid him about it. "When are you gonna get out of the league?" I say. "When are you gonna give me a chance?"

The Phillies beat Doc in the first game, denying him the honor of nailing it down for us. The second night they shellacked Roger, who had relieved Bobby O., and won, 6–5. On Sunday afternoon, they knocked Sid out after four innings. The final was 6–0. We took our champagne to St. Louis.

And lost again.

This one went thirteen innings. The final was 1–0. R.J. and Jesse shut them out for eleven innings, and Roger was fine until the thirteenth, when he walked Curt Ford with the bases loaded, forcing in the game's only run.

The following night, the 16th, we finally won, and I finally did

164

•

some hitting. Aggie won it, J.O. saved it, and I went three for three, with a double. The win clinched a tie for the championship. We took our champagne home to New York.

It was a seven-game home stand. We were going to win our title in Shea after all, which was nice, in a way. The front office had mixed feelings. In 1973, the Mets had clinched at home, and the happy crowd had torn the field to pieces. Our fans this year had been pretty exuberant, and you couldn't help wondering what would happen when the big moment arrived. The ball club pleaded for restraint and good manners in the newspapers, and the night of the 17th, as Doc pitched against the Cubs, the pleas were repeated on the Diamond Vision screen and over the PA system: *"Please refrain from going onto the playing field."* It was like looking up a mountain and asking an avalanche not to happen. The stadium was stuffed with 47,823 people.

Doc went nine, gave up six hits, and won, 4–2. Young Dave Magadan, who'd come up from Tidewater in September, started at first base because Mex had a wicked case of the flu. Magadan had a big night: three hits and two RBIs. Sick or not, Mex wanted to be on the field when we clinched. He went out for the ninth. As Doc was pitching the ninth, the PA announcer had begged and pleaded. We had our hunch as to what would happen and were all poised to make a run for it the moment the last out was made. It was a ground ball to Wally. And by the time Mex squeezed that throw, the playing field was bedlam.

They came over the barriers like water over a dam. It was a flood. They were everywhere. It was as exciting as some wild storm, happy crazed people swirling around, buffeting us, sweeping us along. They felt part of this—of the season, of the team—and wanted to be in on the celebrating.

And they did celebrate. They hollered and pounded us on the back. As I plowed toward the dugout, my helmet disappeared. Hands grabbed at my arms, my shoulders. I was carrying my mask and mitt; a hand tore the mask from my grip. I clutched the mitt hard. Hands tugged at it, but I held on. I'd been shouldering and pushing but still hadn't reached the dugout, and now Sam Perlozzo, our triple

A manager, who had joined us for September, knocked someone out of my way, clearing a gap for me. Sam shielded me as we shoved our way to the dugout. He held on to me, pulled me down the dugout steps, and delivered me to the runway.

Sandy and the girls had flown up for the game. They were in box seats behind home plate. When the fans rushed the field, people dropped from the upper deck to the overhead screen and rolled to the field. It was terrifying, Sandy said. The screen sagged, threatening to give way.

The only casualty was Aggie. The fans knocked him down, and someone jumped on his shoulder. Aggie missed a start, but was all right after that. The ball field was destroyed. They carried away the bases, the plate, and the turf. You've heard of bat day and cap day, when the ball club hands out bats or hats to all customers? September 17 was turf day. Thousands of people went home with hunks of grass and sod. I wonder if they planted it in their back yards. Think of it: Shea Stadium grass sprouting all over New York, New Jersey, and Connecticut.

The front office was furious. Pete Flynn, the head grounds keeper, took one look after the celebration had finally washed out into the parking lots and streets of Queens, and nearly fell over from shock. The ball field had been transformed into a grassless wasteland. It had been chopped, dug up, and trampled like a battlefield. And the next day, at 1:35, we had a game to play. It was up to Pete and his men to create a baseball field. They had about twelve hours.

When the Astros beat us in the fourth game of the League Championship Series, insuring that the series would end, one way or the other, in Houston, the Mets' front office was relieved. Flynn and his crew had given us an instant field to play on, but, for all Pete's skill, it wasn't a perfect field. It was spongy in places. The turf wasn't fastened down real well. The field slowly got better, and was adequate by the time postseason play began. But if we'd beaten the Astros at home, and if the crowd had attacked the playing field the way they had on September 17, Shea would have been a sorry place for a World Series.

12

I had the privilege in October of playing in two of the finest and most memorable postseason games in baseball history. There had been the sixteen-inning epic in Houston. And on Saturday night, October 25, there was the sixth game of the World Series. The Sixth Game. There was a man on the field, Dwight Evans, who had played in another sixth game that had been rated by some as the greatest of all World Series games. The year was 1975. In Fenway Park the Red Sox had fought from behind to tie the Cincinnati Reds, and gone into extra innings, great play following great play, surprise following surprise, until Carlton Fisk had ended it with a home run over the famous wall. Our sixth game may have been as good. It may have been better. I'm sure of one thing: no final inning in World Series history was ever as improbable, or as astonishing, as ours.

On Friday, the off-day, Sandy and I discussed, long and hard, the upcoming trip to Japan. We took a nagging weight off our shoulders and decided we wouldn't go. Ten more days away from my family, ten more days of traveling, ten more days of baseball: I couldn't face it. I hated to cancel. I always honor my commitments. But I couldn't face the trip, which had seemed such an easy thing in July, and I called the office of the Commissioner of Baseball. I got an assistant who'd been helping to organize the exhibition tour, and laid it out as persuasively as I could. I said I was exhausted, mentally and physically. I told him I hadn't seen my son since August. I said I was still willing to make the trip, but would be very grateful not to have to go. He said he understood, no problem, they'd find someone else. I asked him if he was sure; he said he was. I felt relieved. The end of the season, truly, was at hand.

I got out from under the shadow of that trip around the world just in time. I've said that the pressure of the League Championship Series was greater than that in the World Series—until the sixth and seventh games. The first five games had been emotional and tiring, but I hadn't felt the relentless pressure I'd felt playing the Astros, that desperate desire to hit, to excel. Against the Red Sox I'd played relaxed. I'd played comfortable. It was going to get tougher now. The Japan trip had been a worry. This was no time for worries.

The house was full again. Doug and Debbie, Gordy and his wife and, of course, my father. On Saturday afternoon Gordy and I went out and bought steaks, which he cooked on the grill in the back yard. The day was cool and overcast. Everyone was on the quiet side. You didn't have to be playing that night to feel the tension. If we lost, it was over. I couldn't imagine it. I couldn't imagine coming home a loser. Not this year.

It ain't over till it's over. Memorize it. Write it on a three-by-five card and take it to the ballpark with you. In the bottom half of the tenth inning of the sixth game, with two out, none on base, and the Red Sox ahead by two, the operator of the Diamond Vision screen pressed a wrong button, and for a few seconds congratulated Boston on winning the World Series. Up in the press box, the writers put their heads together and named Bruce Hurst Most Valuable Player. In the Red Sox clubhouse, somebody was pulling corks out of champagne bottles. One of the writers jotted Hurst's name on a slip of paper; the paper was given to Vin Scully and Joe Garagiola in the NBC booth. It was my luck, my *good* luck, to be the hitter. The Red Sox had all climbed to the top of the dugout steps. The relief pitchers hung over the side of the bullpen. Calvin Schiraldi, my teammate last year, my battery mate, threw me ball two, outside.

It had been a good game, an exciting game, already. If the game had ended then, if Schiraldi had gotten me, it would have been no ordinary ball game. A tie after five innings. A tie after eight. Extra innings.

Early in the game, with the Red Sox at bat, a parachutist had come floating down onto the ball field. No one heard an airplane; the guy just materialized out of the night, wearing a big flag that said: LET'S GO, METS! The crowd roared. The skydiver landed near the first-base line, where the police were waiting for him. The cops led him away through our dugout. The parachutist really fired us up.

The Red Sox had broken ahead with single runs in the first and second. Bobby O. was pitching for us, and, after the rocky beginning, he was magnificent. Boggs began the game with an infield hit pushed to Ray at third. Bobby got Barrett and Buckner to lift easy fly balls to Lenny. He walked Rice. Then Evans, who seemed to pounce on every mistake, every bad pitch we threw him, did it again, driving a double between Mookie and Lenny. Gedman hit a fly ball to Darryl.

Red Sox 1, Mets 0.

And now Clemens. The big kid started strong, sending in his fastball at terrific speeds, over and over, as if he could throw it all night. He struck Lenny out, a called strike three, to begin the bottom of the first. Wally looked at a called strike three. He had a virus, and he felt sicker and sicker as the game went along. Mex hit a fly ball to Henderson, and we were gone, in order.

Owen singled with one out in their second. They were attacking Bobby O. Clemens struck out. We were playing without the designated hitter, which removed Baylor from their line-up. The years of not batting showed on their pitchers all through the Series, though our guys didn't exactly tear the cover off the ball. Boggs pulled a single to right field, and Marty Barrett did it again, base hit to left, bringing Owen home.

Red Sox 2, Mets 0.

We weren't panicking, but we knew we had our work cut out for us. The dugout was a solemn place that night, everyone anxiously watching the game unfold. Talk was quiet, brief.

I led off our second. I made Clemens labor a bit; the count went to three and two, and I fouled off a bunch of pitches. It didn't seem important at the time, but Clemens threw a lot of pitches to me. A lot of us were nicking his rising fastball, sending it back foul, making him throw again. I got pretty good wood on the ball that first time, hit it hard to Henderson. Clemens walked Straw—more pitches— then fanned Ray. Mookie looked at strike three.

Bobby O. put them down in order in the third. He struck out Rice, and again he struck out his friend Rich Gedman.

In our third, Clemens fanned Raffy. He struck out Bobby O. He'd now struck out four in a row, a total of six in three innings. They must have loved it up in Boston, but Clemens would have been better off if we'd been hitting his first or second pitch for ground balls or pop-ups. After the two strike-outs, Lenny hit a ground ball to Owen, and we were gone in the third, and still hadn't scratched a hit.

In their fourth, Owen—the little guy was almost as much trouble as Barrett—singled to center field with one out. Clemens tried to drop a sacrifice bunt and popped a little foul ball behind the plate, which I got to. Again, a Red Sox pitcher had done nothing with the bat. Hurst had struck out three times in game one. In game two Clemens had succeeded in putting a couple of bunts down, but Stanley had struck out trying to bunt. Clemens's pop-up kept Owen at first, and Boggs hit a ground ball to Raffy, who threw to Mex, and the inning was over.

We went out in order in the fourth, but with one difference: Clemens didn't strike anybody out. I ended the inning with a ground ball straight back at Clemens. In their fifth Barrett hit *another* single, and, with two out, Evans walked. Gedman hit a fly ball to Mookie, and they were gone. In the bottom of the inning, we drew some blood.

For the second time, Darryl walked. And for the second time, with Ray at bat, Straw stole second. Ray then hit one on the ground into center field—base hit—and Straw flew home with our first run. Everyone on our bench was up and yelling. Next, a big play: Mookie pulled a ground ball into right field. Evans, one of the game's best outfielders, charged the ball hard, scooped it, dropped it, as Ray legged to third. Runners at the corners, no outs.

Raffy was due to hit, with Bobby O. on deck. Here, Davey made his first strategic move, and it was to have lasting consequences. All of Davey's moves were meaningful in the sixth game, and all of McNamara's. It was a good game for second-guessers. Davey sent Danny to the plate in place of Raffy. Danny bats lefty and is strong; Clemens throws right-handed. Davey wanted the run. A decent fly ball would do it. And if Danny could get the base hit, or launch one off a wall, it might light a big inning.

Danny did get the run in, but not the way Davey wanted. Clemens kept the ball down, and Danny bounced one to Barrett, double play. Ray scored. The rally had evaporated, so Davey let Bobby O. hit for himself; he grounded out to Barrett.

Mets 2, Red Sox 2.

With one out in their sixth, Owen beat out an infield hit, his third single of the night. Clemens bunted, tapped it to Mex, who had time to get Owen at second. We were always glad to see a Red Sox pitcher at the plate. Boggs grounded out.

Clemens struck out two of us in the sixth: Lenny and me. After Lenny's strike-out, Wally and Mex singled. Runners on first and third; a big RBI opportunity for yours truly. Clemens struck me out looking. Darryl grounded out to end the inning, but again Clemens had thrown a lot of pitches.

So had Bobby O. He was tiring, and Davey brought in Roger. It was the end of Bobby O.'s season, the best of his life. He'd won eighteen games, and would finish fourth in the voting for the Cy Young Award; too low, in my opinion. He'd pitched his heart out in the play-offs and in the Series.

Barrett led off against Roger and walked. We could *not* get him out. He took second on a ground ball by Buckner. Rice hit a ground ball to Ray, who gloved it and threw wild to first. Then Evans hit a

171

•

ground ball—to Wally, who tossed to the new shortstop, young Kevin Elster, too late to get Rice, who was running with the pitch. Kevin threw to first, anyway, and got Evans. Barrett scored.

Red Sox 3, Mets 2.

Gedman dropped a base hit into left field; Mookie rushed the ball, and Rice kept coming. They all knew about Mookie's shoulder operation. Rice came, and Mookie let go a good throw, in the air, to me. I blocked the plate. Rice tried to slide around me; I took the ball to him, tagged him in plenty of time. The inning was over, and Mookie had done it with his throw; Mookie, the guy who waited, the guy who didn't gripe when he had to ride the bench.

Red Sox 3, Mets 2.

Clemens had one more inning in his tired arm. At least, that's what John McNamara thought. Clemens put us out in order in the seventh. Kevin Elster made the third out, a fly ball to Henderson. The kid had begun the season in double A ball in Jackson, Mississippi, and here he was in a do-or-die World Series game in front of more than 55,000 spectators.

On to the eighth inning. Henderson started it with a ground-ball base hit flagged down by Elster. Owen bunted, a good one, the sacrifice working, for once. And here, to our surprise, McNamara sent the kid, Greenwell, to bat for Clemens. McNamara wanted the run, understandably. But Boggs was on deck, and then Barrett. McNamara said afterward that Clemens had raised a blister on the first finger of his pitching hand; we were glad to see him leave, blister or no blister. Roger struck out Greenwell.

Boggs's turn. There's no one more dangerous with a runner on second. The percentages, too, were with Boggs, a left-handed hitter against a right-handed pitcher. Davey yelled to us to walk him. Good move. The only problem was, we then had to pitch to Barrett. Roger pitched carefully to him. He'd driven us crazy slapping the ball up the middle and into right field, but he'd shown us he could yank the ball to left, as well. Roger pitched carefully and lost him. Barrett got the walk. Bases loaded.

Buckner up, a left-handed hitter. He hadn't done much—surely the bad ankle had taken some of the sharpness out of his swing—

but he was still McNamara's number-three hitter, and he was a battler. Roger hadn't pitched too badly—the error had hurt him in the seventh—but he was laboring. It was late, and we were losing by a run. We had to get Buckner. Davey went out and summoned Jesse. Lefty against lefty.

Did Davey remember that Elster had made the last out for us and that the pitcher was the first man up in our eighth? Probably. Davey doesn't forget much. J.O. did get Buckner, on a harmless fly ball to Lenny. But, losing by a run, Davey had to pinch-hit for J.O. We were losing, it was late, and both our bullpen aces were through for the night.

McNamara brought in Schiraldi, his main guy in the pen. Mac had great faith in Calvin. He throws a good fastball, but we thought we could hit him.

So there we went, eighth inning, Lee Mazzilli batting for J.O.— Maz, the home-grown Met come home again, up from Tidewater for a trip to the World Series and the biggest at-bat of his career. Maz looked for the fastball, got it, and pulled a base hit into right field. The crowd woke, and cheered. They love Maz in Shea.

Lenny dropped a bunt on the grass. Schiraldi grabbed it and threw, unwisely, to second, where Maz slid—safe. Runners at first and second, nobody out. Tuff, Doc, and Hojo inverted the bills of their hats for good luck. They stood there tense and solemn with their bills stuck up; the superstition had become serious. Wally bunted, and this time Schiraldi threw to first, getting Wally. First base empty. They walked Mex intentionally, and pitched to me.

It made sense, Mex being a left-handed hitter, just as it had made sense when Houston had done it. I still didn't like it. I remembered Darryl talking to me, years ago, it seemed. *"Don't let 'em do it to you, Kid."*

I won't, I thought now. Calvin threw low—ball one. He was low again, and then outside. They wanted the double play, of course. Ahead on the count, I could wait for something nearer my happy zone. After ball three I backed out and looked down at Buddy Harrelson. Buddy went through the signs, touching and rubbing, and I felt a rush of excitement, because Davey was letting me swing.

173

Schiraldi's pitch might have been inside and it might have been high, but I drove it, anyway, to deep left field. By an inch or two I missed getting all of that pitch, or we'd have had four instant runs. As it was, Rice barely moved—the ball was lined right at him—and he made the catch. Maz came home. Mets 3, Red Sox 3. Straw hit a fly ball to Henderson, the inning was over, and we were even again.

Davey made the logical move. He left Mazzilli in the game, and took Darryl out. He brought Aguilera in to pitch, and because Straw was gone, Aggie could be placed in the fifth spot in the order, Straw's spot. This meant that Davey didn't have to worry about his pitcher hitting for a while. Straw was incensed at being lifted. He felt humiliated. But if he'd stayed in the game, Aggie would have been the fourth hitter in the ninth. Davey would have had to pinch-hit, and he'd already used Roger and Jesse. It was hard on Straw, but Davey had done the smart thing. Straw went into the clubhouse, took a shower, and got dressed. He was in there, alone, during the tenth inning.

Aguilera. He had to pitch to their power in the top of the ninth: Rice, Evans, Gedman. He struck Rice out. Evans drilled a ground ball to Elster's left; the rookie scooped it, bobbled it, an error. Gedman bounced it to Wally, easy double play. It was turning into a long Series for Geddie.

We made a little noise in the bottom of the ninth. Ray began it with a walk. Mookie bunted; Gedman chased it, tried to get Ray at second, and threw the ball into the dirt, an error. Hojo batted for Elster. Schiraldi struck him out. Maz hit a medium fly ball to Rice. Lenny hit one to about the same place.

Mets 3, Red Sox 3.

We played the tenth. Henderson was first, the surprise hitting sensation of the Red Sox' postseason. He'd hit that unbelievable ninth-inning home run in California, and hadn't stopped. "Hendu," they called him. Always smiling. Aggie threw a strike past him and then gave him the fastball higher than we'd meant to put it. Henderson walloped it. I mean, he crushed the ball. Home run. I stood up, only half believing it, and thought, Here we go again. One more mountain to climb. Henderson went bounding, pogo-sticking, down to first, and the Red Sox began celebrating. They were all on their feet in the dugout, and they gave Henderson the royal welcome, slapping his hand and pounding his back. The noise didn't stop over there. Oil Can was one of the nearest to me—at least I heard him loud and clear, his nervous voice darting over the field. They smelled victory over there.

Aggie struck out Owen, and McNamara let Schiraldi hit. Aggie struck him out. We'd regained control of the game and were thinking: one run. We're going to have to battle back and get a run.

Then Boggs lined a double into left center.

Up came Barrett, our tormentor, our nemesis. We'd tried everything we could think of, and he was hitting close to .500. This time he punched a line drive into center field—base hit—and Boggs tore around third and scored. Their bench went crazy. They were waving towels, whooping it up; their dugout was a medley of smiles. No wonder: they had their ace relief pitcher on the mound, a two-run lead, and an attack in full swing. Aggie hit Buckner with a pitch. Rice lined one sharply to right, but Maz ran it down, only barely.

Red Sox 5, Mets 3. They romped out to their positions, eager to play ball one more time, to get it over with. The guys left in the dugout were on their feet. The bullpen crew hung over the fence.

Wally, who by now felt miserable from his virus, took the outside pitch to left field, easy fly ball to Rice. Rice gloved it, held it right there for a long moment, as if he were savoring the precious out. I went to the on-deck circle as Mex got in to hit. Mex battled Schiraldi, hit the ball hard to center field, but Henderson back pedaled, took the fly ball, and held it a moment where he'd caught it, like Rice.

At this point they were choosing Hurst as MVP, and the green bottles were being uncorked in the Boston clubhouse. Mex went inside and threw his glove into his locker. He cracked open a beer and went into Davey's office. The TV was on, of course, and it was me he was watching.

175

I was our last hope, and as I took my place and looked out at Schiraldi, all sounds shrank back, and I felt a presence in me, or perhaps beside me, a calming certainty that I wasn't alone. I was not alone, and I was not, so help me, going to make the last out of the World Series. I felt certain of that. It would have been unacceptable, impossible; I would have lived with it all winter, and probably beyond. It might have stalked me for the rest of my career. Schiraldi's eyes were big with excitement, with the adrenaline racing through him, and the sweat shone on his young face.

He threw: pretty good fastball, and I swung confidently and fouled it back. Strike one, but that didn't matter. I was *not* going to make the last out.

He threw the next pitch under my chin, which irritated me. Too close, Calvin. I stepped back and sent him an angry stare, letting the kid know I didn't like being messed with, even now. Especially now.

Both pitches had been fastballs, and I knew that's all I'd see. I'd caught Schiraldi, I knew him pretty well. The fastball is his bread and butter; he had two outs and was going to keep pouring it in till he got the third. He wasn't going to get fancy with the breaking ball.

Another fastball, and I watched it—outside, ball two. Things were looking up. Calvin would want to send it where I'd swing at it, and it would be the fastball. I looked for something up, got it, and in what seemed like a moment of absolute stillness, an instant in which the big crowd froze, I stepped and swung and drove the ball into left field—the biggest, most needed single of my life. I didn't kill the ball; I hit it near the end of the bat, not perfect, not fat wood, but enough. I watched Rice play the bounce as I ran. Uncle Bill was waiting for me; we slapped fingers. The crowd had come awake.

"Just what we needed, Kid," Uncle Bill told me.

And it was, and the burden had passed to Kevin Mitchell, batting for Aggie. World's biggest at-bat ever, but it was hard to think of him as a rookie, he was so sure of himself, so street-wise. World had seen a lot, and knew a lot.

He looked bad on the first pitch, a checked swing that sent the

176

•

ball over our dugout. He looked overmatched. Schiraldi tried the slider, and hung it.

A hanging slider: World busted it into left center field—base hit. I motored down to second and took the shortest turn I ever had, went back and clung to that base for dear life. This was no time to get frisky on the base paths. The noise thickened, everybody in the stadium sensing, suddenly, that this game wasn't over yet. In the Red Sox dugout the chatter and yelling had all but stopped.

Ray was up. I kept a foot on the bag as he planted his back foot and got ready to hit. I cupped my hands around my mouth and hollered at him, urging him, *begging* him, to get a hit. World's single had fired me up; I was wild, beside myself. *Come on, Ray; you can do it, Ray-Ray.* Quickly, Schiraldi threw two fastballs by him, both strikes.

So there we were. Last half of the tenth, two out, two strikes. Afterward, Ray said that concentration is an act of not thinking, of emptying your mind of everything. He's right. It had been like that in my at-bat, the noise far away, a stillness inside and out. Ray dug in; I had a good view from second.

Schiraldi threw the fastball inside; the ball climbed on Ray, and he fought it, swinging short and quick, and nudged it off the bat handle, tucked it just over Barrett's head—base hit. It was tough hitting, good hitting, and I ran like my life depended on it, came hauling around third and down the line, as World sped to third. Red Sox 5, Mets 4, runners at the corners, tying run at third.

The Red Sox who had been lining the top step of the dugout were melting back down into the shadow of the overhang. There was something in the air now, electricity, magic, and we knew it, and so did they. They were beginning not to believe what was happening, you could see it in their faces. You could see it in John McNamara's stony Irish face as he took the slow walk to the mound to get Schiraldi. Mac gave his right forearm a slap: he wanted the right-hander, Bob Stanley.

Stanley's year had been a long way from spectacular, but he'd pitched well in the Series. He hadn't given us a run yet. Mookie's a switch hitter, so McNamara wasn't gaining the percentage with

Stanley. He just thought Schiraldi had had it. I thought so, too. Stanley tossed his eight warm-ups, and the crowd roared a steady cheer, the noise building as Stanley got closer to pitching.

Mookie's at-bat, one of the most famous in baseball history, was vintage Mookie Wilson. What happened next was compelled, created, by Mookie's cleverness and speed—a hitless at-bat that had wizardry in it.

Stanley threw a strike by him, and then came that inside pitch that nearly grazed Mookie's thighs. Mookie jackknifed out of the way, supple and quick as lightning to dodge that ball, which shot past Gedman's mitt. Wild pitch; a run, as World pranced home. Ray took second, and the game was tied. Now, think about it: if the pitch had hit Mookie, he would have gone to first, a meaningless runner, Ray being the winner. The pitch was sailing; Mookie had to know it might get away from Gedman. *Dodging that ball was crucial.*

We were wild, crazy, celebrating this incredible reprieve, this second chance. We'd been one out, one strike, from being dead. We had a new life, and we were going crazy.

In the clubhouse, Mex watched as I, World, and then Ray, banged our hits. When the pitch escaped Gedman and World scored to tie the game, Mex bounded up out of Davey's chair to go get his glove. But he stopped. He decided there was luck in Davey's chair, and sat back down to watch Stanley pitch to Mookie.

Give Stanley some credit. Gedman could have caught that wild pitch. It should have gone into the history books as a passed ball. It wasn't an easy play, but Geddie should have made it. Maybe he lost sight of it for a split second inside the mask. He just didn't stick the mitt out far enough. Give Stanley credit: he pitched Mookie tough. The tide had turned with a vengeance, the Shea crowd was in an uproar, the Sox were stunned by the turnaround, and Stanley pitched tough. His teammates had all sunk to the back of the dugout. Stanley bore down.

He wasn't wild. His pitches were good, on the corners, but Mookie kept fouling them off. He chopped one off his foot. Stanley kept bringing it, Mookie kept himself alive, and then, finally, hit that ground ball to Buckner.

The ground ball to Buckner: I suppose there are people in this country who have never seen a replay of that ground ball, but it's hard to imagine. It became a kind of instant legend: Buckner's Error.

The ball went skipping down to him, not hard; he hobbled to get in front of it, leaned down, and suddenly, incredibly, it was behind him. It was trickling into right field, and not only was Mookie safe, but Ray was coming around third; he was going to score before anyone could *get* to the ball. It took us, and 55,000 fans, a second to comprehend.

And as it sank in that we'd just won the sixth game and had come back from the dead, it sank in also that Mookie had shot past Stanley, who was hustling over to cover first, and that there was a connection between Mookie's speed and the error. Buckner knew who was flying down the line, and he was thinking about fielding the ball and racing Mookie to the bag. Something, maybe just a twitch of his head or of his gaze, convinced me of this. He was distracted, and the ball jumped his glove and was gone. McNamara was criticized by Red Sox fans for letting Buckner play the tenth with that bum ankle; the ankle never affected his glove, but because of it, he may have been worrying about Mookie's well-known speed.

Keith Hernandez could now leave the lucky chair. He hurried out and found bedlam on the field. We were hugging and hollering, celebrating like we'd just discovered how. The Red Sox were sitting like statues over there. They had to be astonished. We were amazed ourselves.

When we finally came piling into the clubhouse, Darryl Strawberry was waiting for us. He held himself apart from the commotion, still brooding about being taken out of the game. He hung around, looking unhappy, until the reporters found him. It didn't take much to start Straw talking. He said he was embarrassed, and that Davey had shown he didn't have faith in him. He said Davey had made a big mistake by lifting him. He said he'd always remember being "snatched" from the World Series.

Davey took it calmly. He didn't want to start trading insults with Darryl, especially in the newspapers. Davey was wise enough to know it would blow over. I also think Davey understood Darryl's

179

•

anger. "It's okay to be selfish," Davey says. He understands wanting to be in the thick of things.

Straw managed to avoid Davey for the rest of the night, and in the hours before game seven. Just before the game, as usual, the starting line-ups took the field as they were introduced over the PA, and stood along the chalk lines till everybody had been brought out. The managers went out first. Everyone would move down the line as he arrived, shaking hands with the guys that preceded him. When Straw came out, he took his place without shaking hands. He was avoiding shaking hands with Davey.

The sixth game spun the Series around and sent it in a new direction. The tide had swung our way—for good. The Red Sox had checked out of their hotel, and after that unbelievable defeat had to go back and check in again. If they'd won, they'd be flying home, with a crowd waiting to greet them at the airport. Instead, they were returning to their hotel. They were unpacking. Again.

The next day was do-or-die for both teams, but we felt like *they* were on the precipice, not us. We'd been there, and fought our way clear. We couldn't wait for the next day.

SATURDAY, OCT. 25 at SHEA

Boston					110 000 100 2 — 5 13 3
Mets					000 020 010 3 — 6 8 2

BOSTON (5)

	ab	r	h	bi
Boggs 3b	5	2	3	0
Barrett 2b	4	1	3	2
Buckner 1b	5	0	0	0
Rice lf	5	0	0	0
Evans rf	4	0	1	2
Gedman c	5	0	1	0
Henderson cf	5	1	2	1
Owen ss	4	1	3	0
Clemens p	3	0	0	0
Greenwell ph	1	0	0	0
Schiraldi p	1	0	0	0
Stanley p	0	0	0	0
	42	5	13	5

METS (6)

	ab	r	h	bi
Dykstra cf	4	0	0	0
Backman 2b	4	0	1	0
Hernandez 1b	4	0	1	0
Carter c	4	1	1	1
Strawberry rf	2	1	0	0
Aguilera p	0	0	0	0
Mitchell ph	1	1	1	0
Knight 3b	4	2	2	2
Wilson lf	5	0	1	0
Santana ss	1	0	0	0
Heep ph	1	0	0	0
Elster ss	1	0	0	0
Johnson ss	1	0	0	0
Ojeda p	2	0	0	0
McDowell p	0	0	0	0
Orosco p	0	0	0	0
Mazzilli rf	2	1	1	0
	36	6	8	3

Two outs when winning run scored

E—Evans, Knight, Elster, Gedman, Buckner. DP—Boston 1, Mets 1. LOB—Boston 14, Mets 8. 2B—Evans, Boggs. HR—Henderson (2). SB—Strawberry 2 (3). S—Owen, Dykstra, Backman. SF—Carter. Game-Winning RBI—None.

	IP	H	R	ER	BB	SO
Boston						
Clemens	7	4	2	1	2	8
Schiraldi (L, 0-1)	2 2-3	4	4	3	2	1
Stanley	0	0	0	0	0	0
Mets						
Ojeda	6	8	2	2	2	3
McDowell	1 2-3	2	1	0	3	1
Orosco	1-3	0	0	0	0	0
Aguilera (W, 1-0)	2	3	2	2	0	3

Stanley pitched to 1 batter in the 10th. HBP—Buckner by Aguilera. WP—Stanley. T—4:02. A—55,078.

•

13

Before the 1982 season, Dick Moss and Jerry Petrie negotiated my new contract. I signed a seven-year contract extension with the Montreal Expos. Yes, it was a good contract, a fabulous contract: close to $2 million a year to play baseball. John McHale, president and ten percent owner of the Expos, was in favor of the contract. Charles Bronfman, who had owned the Expos since their creation in 1969—the Charles Bronfman of Seagram—apparently had his doubts.

He said he did toward the end of the 1983 season. Bronfman put it this way: "I will regret the signing of Gary Carter for the rest of my life." The Expos were in the process of finishing third, eight games behind the leader of the Eastern Division. I was in the process of hitting .270, with seventeen home runs and seventy-nine runs batted in. I'd been bothered all season by tendinitis in my left elbow, an injury left over from 1982. I'd played with considerable pain. I'd taken cortisone shots to enable me to play. The year before, I'd hit .293 and had twenty-nine home runs and ninety-seven RBIs. My somewhat shrunken numbers, maybe, had been a kind of last straw for the owner. Or maybe it was the third-place finish.

That winter, Bronfman called me at home and said he wanted to see me in his condominium in West Palm Beach, near the Expos spring camp. His phone call was long-distance, from Montreal, or someplace far away. He was flying in to West Palm in a day or two. He didn't say why he wanted to see me. He told me when to be there, and I said I would.

Bronfman isn't old—fifty, maybe, at the outside. He's a very powerful, very rich man. He established the Montreal Expos with family money, and I suppose he thinks of owning a big-league baseball team as a kind of hobby. He liked to come out on the ball field during spring training wearing an Expos uniform, number eighty-three, which has something to do with his company.

It was about a week before spring training when I went to see him. He'd told me to be there at eight in the evening, and he kept me waiting for half an hour. I wondered what he wanted. I thought it was going to be a pep talk. I knew he wasn't happy with the year I'd had. He arrived, finally, and invited me into his place.

It was lavish and had a fabulous view of the Atlantic. I sat down with Bronfman, and he lit into me. He seemed to have invited me to tell me what a lousy ballplayer I was. He really laid it on. I wasn't a winner, I didn't hit in the clutch. One line will live forever in my memory: "Whenever you come up with men on base, I head for the bathroom."

The session ground along for more than two hours. The whole time, I felt under attack. I kept trying to defend myself. I told him how much the Expos and the city of Montreal meant to me. I said I'd given myself, heart and soul, to the team and the city. He said he'd wondered about my loyalty, which really burned me up. I pointed out that we'd built a house in Montreal; if I didn't intend to stay, why would I build a house? Three times I'd been Expos Player of the Year; I reminded him of that. Yes, he said, but we hadn't won. He was paying me all this money to get him a championship.

How do you explain to a man like Bronfman what it takes to win a baseball championship? Pitching and more pitching. No team in recent memory has won a pennant, let alone a World Series, without at least one premier bullpen closer. To win requires certain overall strengths: speed, power, depth on the bench. It takes luck to win. It takes a Willie Hernandez coming out of nowhere to win a Cy Young Award for the Tigers in 1984. A John Tudor or a Bobby

Ojeda being reborn in a new league, a new ball park. How do you explain this to Charles Bronfman? How do you tell him? It seems strange that a man can own a major-league baseball team and really understand so little of the game.

After ripping me for two hours, he softened a bit, and we parted on a cordial note. We shook hands. "I'll be pulling for you," he said. I hoped so. I went home demoralized, my pride all bruised. Home to Sandy.

"Honey, I can't believe this," I said. "I spent over two hours defending myself."

I'd been on the All-Star team in '75, '79, '80, '81, '82, and '83. In the 1981 Championship Series I'd hit .421. I'd hit two home runs. What did I have to defend?

"I'm going to have a great season," I told Sandy. "Maybe my best ever."

"You already knew that," she said.

I'd been working harder than ever that winter, lifting weights, running. I was in terrific shape. I didn't like seeing my statistics fall off any more than Bronfman did. I wanted to do better. I did work for the man, after all, and he was paying me well. I wanted to satisfy him, just out of principle.

I played 159 games in 1984. I batted .294, hit twenty-seven home runs, and tied for the league lead with 106 RBIs. It was my best year ever, but it still wasn't enough for Charles Bronfman, because the Expos finished fifth. Jim Murray, the syndicated columnist for the *Los Angeles Times,* once wrote, "Gary Carter is the type of guy who, if he saved a child from drowning, the mother would look at him and say, 'Where's his hat?' " What I did for the Expos was never enough. After the year I'd had in '84, Bronfman decided to trade me.

When I first came up with the Expos, I played mostly in the out-field, because it was a way to get my bat in the line-up. Barry Foote was the regular catcher, but when he wasn't hitting, they'd stick me behind the plate. Our manager for most of '76 was Karl Kuehl, who happened to be my trusted friend, a sort of second father to me. Karl replaced Gene Mauch, who had been fired at the end of the '75 season. (Charles Bronfman has hired and fired a lot of managers.) Karl had coached me in the Instructional League. He'd managed me at Quebec City in 1973 and the following year in Memphis. He had big hopes for me, and he worked hard teaching me to catch, and to hit. He threw me extra batting practice. At Quebec City he fined me a quarter every time I dropped a pitch in a game. I was earning $600 a month, and those quarters added up. Karl believed in me, and I was grateful to him.

Karl was young to be a big-league manager, forty, and he had a sort of childlike awe of his position that caused him problems with some of the older ballplayers. My friendship with Karl stuck out, and some of the guys ragged me, called me his pet, called him my daddy. It was a bad year for the Expos, a horrendous year. We were in the process of losing 107 games and finishing forty-six games out of first place.

That year Ellis Valentine made the ball club. Ellis was loaded with talent. He was an outfielder with an outstanding arm. He could hit, run, and throw. But he didn't push himself as hard as Karl expected his players to, and he wasn't playing to his potential. Karl sent him down to triple A. Some of the guys on the team were annoyed.

Tim Foli, the scrappy shortstop, didn't respect Karl and didn't always listen to him. Foli pretty much did what he wanted, till guys were openly wondering who was running the team. Karl benched him. Foli rode the bench for a couple of days. To the front office it looked like a choice between Karl and Foli, and they ordered Karl to put him back in the line-up. Karl did it, and blew any respect he had left among the players who'd been making trouble for him. On September 1 he was fired. I felt bad for Karl.

Charlie Fox took over and, when he saw me catch, he told me I belonged behind the plate. He said I'd never play the outfield again if he had anything to do with it. Foote wasn't having such a hot year, so I got a lot of catching work for the rest of the season. But Fox was gone as manager by the following year (he became general manager), and Dick Williams became our new skipper.

•

There were problems with the team right from the beginning, but the major conflict occurred in 1977, when Williams decided to let me and Foote fight it out for the first-string catching position. Foote was very close with the veteran pitchers on the team. As their battery mate he'd had a nice rapport with them and was popular with them off the field as well. When I beat him out for the job (he was traded at the June 15 trading deadline), his friends resented it. He knew how to call a good game, and I was still learning, and when I made mistakes, the pitchers griped, mostly behind my back. It was something they could point to—I didn't know the hitters, I called a bad game. But I learned, soon enough.

I don't think it ever was a happy ball club.

We had our drug problems, like a lot of teams, in the early '80s. Tim Raines finally went public with his cocaine involvement. Raines confessed that he'd once gone five days without sleeping, then crashed and slept through a game. I must be naïve, because I never really knew it was going on. I knew Raines acted funny sometimes, but I had no idea why. It's foreign to me. Drinking I understand, but drugs are another language.

I still occasionally experienced the awkward silences in the clubhouse when I walked in, and the verbal jabs. "Camera Carter." "Teeth." "Hey, Teezo." I tried with Andre Dawson; I made a point of going to dinner with him, to the movies. We got along, but I guess it was just on the surface. Warren Cromartie was a great friend of Andre's, and I think he fueled Andre's resentment. Cromartie was a good ballplayer, but a divisive guy. His mind was quick, witty, and he used it like a needle. Sometimes he was plain nasty.

Dawson and Raines are close friends. The Raineses even named a son Andre Dawson Raines. Raines lives in Florida, not too far from me, and before the '84 season, before my meeting with Bronfman, I called him. I said I thought Andre resented me, and I wanted to find out if there was a problem. Tim said he didn't think Andre felt that strongly against me, but, hey, why not go see him? So I did.

I called Andre, down in Miami, and arranged to meet him. He must have figured out what I wanted. Maybe he'd talked to Raines. I drove down, and we met for lunch in a nice restaurant. After some

185

•

small talk I laid it out straight. "I get the feeling you don't like me," I said. "I want to know what the problem is." I said I wanted to put it behind us, and that I thought we could win the pennant.

Dawson, Raines, and some of the others on that ball club wouldn't tell me they disliked me; they'd never spelled it out to me. Andre said now that he didn't hold any grudges or have any bad feelings about me. I tried then to form a kind of partnership with him, to plan how the two of us could help the Expos win in '84. We had just learned that Pete Rose had signed with the Expos, and I was looking forward to being his teammate. Andre had been hot in '83: .299, thirty-two home runs, 113 RBI's. He'd broken my team record for home runs, thirty-one.

"What do you think we need to do?" I asked. "Is it up to us to lead the ball club?"

He said he thought it was, and that we were already pretty much doing it.

I thought it was going well, and talked some more about winning the next year. I said, in a relaxed sort of way, that we all ought to forget about the aggravations of living outside our own country, the language barrier, the inconvenience of going through customs, all those small things. It only pulls us down, I said, worrying about them. Andre agreed.

After lunch we did some browsing and a little shopping. Then I went to his house and said hello to his wife, Vanessa. He showed me his awards and trophies. I liked his house and told him so. Toward the end of the afternoon, I headed home. I thought I'd accomplished something. I felt like I'd come out from under a shadow, and that the sun would shine on the new season, the way it's supposed to on baseball.

When I next saw Andre, it was at spring training. He seemed glad to see me. I thought we really had put the bad times behind us. I felt more comfortable doing things with him off the field.

But as the season got rolling, I began hearing the old barbed remarks, the secondhand complaints about my style of play. The ball club, as I mentioned, finished fifth. We were eighteen games behind

•

when the sad season ended. The manager, Bill Virdon, had been fired. A rumor floated around that I was going to be traded.

I did a poster ad for Sasson designer jeans, and to sweeten the deal Sasson gave me jeans to give to my teammates, their wives, and even their kids. And when I did some ads for Dominion Textile, the company gave me a batch of sweatshirts and turtlenecks, which I gave to the guys on the team.

One winter I bought everybody on the team a director's chair. I had each guy's nickname put on the back of the chair—Hawk, Rock, Yak Yak, Tito, Eli, and so on. I had the idea, crazy maybe, that this would open communication around this divided team—that it would, if only in some small way, unite us.

Some of the guys thanked me. Later someone asked Andre why he hadn't said anything to me about the chairs. "Oh," he said, "I thought he got those things free from one of his endorsements. I didn't know he *bought* them." Even if I had picked them up for nothing, what did it matter?

I was traded in December. Surprisingly, Andre called me the night of the trade. Jeff Reardon called the next day, and Gary Lucas called later. They were the only ones. My former teammates refrained from talking about it to the press until spring training. The writers wanted to know how they felt without me in the middle of things. Some of the guys let me have it. Not only those I knew hadn't liked me, but some who, I thought, felt okay about me. They said things like: it was the best thing the ball club could have done; he didn't fit in; the clubhouse was a bad scene with him there; now we can relax, we can be ourselves; we couldn't win with him here.

That year, the Expos' first without me, they finished in third place, sixteen and a half games behind the Cardinals, thirteen and a half behind the Mets.

I would have been happy to finish my career in Montreal. It was one more goal I'd set, to stay, to carve a place in the history of the

187
•

ball club. Not many ballplayers have done it. Carl Yastrzemski, Mickey Mantle, Ted Williams, and Johnny Bench leap to mind. Even Willie Mays and Pete Rose went elsewhere. I wanted to be a franchise player—like Ernie Banks.

But soon after the '84 season, my most productive year, the rumors began traveling around. I realized it just might happen, I might be traded. It's a jolt to the ego. It's like being benched. It can be explained a dozen ways, logically, but in the end it's because they want someone else more than they want you. The rumors flew, and, finally, just before Thanksgiving, I called my friend John McHale in Montreal to find out when he would be back at his house in West Palm Beach for the holidays. He promised to call when he returned. He never did. Finally, I called him.

"I was about to call you," he said.

Maybe so.

I said, "I really want to talk to you. Could we get together tomorrow?"

"I'm afraid it's an impossibility."

I was beginning to feel as if my whole career had never happened.

"I've got to see you," I said.

"I'll call you, Gary. I'll let you know. We'll get together *soon.*"

I was feeling a little crazy. Hadn't I come through this season? Hadn't I lived up to Bronfman's expectations? What more did they want? Over the weekend, John's son, Kevin, called to tell me his father was out of town and would be flying in on Sunday. He said his father wanted to sit down with me on Monday morning.

"That isn't any good," I said. "I've got a golf game."

I was supposed to play with my pastor and his associate, and with my good friend Tommy Hutton, who had been an Expos teammate and now broadcasts their games. I'd canceled playing with my pastor a couple of times already. It was getting embarrassing.

"I don't know what to tell you," Kevin said. "My father's flying out again at one on Monday. He wants to see you at ten."

I was supposed to play golf at eight, yet I had to see McHale. The rumors were eating away at me.

"All right," I said. "I'll be there at ten."

188

•

"Sorry, Gary," Kevin said.

I didn't blame him. I didn't blame John. The McHales weren't running the ball club. I played nine holes of golf, then left, full of apologies. I was at McHale's office at ten, where I waited half an hour for him to show up. We had exactly half an hour to talk, not enough to cover it all, in my opinion. I wanted to talk about my career. I wanted to talk about staying in Montreal.

I got right down to business. Was Charles Bronfman still unhappy with me and my contract, and did he want to trade me?

John said the answer was yes, to both questions. It hurt, of course, but I wasn't surprised. I turned it over in my mind, trying to get used to the idea. They were going to trade me. *Me*, Gary Carter. Their All-Star catcher. I felt withered inside, humbler than I'd ever felt. Then I saw one chance to feel a little better.

"John," I said, "if you had the choice, would you trade me?"

"I wouldn't trade you," he said. "No way. I was the one who stuck my neck out in '82 and told Charles to sign you. I said, 'Get him, whatever it costs.' If we were ever going to win it, I thought you were the guy we needed."

"Well," I said, "I appreciate that." And I did; I respected John. He knew baseball.

"It's not me," he continued. "Charles isn't in favor of keeping you, and, to tell you the truth, the consensus on the board of directors is the same. They feel they don't want to pay that kind of money."

I turned this over in my mind, then said, "Do you think it's best if I leave?" I'd been with the club for ten years, and had earned the right to veto a trade.

After a moment or so, he said, "Probably."

I saw that he was right. I thought of the clubhouse animosities. Certain guys were going to resent my contract for as long as I was here. It wasn't ever going to change.

"All right," I said, "I'll do what's best. I'll consent to a trade. But I don't want to go just anywhere."

"I understand."

"I want to stay in the National League."

"All right."

189

•

"Los Angeles is a possibility," I said. "I wouldn't mind going home."

"We'll look into it," he said.

"Atlanta is another idea." We had the house in West Palm Beach, where Atlanta shares spring-training facilities with the Expos.

"We'll look into it," John promised.

If he'd asked me, I would have said I'd love to go to New York. But I wasn't thinking of Eastern Division teams. It didn't occur to me they'd be foolish enough to trade me to a club in their own division, especially a contender.

The winter baseball meetings were held in early December. It's a week when all the owners get together to wheel and deal, and to make trades. I was going to be traveling that week in Canada, but I left my itinerary with John McHale's secretary. If they were going to trade me, I wanted to be the first to know.

They did talk to the Dodgers. Playing for the Dodgers wouldn't be the sentimental journey it would have been ten years earlier, but California was still, in a sense, my home. My family was there. But the Dodgers didn't want to pick up my contract. They said it would disrupt their salary scale.

Instead, a deal was made with the New York Mets. I had to agree to the trade, but it was one of the easiest decisions I ever had to make. The Mets' star was on the rise. Davey Johnson had arrived, and the team had finished second. Dwight Gooden, Darryl Strawberry, and Keith Hernandez had arrived. The team was going places. And there is nothing like playing baseball in New York City. The trade was announced on December 10, 1984.

No single player takes a team to the World Series. It can seem that way: Carl Yastrzemski in 1967, Reggie Jackson in the late 1970s, Pete Rose in 1980. What can be said is: their teams would not have gotten there without them. But they didn't do it alone. The pitching was there, and the bench strength. The luck held. In a pennant year, inspiration takes over, that magic, and it touches everyone.

It is different in kids' dreams, simpler. *Seventh game of the World Series. Ninth inning. Two down. And here comes Mickey Mantle. One home run coming up.* In the alley fantasy, there are enough men on base to enable the hero at the plate to win the game with a home run. In kids' dreams it's all beautifully arranged. The stage is set for that one epic swing of the bat.

In real baseball, big-league baseball, it takes many at-bats, many swings, and they are almost never the one perfect swing kids dream of. I got my dream at-bat at the age of thirty-two, in the sixth game of the 1986 World Series. Two were gone, no one was on base, and we were losing by two runs. A gigantic home run was of no more use then than a bloop single. I did get the single. I didn't smash it, didn't get real good wood, but hit the ball toward the end of the bat, a short line drive into left field. It wasn't epic, but it was major-league. I came through.

Kevin Mitchell followed me. He didn't tear the cover off the ball, but he came through. Ray Knight pushed the littlest single you could imagine over Marty Barrett's head, and *he* came through. Mookie Wilson, all speed and agility, went oh for one, and won us the game.

It takes more than one swing, more than one guy, to win in the major leagues.

It wasn't all bad in Montreal, not by any means. I'd spent a third of my life there, and I left many friends and many good memories. In 1975 the Expos' batting instructor, the great Duke Snider, introduced me to Jerry Petrie, who became my agent and best friend throughout my years in Montreal. Jerry was ten years older than I, and wise in the ways of the world. He helped me mature and showed me how to conduct myself off the field. "Kid," he said, "appearance is almost everything." Dress well. Be courteous. Show people you like them. Learn some French; get involved. I had Jerry to thank for all those endorsements. Christy was born in 1978, and we asked Jerry to be her godfather.

One of Jerry's agency's clients was Rusty Staub. Rusty had been with the Expos from 1969 till 1971, and the city had opened its heart

191

•

to him. "Le Grand Orange" had earned this affection, and Jerry held him up to me as an example. In 1979 Rusty was traded back to the Expos. There he was, the guy I'd been using as a model, my teammate now. Rusty was a class act, and it was a pleasure playing with him. We played a final year together in 1985 in New York, another city that loves the big redhead.

Another good friend was Tony Perez, who played three years with the Expos, beginning in 1977. It was my good luck that Tony's locker was adjacent to mine. His nickname was Doggie, because when he was at the plate with men in scoring position he was tough, he was like a dog. Tony was a quiet, strong man who was above the bickering in the clubhouse. He was a calming influence, a mediator. His lovely wife, Pituka, became a good friend of Sandy's.

An early memory was Duke Snider. What ballplayer wouldn't admire Duke? He took me and Larry Parrish under his wing that first year. He liked us, I think, because we were power swingers, like him, and we loved the game. When Duke made a suggestion, I listened. The following year, '76, he became a broadcaster.

There were other memories, other friends. I can't leave out the Spaceman, Bill Lee. Space put new meaning in the word *eccentric*. He came over from the Red Sox and was with us from '79 to '82. He was a good left-handed pitcher—when he concentrated on it. He was a rebel, a hippie. He grew a long beard, and it went unkempt. He sprinkled marijuana on his pancakes. He talked in riddles that sounded deep and wise, and perhaps were. Who knew? Space himself may not have known.

The ball club laid down a dress code, but Space had his own dress code. I remember his getting on a plane wearing a dirty T-shirt, cut-off jeans, and sandals, with no socks. He had the longest, boniest, ugliest feet you ever saw. Put on some socks, Space!

One time in San Francisco, Space vanished without a word. No one knew where he'd gone. The team was flying to Los Angeles for a series with the Dodgers, and Space was supposed to pitch the first game. We got to L.A. the night before the game. Space didn't show up in his hotel room. Later, we found out he'd gone to Tijuana,

Mexico. He hitchhiked from Tijuana to Los Angeles, arriving in time to play.

The usher didn't want to let him into the ball park, and no wonder. Here was this bearded hippie who looked as if he'd just come in off a desert, saying he was pitching tonight against the Dodgers.

He was wacky, but he was also intelligent, and never unkind. He never entered any of the quarrels, or contributed to any of the unpleasantness. Space was everybody's friend, including mine. I liked him, and, though we are as different as night and day, I respected him. There was nothing fake or dishonest about the Spaceman.

I first returned to Olympic Stadium, as a Met, on June 14, 1985. I'd thought a lot about it, naturally. I wondered how I'd be received. Affectionately, I hoped. I didn't see why not: I'd put in ten years there, had reached out to the city and been accepted by it. The Montreal writers built up my return in the papers, and summoned me to a press conference before the first game of the series. They tried to extract some anger or bitterness from me, but all I gave them was that I had many fond memories of Montreal and was happy to be back. It was true.

The first time I strode to the plate, the crowd gave me a big cheer. It was a nice feeling. I was still their guy. I responded with a base hit, and they cheered the hit. I was feeling comfortable about the whole thing, but the next time I came up they booed me. They really gave it to me. The truce was over. I heard some scattered shreds of cheering, but mostly it was one storm of boos. The organization, I think, had given out the impression that I had wanted to be traded.

I answered the boos with two more hits and two walks. Still, the Expos beat us. They beat us twice more, to sweep the series and lift themselves, for the time being, into first place. We'd come into Montreal in third place, two and a half games out, and we left in fourth, three and a half out. Charles Bronfman must have been a happy man. The Cardinals hadn't gotten hot yet.

They continue to boo me in Olympic Stadium. It has faded, but it's always there. In 1986 we beat the Expos on October 1 and 2 in Olympic Stadium to begin our closing five-game winning streak. I'd driven in ninety-eight runs, and had been laboring a bit chasing that big hundredth RBI. On the 2nd, Floyd Youmans was on the mound for the Expos. He had been one of the four guys who had come in the trade for me. In his previous game, he'd pitched a shutout and struck out fifteen. Not the ideal guy to face when you're in a quest for RBIs.

In my first at-bat I singled home a run, number ninety-nine. I batted for the third time in the seventh inning. There were two men on base. I hit Youmans's first pitch, a fastball, out of the ball park, a home run and three RBIs. I had that hundredth RBI, plus two more.

In the bottom of the inning, Andre Dawson batted. Andre dug in, and just before he focused on the pitcher, he half glanced at me, and spoke in his quiet way, barely moving his lips.

"Way to go, man," he said.

14

♦

It rained in New York on Sunday, October 26, and they postponed game seven till the following night. This rainout could have turned the whole thing around. We were red hot, eager to ride the momentum of the previous night's tenth inning right through tonight. We were excited, and we wanted to play ball. The Red Sox could only have been stunned by what had happened to them. The rainout gave them time to recuperate a little. It put some distance between them and game six. It brought us down to earth.

It had another consequence that wasn't at all psychological. If we'd played Sunday, the Red Sox' man of the hour would have been Oil Can Boyd. We'd roughed up Oil Can in game three, and we had every confidence we could beat him again. He'd had that crisis before the All-Star game, and it must have been hard on him to lose to us in Fenway, especially after boasting. Now he'd be pitching in Shea, with the tide and the crowd against him. The rainout changed all that. It gave Bruce Hurst the day's rest he needed to pitch again. So it would be Hurst, who had owned us, instead of Boyd, whom we'd hammered.

Our pitcher was Ronnie Darling, either way, Sunday or Monday. Why not? R.J., Doc, Bobby O. —all were so good. And we had a starting pitcher working out of our bullpen, Sid Fernandez, who'd gotten Cy Young Award votes—in fact, all four had received Cy Young votes. What a great staff! R.J. had been masterful in game one of the Series, and he'd shut the Sox out for seven innings in game four. In fourteen World Series innings, he'd given up one unearned run.

We hated waiting, but we were still loose and confident on Monday. The papers had been noisy about Darryl's little feud with Davey, and before the game Straw avoided him. Then he joined us on the field when the line-ups were introduced and didn't shake any hands, and I finally got irritated. I thought, We don't need this. Not now. Straw was hitting after me, as usual, and he stood beside me as though Davey didn't exist, looking proud and not at all sorry. What a young team we were. For the last time that year, the national anthem played. For the last time, we scattered out to our positions to begin a ball game. The night was cold, still with a wetness in the air. It was a long way from that soft April afternoon when we'd opened at Shea against the Cardinals.

Quickly, the Red Sox drew blood. R.J., who had pitched so well, wasn't getting his pitches where we wanted them. Boggs began the game by driving one straight at Raffy, a lucky out. Buckner did get a single, but we escaped the inning.

Hurst began where he'd left off. Mookie hit a ground ball to Barrett. Tuff hoisted a pop-up to Barrett. Mex went out on a fly ball. I've been told that Hurst has been accused in his own league of not having the guts to pitch in the majors. Take it from me: Bruce Hurst can pitch anywhere.

In the second inning, the Sox let loose. With the count three and two, Evans slammed one of his line-drive home runs over the fence in left. Ronnie went ahead of Gedman, one and two, then let the pitch sail too high, and Geddie belted it high and deep to right, just in our bullpen. Straw got to the ball, got his glove on it, but it fell in. Henderson walked. We got Owen, and Hurst finally succeeded in putting down the sacrifice bunt. Boggs singled up the middle, bringing Henderson around. Barrett dropped a bunt single. We got Buckner to hit a fly ball to Mookie in center field.

Red Sox 3, Mets 0. It seemed like a lot of runs with Hurst pitching.

I led off in our second. I tried to bunt, and tapped it so near to Hurst that he threw me out with no trouble. I bunted because I'd been so frustrated by the guy. In game five I hadn't hit a ball out of the infield. I kept chopping them into the ground, near the end of the bat. I thought a bunt might get me on base to get things going. Ray hit a single that inning, but otherwise we were quiet.

Rice helped us in their third. He drove the ball to the fence in left—base hit. World took the carom and threw in as Rice tried to stretch the hit to a double. The ball beat him to second by plenty. One out. Evans hit an easy fly ball, and Gedman bounced one to Mex. Hurst put us out in order in the third.

In the fourth, R.J. ran out of gas. He hit Henderson with a pitch. Owen went out on a fly ball, and Hurst astonished us with a second decent bunt, sending Henderson to second base. Man on second, two gone, with Boggs and Barrett coming up, both so dangerous. We didn't want to fall another run behind. Davey went out and took the ball from R.J. Mr. P. got the ovation he deserved. Nice job, Ronnie. Nice year.

Sid jogged in from the pen, and when Davey handed him the ball, the game, the World Series, was settled. It was over for the Red Sox when he started pitching. He gave us two and a third innings, and he smothered the Sox, giving us time, all we needed, to get hot. It wasn't just that he held them off; he overwhelmed them. They couldn't catch up with his climbing fastball. It soared high when they swung at it. They hacked at his floating curve ball, missing.

Boggs, his first man, walked. Runners at first and second, and Barrett at the plate. Dukey got him on a fly ball to Straw. In their fifth, he struck out Rice and Evans. In their sixth, he struck out Gedman and Owen. You could feel the game turning. Hurst was perfect in the fourth and fifth; we were still losing, 3–0, and yet you could feel this game turning, for good.

The feeling became certainty in our sixth. Hurst got Raffy on a ground ball, and Davey had to lift Sid for the pinch hitter. He chose

Maz, who had done it for us in game six. He did it tonight: base hit to left field. Mookie pulled a single to left. Tuff walked. And Hurst was in trouble.

Davey sent Wally to run for Tuff, who left to a great cheer. Right then that unhappy July night in Houston must have seemed long ago.

The feeling was growing. Hurst pitched cleverly and courageously to Mex, slipping two strikes past him. But then he threw a fastball in, and Mex drove it to left center—base hit—a sensational hit that turned the momentum in our favor. Maz romped home, Mookie scored on his speed, and Wally made it to third. My turn, with runners at the corners. The crowd was roaring, and we were only down by one run.

I was one for ten against Hurst, but the main thing then was to send the ball deep enough to bring Wally home. Hurst was still keeping the ball low on me, and I reached down and got one, *still* near the end of the bat but a soft line drive this time, between Barrett and Buckner. Evans charged hard, dove, rolled, and the ball vanished beneath him. Mex could only go halfway to second and wait to see if Evans had made the catch. The umpire out there was Dale Ford, and Ford wasn't helping us. Evans flopped to his knees, and I saw he hadn't caught the ball. It was a base hit—if Mex could get to second. I yelled at him to go ahead. It was too late. Evans jumped up with the ball and, with that fine arm, threw to Owen, forcing Mex, who'd been waiting around for Ford to give him the signal, catch or hit. Wally scored easily. I stood on first—fielder's choice, run batted in.

Mex was furious. He hollered at Ford, gesturing dramatically. Uncle Bill steered Mex off the field—we didn't want to lose him—but Mex kept yelling. He continued to tell Ford what he thought from the dugout. I wasn't happy about it either. If the umpire had made the call promptly, Mex would have had second, and I would have had a base hit. The rally might have snowballed. Later, I realized something else: a base hit then would have been the difference between a Series batting average of .276 and one of .310. Straw hit a fly ball to Rice, and the inning was over.

198

•

Mets 3, Red Sox 3.

I can say, honestly, that I was convinced by then that we would win. I knew it. Schiraldi was warming up in their bullpen.

Davey summoned Roger to pitch the seventh. Hurst was due to lead off, and McNamara sent in a pinch hitter, Tony Armas. Hurst had to have been tired, or McNamara would have left him in the game. He had pitched beautifully, and in our hearts we applauded him respectfully. He'd been prematurely named Series MVP, and if the Sox had won, he would have had that award hands down. We were as happy to see him leave as we were when Clemens departed from game six. We looked forward to hitting against their bullpen pitchers.

Armas hadn't appeared in the Series. Not long before, he'd been a premier outfielder, a slugger with a pretty good glove in center field. Then he'd hurt himself in the play-offs against the Angels, and suddenly Henderson was a hero and their center fielder. Armas came off the bench rusty, maybe down over losing his job, and Roger struck him out. Boggs grounded out. Barrett grounded out.

Mets 3, Red Sox 3.

Schiraldi. McNamara still believed in him. He'd gotten the Sox here, and Mac stayed with him. On this night, though, he couldn't handle us. Probably no one could have. The game was tied, but we'd felt it turn so decisively in our favor that we were as relaxed and confident at the plate as if we were leading by ten.

Ray greeted Schiraldi with a home run over the fence in left, probably the biggest home run of his career. We and the fans went nuts. Lenny batted for World and shot a base hit into right field. Shea was rocking; everyone was beginning to smell it. Schiraldi bounced a wild pitch past Gedman, and Lenny scooted to second. Raffy, the quiet guy, drove a hit into right, bringing Lenny home. Rafael Santana: another unsung hero. He's Dominican, the only Spanish-speaking guy on the team, and yet he doesn't let it isolate or upset him. He was another one who had done a lot of sitting early in the season. He was patient, and his time came around. Mex and I tell him constantly not to worry about hitting. We tell him, "The way you field, you don't *have* to hit." It's the truth. Now he stood on first, and we were leading by two.

Schiraldi had pitched to three men: home run, single, single, with a wild pitch added in. The kid's confidence must have been mangled, and you can't pitch without confidence. Davey let Roger bat, and Roger put down the sacrifice bunt, the first out of the inning. It was the end for Schiraldi. McNamara went out to get him, and Calvin took his last long walk of the year.

McNamara brought in Joe Sambito, who'd had terrible luck against us in game three. Raffy was at second, first base was empty, and they decided to walk Mookie intentionally. Unintentionally, Sambito walked Wally. Bases loaded. Mex knocked a fly ball to Henderson, easily deep enough to allow Raffy to score.

Mets 6, Red Sox 3.

McNamara didn't want the lefty to pitch to me, so he called for Bob Stanley. Out went Sambito, in came Stanley. Straw and I chatted at the on-deck circle while Stanley tossed his warm-ups.

When I was about to go up there, Straw said: "Get a hit, Kid. Add to what you've done. You're the MVP; go add to it."

I looked at him; I felt a rush, a thrill. Maybe Straw was right. To play in a World Series, to win a World Series, to be Most Valuable Player: dreams piled upon dreams.

With Straw's words swimming in my brain, I tapped a ground ball to Owen, who easily threw me out. Still Mets 6, Red Sox 3. MVP or not, our team was going to win the World Series.

The Sox made one more run at us in the eighth. It didn't scare us. We'd gotten into their bullpen, and we were confident we could score as many as we needed. Their bullpen ace was gone, shelled. Sambito was gone. The deeper we went, the more confident we'd feel.

Buckner pushed a single to left, Rice drove the ball up the middle—base hit. Evans, for once, didn't pull the ball, but banged it to right center beyond Lenny and Darryl, a long double that sent both runners home. Suddenly, we were leading by just a run, and the tying run was on second with none out. Davey called, one more time, for Jesse.

•

I still felt good about things. We were leading. Even if they did get Evans in, we were going to add some runs. We would add as many as we needed.

Gedman was first. J.O. threw a slider, and Geddie swung early and hit a soft line drive off the end of his bat to Wally. One out. Henderson. J.O. struck him out. Owen was due to hit, and McNamara chose the moment to use Baylor, a weapon he'd been deprived of in all four games in Shea. It must have been hard on Baylor, to have it all boil down to this. J.O. pitched him tough, and Baylor hit a ground ball to Raffy, easy out. The Sox had left Evans at second.

Mets 6, Red Sox 5.

Stanley didn't come out in the eighth. McNamara brought in Al Nipper, the starting pitcher in game four. His first task was to pitch to Darryl, righty to lefty. No balls, two strikes. And then Straw got all of one, a towering right-field blast—home run. He'd been looking for it all Series, and I was happy for him. He cruised the bases slowly. Ray was on deck, and when Straw finally crossed the plate, Ray stopped him, gripped him with both hands. He told Straw to make it up with Davey. He told him to go shake Davey's hand.

Straw didn't say he would and didn't say he wouldn't, but it didn't matter. Grinning, Davey said, "He's gonna *have* to shake my hand," and placed himself where Straw couldn't avoid him. He came down the dugout steps to a bouquet of hands. Davey moved in front of him. They traded grins, shook hands, and the feud was over. There's nothing like hitting a home run in the World Series to make a guy forgive and forget.

We weren't through yet. Ray singled to center, his third hit of the night. He took second when Lenny grounded out. They walked Raffy intentionally, mainly because Jesse was up next. But J.O. poked a hit up the middle, the first base hit by a pitcher all Series, and Ray scored from second.

Mets 8, Red Sox 5.

The excitement grew and grew. It felt inevitable, like counting down the minutes on New Year's Eve.

They brought in Crawford to try to stop the rally. Crawford did, after plunking Mookie with a pitch. I was in the on-deck circle when the last out was made, Mex's ground ball to Barrett.

So Jesse, who'd been on base, went to get his glove and pitch the inning we'd all been living for. J.O., too, had seen some hard times in the early days of this dream season. He'd been having trouble getting his slider to break hard and to drop. We'd stopped relying on it, going instead with the fastball. J.O. was going with mostly hard stuff, and the hitters were waiting for it, and hitting it. Davey began using Roger more, J.O. less. Then J.O. figured out a nice, tricky change-up, a fork ball, and the hitters couldn't count on getting the hard stuff at any particular time. J.O. regained the edge, and had a fine second half. And there he was. The huge crowd, and maybe half of New York City, was on its feet.

Romero, Boggs, and Barrett. Romero was the backup shortstop. He was in there because Baylor had hit for Owen. Romero bats right, so McNamara let him hit. The noise kept building. The air shook. Streamers were floating down out of the upper decks.

There was no more magic left in this magical World Series. The magic had at last run dry. In the Boston dugout the guys sat motionless, staring sadly at these final moments of their season. It was a quick, very ordinary half-inning. Romero fought a pitch off, punched it up in the air foul, near first. Mex took it. One out.

Boggs pulled a ground ball to Wally. Two gone. The streamers hung, arcing, on the heavy air. Lord, it was noisy. A smoke bomb bounced on the grass in left field, squirting red smoke and delaying the finale. I saw that policemen had quietly ringed the field. Someone took away the smoke bomb, and we pitched to Barrett.

He's so good, Marty Barrett, so tough, but everything was working against him: odds, momentum, the crowd, the *feeling* in the huge bowl of Shea. The game had been decided, and we were all going through the motions. J.O. poured in the strikes. The noise kept building. Two strikes. J.O. threw a fastball, inside. Barrett swung and missed.

We were World Champions! The new year had arrived.

J.O. had struck out Marty Barrett, just as he'd struck out Kevin Bass to win the pennant, and I had the ball. Again I had the ball, and I thought of it, registered it, as I charged Jesse. The ball was in the deep pocket of my mitt, and I closed my fist on it, squeezed it. J.O. threw his glove in the air, high as a glove can go, then fell to his knees and shot his arms up in a V. The scene was a replay of the celebration in Houston, only wilder, more delirious. We converged near the mound, crashing together. The pile kept growing; bodies kept flying. The cops kept the crowd off the field, so it was all ours. We hugged, jumped on each other, wrestled, fell down, got up, and laughed till we wept. And I held on to that ball. I'd given the other one to J.O., but this one was mine. You can keep the World Series ball, Mex had said. And I did.

The clubhouse was packed, hot with the white lights of the TV crews and so noisy you couldn't hear yourself speak. Champagne foamed over heads and shoulders. They sprayed it around, they painted the tables with it. I didn't recognize a lot of faces, and wondered who they were. Everyone smiled as if he belonged right there. I hugged Mex, Straw, Raffy, everybody I saw. Wherever I went, champagne was dashed on me. I was wet all over and it felt great.

Then Sandy arrived, and my father and Gordy, and I went outside. She wore blue suede and a radiant smile. I know, said the smile. I understand. We embraced, and I held her for the longest time, pressing champagne into blue suede.

Gordy was next. "You did it, Gar," he said, and he hugged me. He hugged me hard, and suddenly he was weeping. They were happy tears, and genuine, and I knew that what he felt was bigger and deeper than everything that had ever come between us. I felt swept up by love—for Sandy, for Gordy, and for my father, who was standing waiting for *his* hug.

He got it, my creaky dad whose back was still killing him. How I love him! He must have been thinking the same thing I was, which was: how he'd coached me in Little League, and here we both were, World Series winners. Doug and Debbie had come down, too, with my friends Sam and Mickey McRoberts, and, of course, Mead.

203

•

Then I did an interview with Fran Healy for his cable station. We talked about the game, and I tried to make my mind work, to analyze things. While we were talking, I saw Ray Knight get up on the raised platform to talk into the network microphones, and I wondered if that meant he was MVP. I guessed it did. After we'd talked a while, Fran asked me if I was MVP. I said I didn't know, but didn't think so.

"Well, you deserve to be," Fran said. "Let's go find out."

It was Ray. They were announcing it. I felt a small pang: I would have loved it. But Ray had played superbly, and I couldn't argue with the choice; I was genuinely happy for him. It culminated a great year—Comeback Player of the Year and now the MVP.

I went back into the clubhouse, and the first guy I saw was Mex's brother, Gary. Mex's locker is in the corner by the door. We gave each other big greetings.

"Hey," Gary said, "when I said you'd be Series MVP, I was pretty much on target, wasn't I?"

"Pretty close," I said.

"You missed by one guy," he said. "If it hadn't been Ray, it would have been you."

I thanked him.

Then he said, "I can't tell you how much your phone call from Houston meant to me. I'll always remember it."

"I won't forget it, either," I said. "Don't ever lose what you and Keith have."

I left him, and brought Gordy and Doug into the clubhouse. Doug was in seventh heaven. He's a young businessman, and enthusiastic about everything he does, whether it's a night on the town or going to a ball game. He and Gordy wandered around, and Doug kept saying, "Would you want to be anywhere else right now? Would you want to be anywhere else?"

Bob Costas of NBC pulled me over for an interview. It was then that I gave thanks, and credit for all of this, to the bestower of all blessings, Jesus Christ.

They'd hung clear plastic sheets over our lockers to keep our clothes dry when the champagne began to fly. When I finally got to mine, I unbuckled my armor—shin guards and chest protector—and shoved them deep inside the locker. I stuck the precious baseball as deep as it would go and wadded clothes around it. There were so many strangers milling around that I had a hunch little things might vanish before the celebration ended. I was right. The ball club had given us T-shirts emblazoned 1986 WORLD CHAMPIONS, and mine was swiped. A lot of things were swiped. Some of the reporters I knew asked me for souvenirs—a sweat band, a batting glove, anything—and I gave away the sweatbands from both wrists, and a T-shirt. Strangers, too, asked me for things. I soon ran out of small dispensable items, and I suspect that some people got their souvenirs other ways. Later I heard Charlie Samuels, our equipment manager, say he'd found someone digging into Dwight Gooden's trunk. No one stole my protector or shin guards, and no one got the baseball.

There were twenty-four cases of champagne in the clubhouse. Quite a few gallons were spritzed in the air and dumped on heads, but enough was drunk to make that clubhouse the happiest, loudest, wildest room I've ever been in. I got my bottle. I didn't spray it around; I drank it. There's no taste more thrilling than the sweet, fizzy taste of champagne. Victory in a bottle. The celebration grew, the hollering, the singing. The writers were slipping away to knock out their stories. The TV crews were finishing up. Slowly, I peeled off my champagne-doused uniform.

It seemed like a long time before I'd be pulling it on again. It always does after that last autumn game. The months till spring seem like so many years. At my age, you know there won't be too many more new seasons, and each season's final game brings you closer, and makes you think. It's a kind of rehearsal.

I would like to go out with dignity. I don't want anyone feeling sorry for me. I'll announce my retirement while I can still get around on the fastball. I'll finish like Johnny Bench. Toward the end of his final season, he was honored in Riverfront Stadium, Johnny Bench Day. He hadn't caught much for the past two seasons, his body couldn't take it anymore, but that day he caught, and caught well. He wanted to remind them that he was one of the greatest catchers of all time, and he showed them that day that even though he was about to retire, he could still catch. And in his last at-bat in that game, he hit a home run. That is how I would like to finish.

I left my uniform in a soggy pile and went to the shower. The hot water felt good. Everything felt good. I stayed in the shower a long time, and when I finally came out, the room had thinned out considerably. The media people were gone, and all those mysterious strangers. I'll never know who they were. Maybe nobody will. Some of the guys were talking about moving the celebration somewhere else. Bobby O., Lenny, Straw. Somebody came up with a restaurant on Long Island called Finn McCool's, and about fifteen guys said let's do it, let's meet there, and it was decided. Long Island suited me fine.

The guys were leaving in twos and threes, trailing laughter, most of them feeling no pain. I was one of the last to leave. I drew it out, held on to it.

The players leave Shea through the bullpen and out the runway in right field. Fans can watch us from the grandstand above the bullpens, and they can gather outside the ball park where we drive out. This season, as we pulled away from the rest of the Eastern Division, the fans took to waiting for us after almost every game. They'd holler at us, they'd whack our cars with their hands as we slid by. Tonight, hundreds had waited for us. It was late, the night was half over, but they'd waited. They banged on our cars, they showed us the V for victory sign, and they sent us off with our battle cry: Let's Go, Mets!

Off we went, horns blaring, to Finn McCool's. At the restaurant, a crowd had assembled—I don't know how they knew we were coming. Some policemen made a corridor for us to walk through the restaurant door. The restaurant had reserved a section for us, our wives, and our friends. The best champagne was brought. I settled for champagne and a hamburger; a big, beautifully cooked hamburger that tasted better than the best filet mignon I'd ever eaten. That night I ate the world's most perfect hamburger.

There was no game tomorrow, or the next day, or the next. There was our parade—but you don't have to rest for a parade. You don't have to worry about tired legs and the ache in your throwing arm. No game tomorrow, no need to watch the clock. We were still pinching ourselves, but the magic and the dream had become reality. We *were* the World Champions, and we couldn't stop reminiscing about the games. We didn't break up till four in the morning.

MONDAY, OCT. 27 AT SHEA

BOSTON (5)					METS (8)				
	ab	r	h	bi		ab	r	h	bi
Boggs 3b	4	0	1	1	Wilson cf	3	1	1	0
Barrett 2b	5	0	1	0	Teufel 2b	2	0	0	0
Buckner 1b	4	1	2	0	Backman 2b	1	1	0	0
Rice lf	4	1	2	0	Hernandez 1b	4	0	1	3
Evans rf	4	1	2	3	Carter c	4	0	0	1
Gedman c	4	1	1	1	Strawberry rf	4	1	1	1
Henderson cf	2	1	0	0	Knight 3b	4	2	3	1
Owen ss	3	0	0	0	Mitchell lf	2	0	0	0
Baylor ph	1	0	0	0	Dykstra cf	2	1	1	0
Nipper p	0	0	0	0	Santana ss	3	1	1	1
Crawford p	0	0	0	0	Darling p	1	0	0	0
Hurst p	0	0	0	0	Fernandez p	0	0	0	0
Armas ph	1	0	0	0	Mazzilli ph	1	1	1	0
Schiraldi p	0	0	0	0	McDowell p	0	0	0	0
Sambito p	0	0	0	0	Orosco p	1	0	1	1
Stanley p	0	0	0	0					
Romero ss	1	0	0	0					
	33	5	9	5		32	8	10	8

```
Boston _____ 030 000 020 — 5  9 0
Mets   _____ 000 003 32x — 8 10 0
```

LOB—Boston 6, Mets 7. 2B—Evans. HR—Evans (2), Gedman (1), Knight (1), Strawberry (1). S—Hurst 2, McDowell. SF—Hernandez. Game-Winning RBI—Knight (1).

Boston	IP	H	R	ER	BB	SO
Hurst	6	4	3	3	1	3
Schiraldi (L, 0-2)	1-3	3	3	3	0	0
Sambito	1-3	0	0	0	2	0
Stanley	1-3	0	0	0	0	0
Nipper	1-3	3	2	2	1	0
Crawford	2-3	0	0	0	0	0
Mets						
Darling	3 2-3	6	3	3	1	0
Fernandez	2 1-3	0	0	0	1	4
McDowell (W, 1-0)	1	3	2	2	0	1
Orosco (S, 2)	2	0	0	0	0	2

McDowell pitched to 3 batters in the 8th. HBP—Henderson by Darling, Wilson by Crawford. WP—Schiraldi. T—3:11. A—55,032.

New York is the most exciting city in the world, and the parade was the greatest, most exhilarating tribute ever paid to any team, in any sport. They said that it was the second-largest massing of people in the history of the city, the first being the turnout for the ticker-tape parade at the end of World War II. They said that the blizzard of computer paper and confetti that fell on us as we drove up Broadway weighed more than any other except the one that came down on the men after the war. They said that some 2.2 million people flocked to Broadway to watch us roll by.

We gathered at Shea at about nine, with our wives. Two buses took us to the bottom of Manhattan to begin the parade. At ten o'clock we pulled out of the parking lot. We had a police escort: ten motorcycles, three cruisers, sixteen cops. It seemed like more, like a little army. Now I know how great statesmen travel. Those long limousines, with the little flags whipping in the wind. If the police want to get you someplace fast, it can be done. I mean, we flew into Manhattan and all the way downtown: buses, motorcycles, police cars with their blue lights twirling and their sirens wailing. The motorcycle riders went out ahead to stop the traffic at intersections. They stopped cars and sent them to the side of the road to let us through. Incredibly, magically, no one minded. They smiled, they honked their horns, they jumped out of their cars and pumped their fists like Mets who had just hit the long ball. That drive, from Shea Stadium to Battery Park, will usually take forty-five minutes. We made it in about twenty.

At the park a fleet of convertibles waited to take us to City Hall. Each convertible had a player's name written inside. Mine and Sandy's was a 1931 Model A Ford. Somebody, I don't know who, handed each of us a scarf as we came down out of the buses. I LOVE NEW YORK, said each scarf. I threw mine around my neck. In the near distance, the Statue of Liberty raised her arm. There was a lot of confusion, but finally we all got into our cars.

Davey led off the parade in a car that also carried Ed Koch, the mayor of the city, and Governor Mario Cuomo. Sandy and I rode in the ninth car. The cars slid out of the park and fell in line for the long, slow crawl uptown. Ahead, a marching band struck up. The route was fenced with barricades, and policemen walked beside each car. Off we went, walled on both sides by one continuous, deafening cheer. The crowds were solid along the way, and the side streets were stuffed with people. Sandy and I sat on top of the car; we wanted to see everything, to hear everything. I'd dressed to look good in a suit and tie. Sandy was lovely in a blue sequined sweater.

We'd been told not to look up. They said the computer paper could cut your eye if it caught you just right. But I didn't care. I looked up. I looked everywhere. I sat as high as I could and let the noise wash over me, inhaling it, swallowing it like champagne. I wore a smile from one ear to the other, a single smile that never broke. "Ga-ree! Ga-ree! Ga-ree!" They sat on second-story ledges, they perched in trees, they clung to the tops of traffic lights. I'd look in one direction, yeah, and give them the raised fist. Sandy would tap my shoulder and point somewhere else, and I'd give them the fist. I could see them smiling at me. I could read their lips yelling my name. I didn't want it to end.

A couple of times people spilled over the barricades and around our car. Smiles; faces lit with excitement. It was a little scary, the sheer energy of such masses of people—like a clumsy loving giant that didn't know his own strength. When they came over the barricades and past the cops, I leaned down and swatted high fives with them. "Yea, Gary . . . Ga-ree!" "Aw-right . . ." Hands clutched at Sandy and me, and my scarf was whisked away. People everywhere. A cop burrowed after whoever had taken the scarf, and came jogging back with it moments later. It was a little scary, but it was all right, because I knew they wanted to join in, to become part of this. They wanted a piece of it.

The parade crawled on. I have no sense of the time it took to get to City Hall. Twenty minutes? Forty? It was over too soon, a wild sweet flash of time that could not be relived or brought back, even if we were to win again. The next time will be wonderful, too, but it will be different. This was like first love.

At City Hall the Mayor gave each of us a symbolic key to the city. The crowds surrounded us; they packed the wide steps and blanketed the street below. They shinnied up sign posts. The Governor and the Mayor made little speeches. The Mayor was flowery and went on for a while, and you could hear a faint rustle of impatience.

Today, the people didn't want to hear Hizzoner. They wanted to hear Ray, Mookie, Mex, and yours truly. Koch finally wrapped it up, and we were introduced, starting with Buddy Harrelson, shortstop for the 1969 World Series winners.

Some of us spoke. Ray, Mex. Mookie said that 1986 was the year of the Mets, and that 1987 would be the year of the Mets. And 1988, and 1989, and at that point a cheer rose, drowning Mookie out. Mookie had come up in 1980 and had seen some lean years.

I spoke last. They gave me a nice ovation. It rose and fell back. I made it short and simple. I said, yes, it was a fabulous year, and thanked them for being so supportive. We'd achieved the ultimate, I said. And:

"Thank you for helping to make the dream come true."

I'll always be grateful for the dream season of 1986. In a corner of my mind I will stand forever with my bat cocked, waiting for the two-one pitch from Calvin Schiraldi. It is the bottom of the tenth inning, two out, nobody on base. It is the sixth game of the World Series. I've been there now. I'm one of the lucky ones. I keep thinking about Ernie Banks.